Publishing a New International Journal from the University of the Ryukyus

Okinawa and its neighboring pacific island countries have been uniquely investigated through their rich histories, cultures, natures, and economies. In the booklet outlining our university, I once touched briefly on how the University of the Ryukyus had a markedly different history from those of other national universities in Japan and described the many ordeals we have overcome to stand here today. These problems have mainly been of a political or cultural nature with Japan, China, or post-war America, in the face of which both Okinawa and the university have remained undaunted. In fact, from the birth of the Ryukyu Kingdom and through its subsequent administration, Okinawa has maintained close links with the surrounding region through overseas trade and exchange. Successful trade relations flourished particularly between the 14th and 16th centuries, with Asian nations ranging from China, Japan, Korea, the Philippines, Thailand, Malaysia, and Sumatra — all countries linked from pre-history by waves of human migration from continental Asia to the chain of islands along the continental edge and the Pacific islands. In continental narratives, Okinawa and its neighboring countries are culturally marginal; however, if we look at them from the sea, islands are rather creatively and imaginatively centered.

The purpose of publishing a new international journal in Okinawa today is to encourage study of these islands and their neighboring regions and the ocean which joins them, from historical, geographical, sociological, ethnological, and cultural perspectives. I firmly believe that this new journal will meet all our expectations and play a central role in the coming years.

IWAMASA Teruo
President
University of the Ryukyus

新しく国際誌を発刊するにあたって

　沖縄は海で囲まれた島嶼亜熱帯地域にあります。周囲には同じように広い海でつながる島々や国があり、そこでは歴史、文化、自然そして経済活動について興味ある研究が展開されてきました。日本の国立大学は、太平洋戦争以前からあった旧制度の大学や高等学校等を母体として出来ていますが、私共の琉球大学はそのような他の国立大学とは全く異なる設立の経緯と理念を持ち、多くの困難を克服し今日に至っています。日本、中国、太平洋戦争以後のアメリカなどとの間に種々の困難な問題が大学だけでなく沖縄に存在しています。他方、歴史的に見ますと沖縄は広く海でつながる多くの国々、中国、日本、韓国、フィリピン、タイ、マレーシア、スマトラなどと交易し、人々の移動にともない繁栄し琉球王国の成立をみています。

　今日、沖縄と周囲の海でつながる島々や国は、大陸からみれば文化的に周縁と考えられたり、政治的には国境としての重要性が考えられていますが、そのような大陸側からの一方的な見方ではなく、視点を変え島や海の側から見ることや考えることが重要で、より創造的でありイマージナティブであると考えます。新しく沖縄を中心とする島嶼圏の文化、歴史、社会、民族、自然などの研究を深め発展することを期待し、国際誌を発刊いたします。

国立大学法人琉球大学

学長　岩政　輝男

From the Director of the IIOS

Katsunori Yamazato

The International Institute for Okinawan Studies (IIOS) was established in April 2009 by combining the existing research centers — the American Studies Center, the Migration Studies Center, and the Asia-Pacific Island Studies Center — at the University of the Ryukyus. In addition to combining these centers, IIOS created two new research sections, Ryukyuan-Okinawan Studies and Contemporary Okinawan Studies.

IIOS aims to do research on Okinawa and areas that have a close relationship with Okinawa. To accomplish this aim, the Institute will carry out interdisciplinary research and projects in addition to research conducted by individual researchers at the Institute. The Institute hopes to be an international center for such research and to contribute to mutual understanding and promotion of research. To accomplish such an aim, we will publish a journal once a year.

This is the premier issue of *The International Journal of Okinawan Studies* (*IJOS*), which reflects the realization of a long-standing dream of Okinawan scholars to create a forum in which historians, literary critics, philosophers, political scientists, economists, natural scientists, and other analysts can present various perspectives on the culture, nature, and society of the Ryukyus and areas related to this region.

IJOS aims to be an international journal and thus invites articles from the international community of scholars. It is our strong desire to encourage multiple perspectives and promote serious discussion and debate in *IJOS* about Okinawa and areas that have close relationships with Okinawa, ultimately hoping that this journal will serve as a site for production of new knowledge.

『国際沖縄研究』の創刊にあたって

　国際沖縄研究所は、沖縄と沖縄に関連する地域と研究分野の個別的、学際的研究及びプロジェクトを推進し、国際的な研究拠点として、研究の進展と相互理解に貢献することを目的として、2009年4月1日に設立されました。本研究所は琉球大学に設置されていたアメリカ研究センター、移民研究センター、アジア・太平洋島嶼研究センターなどを統合し、さらに新しく琉球・沖縄の領域を研究する研究者が参加することで、沖縄と沖縄に関する地域の総合的な研究と新たな知の創造を目的としています。

　もっと具体的に言えば、研究所は以下の特徴を持つ共同研究拠点となることを目的としています。
（1）　総合的・学際的な共同研究の推進
（2）　理系とのコラボレーションによる文理融合型研究の推進
（3）　国内外の研究機関・研究者の連携・交流を促進するネットワーク型の拠点形成
（4）　沖縄から発信する新しい学知の形成

　また、国際沖縄研究所は、以下のような研究分野に関して、国内外の研究機関・研究者の連携のもとに、学際的・融合的に共同研究を推進します。
（1）　琉球／沖縄研究
（2）　現代沖縄研究
（3）　太平洋島嶼研究
（4）　アメリカ研究
（5）　アジア研究

　このように、本研究所は、沖縄と沖縄に関連する地域と研究分野に関する国際的な共同研究の中核拠点を形成し、アジア・太平洋地域における「知の津梁」としての役割を果たすことを願って設立されました。

　このような目的を達成するために、研究所は『国際沖縄研究』を発行します。本号はその創刊号です。さまざまな分野の研究者が、沖縄と沖縄に関連する地域に関して議論をする国際的なフォーラムの役割を担った国際学術誌を想定しています。ですから、掲載される論文は日本語と英語で書かれたものであることを条件とし、厳格な査読により高い水準を有するジャーナルとして、研究者が新しい学知の創造に共同で参画するものでありたいと願っています。

国際沖縄研究所
所長　山里　勝己

Okinawan Studies and Its Interventions

Gary Y. Okihiro*

介入する沖縄研究

ゲーリー・Y・オキヒロ

本論考は、流動するフィールドとして沖縄研究を記述することにより、島々を主題とする沖縄研究が大陸という神話に抗して叙述を行うことを争点化する。地域的隔たりをまたぐ場所としてのこの領域は地域と地域研究の双方を歴史化する。さらには日本とアメリカ合衆国の周縁である沖縄は国民／民族および均質性についての語りを再想像する場である。まとめて言うならば、沖縄研究とはこれら根本的 (foundational) とされてきた空間的・社会的カテゴリーおよび人間の生活条件に関する複数のとらえ方を疑問に付すものである。

Islands, like debris deposited along the curving bank of a vast river in the sea, the Kūrōshio current, trace the peaks called the Ryūkyūs. The summits rise along the eastern fringes of the Eurasian tectonic plate in a gentle bending arc, and press southward and eastward with the earth's mantle against the northward thrust of the Indian-Australian plate and the westward probing of the Pacific plate. Marine life—corals, seaweeds, mollusks, and fishes—percolating from the fecund Indo-West Pacific, navigate Oceania's currents to settle and make homes in Ryūkyūan waters. Those spatial formations of land and water and their movements, including their biotic communities, distinguish the discursive and material contours of what I propose constitutes Okinawan studies.

Situated at the tip of that triangle of oceanic life, the Ryūkyūs are connected with Indonesia at one corner and the Philippines at the other and all of the lands and waters hemmed therein. The islands' spread is more capacious, though, through mobilizations, which extend their reach beyond the Indo-West Pacific to the rest of Oceania and to the Eurasian continent and plate of which the islands form outposts along its easternmost frontier. Moreover, mirroring its liminal location bordering two of earth's edges, the Eurasian and Pacific plates, Okinawa and its study proceed in multiple directions and intervene in reductivist notions of landmasses, regions, and nations. In this essay, I cite some

---

* Professor, Columbia University コロンビア大学教授

of those provocations posed by Okinawan studies to spatial and social formations and thereby reference some of the intellectual gifts of this field to scholarship broadly conceived.

1. Nations[1]

The modern nation-state, a European configuration of relatively recent vintage, was conceived of as coterminous with a people. That is, originally, conjured kinship or "blood" tracings delimited the members of a nation-community, and insofar as people constituted a nation, the nation defined the people who were commonly referred to as "races." In that way, we came to know the British race, the German race, and so forth; the very term "nation" derives from the Latin for "birth," indicating a common ancestry or descent and hence blood and thus race. That mutual identity and identification is central to the idea of a nation/people. And as a creation of self (nation/people), it set and found itself against those the self was not, its other (other nations/peoples). Nation/people then, like the idea of race, assumed the natural order—timeless, universal, and absolute distinctions, which emerge from equally constant, certain, and peculiar others.

In reality, those inventions of nation/people are historical, arising in place and time through human agency, and their borders are fluid and under constant challenge and violation. Conquest and expansion altered those margins, incorporating novel lands and diverse peoples not originally designated as community members. Migration likewise produced new subjects albeit not always equal or welcome. Indeed, those transgressions of place, together with the imperial expansion of the idea of the "nation," exposes the simple mindedness of the original notion of an undivided, homogeneous nation and people.[2] Consider "Japan" and the "Japanese" as a nation/people.

A founding history recounts that "Japan" was the homeland created for a people, the "Japanese," who were descendants of Amaterasu, the sun goddess. As the fourteenth-century text, *Jinnō Shōtōki* or *Records of the Legitimate Succession of the Divine Sovereigns* declared: "Japan is the divine country. The heavenly ancestor it was who first laid its foundations, and the Sun Goddess left her descendants to reign over it forever and ever." And "Japan" was unique because it differed from "foreign" lands and peoples, its others. "Japanese," another document explained, were originally "of one blood and one mind," forming the "Yamato race," and later, absorbed and subordinated others of alien "blood" became "Japanese" as subjects of the emperor.[3]

That version of its origin gained traction with the transformation of Japan into a modern, European nation-state—the kokutai (national polity). As we know, following the Chinese worldview, kuni (country) once referred to a local domain or region that was familiar and orderly in contrast with the foreign and disorderly outside that domestic sphere. But under Western influences and maps, Japan came to see a larger world, an array of competing nation-states arising mainly from continents and their races arranged in a hierarchy of beauty, merit, and worth—white Europeans, yellow Asians, black Africans, red Americans, and brown Pacific Islanders. Those Enlightenment ideas were introduced to Japan by Westernizers such as Fukuzawa Yukichi in his *Sekai kunizukushi* (1869) or *Account of the Countries of the World*.[4]

Troubled by Russian expansion to its north in Kamchatka and the Kurile islands and to its south by Europeans in China and Southeast Asia, Japan sought to delimit and consolidate its borders. Ezo or Ainu lands and the Ryūkyū islands, formerly considered ikoku or "foreign countries" as listed in the *Wakan sansai zue* (1712) or *Japanese-Chinese Illustrated Encyclopaedia*, became parts of Japan as Hokkaido in 1869 and Okinawa prefecture ten years later. Further, assimilation or Japanization along with the suppression of Ainu and Uchinanchu language and culture were official policies of the Japanese state.[5]

Still, those of unrelated "blood" from the Ainu of Japan's northern frontier to the Uchinanchu of Japan's southern extremity stretched the physical area known as "Japan" and confounded the idea of its people, the "Japanese." The former regime of discrimination based upon jinshu or physical type fell to the new order of Yamato minzoku or folk by the late Meiji period. Although different (and inferior) minzoku discourse held, Ainu and Okinawans were Japanese insofar as they shared a national (Yamato) history and culture. In our time, the myth of "Japonesia," as proposed by novelist Shimao Toshio in his *Japonesia no nekko* (1961), helps to suture those fractures at both ends of the reconstituted nation/people. "Japan," Shimao claimed, formed a unitary racial, linguistic, and cultural sphere from Hokkaido to Okinawa, giving rise to the "Japanese" who are distinctive from their kindred others in Indonesia, Melanesia, Micronesia, and Polynesia of the same, as some believe, Austronesian language family.[6]

Like the Meiji contexts of imperialism and national constitution, Shimao's Japonesia emerges from a contemporary condition of kokusaika or internationalization. Amidst an increasing traffic of labor, capital, and culture, including migration and language shifts, anxieties over losses of identity and distinctiveness can easily translate into political capital. Thus in a July 1985 speech, then prime minister Nakasone Yasuhiro claimed that Japan's eternal racial purity advanced an "intelligent society" whereas the mixed and colored populations of the U.S. could only produce a dull, superficial nation.[7] And the International Research Center for Japanese Culture or Nichibunken, established in 1987, bankrolls research projects devoted to the promotion and preservation of a singular Japanese culture. Accordingly, like the Kokugakusha or National Learning scholars of the eighteenth century who insisted upon Japan's pure essence undiluted by Chinese contaminants, intellectuals continue to promote state ideology to reach a popular consensus and commonsense.

Vexing, nonetheless, are the contradictions posed by those at the nation's margins like the Ainu and their sustained movement for identity, culture, and indigenous rights and the Okinawans and their resilient drive for self-determination, anti-militarism, and peace.[8] At the same time (and I'd like to address briefly the twists and turns of Okinawan historiography), those resistances posed by subject peoples to their condition are often complicated and are at times oppositional while in other moments, complicitous. And yet, their interventions help to historicize invented traditions and trouble the placid waters of the national narrative.

Assimilation might have begun with Ryūkyūan Queen Shō Nei's poem, the last entry in the *Omoro-sōshi* (1610) and a year after the Satsuma invasion, which refers to "when the northerly wind blows." The myth of Amamikyu, possibly of Japanese derivation, traces the Okinawan peoples to divine origins and legitimizes the Shō rulers (1422–39, 1470–1879) who turned the kingdom from a southerly orientation toward Japan especially during the Tokugawa, which annexed the kingdom and transformed it into a prefecture in 1879.[9] Ifa Fuyū (1876–1947), the "father of Okinawan studies," believed that Okinawans came from Kyushu, following the tradition of Ryūkyūan historian, Haneji Chōshū (1617–75), who cited language and race as indicative of a Japanese descent and a migration southward.[10]

The Amamikyu creation story, according to Ifa, comes from the Amabe clan of Japan's Inland Sea who, in the third century, were in service to the Yamato. The Amabe, with their migration to Okinawa, became associated with the creator diety, "Amami person," who visited Okinawa from over the eastern sea. That eastern homeland, the nirai-kanai, was a great island of abundance and happiness and the source of all knowledge, including agricultural arts.[11] In those ways, Japanese culture seeped into the Ryūkyūan fountainhead, the *Omoro-sōshi*, with the complicity of some Okinawan intellectuals and rulers, thereby legitimizing Yamato political and cultural hegemony.

By contrast, on islands off Okinawa island, including Kouri, Miyako, and Ishigaki, the origin story is less grand. Their founders, a brother and sister, as in other Oceanic creation stories, are human, not divine. In addition, the sister-brother ancestors escape a flood to become the progenitors of a people, a narrative common to Southeast Asia and Oceania. "A long time ago, a long, long time ago," a Miyako island deluge account begins, "there were the Bunazee siblings. One fine day, the brother and sister went out to the fields to work. Suddenly from far off in the ocean, they saw a mountain-like wave . . . . The brother, concerned for his sister, [carried her] with great difficulty up a high hill . . . . The tsunami swept away all life from the land. Resigned, brother and sister built a grass hut and pledged to be husband and wife." The sister gave birth to the ajikai mollusk at first, and then to a human child. Gradually the island became filled with people who descended from the sister and brother and honored them as the kami who regenerated the island.[12]

Other suggestions of Okinawa's southern exposure is the ryūka or five-tone, musical scale, which resembles the widely influential Indonesian gamelan scale, the Okinawan liquor, awamori, which some link with the Thai drink lao-lon, and the South Asian use of banana fibers (bāsho) to weave textiles, bashōfu.[13] And Okinawan traders, at least since the mid-fourteenth century, frequented ports in Korea, Japan, and China, but also Java, Thailand, Viet Nam, and other places in Southeast Asia. That "South Seas" traffic was enabled by Ming China, which secured Okinawa (Chūzan) as a tributary state in 1372.[14] Chinese diplomats and merchants settled in Kumemura near Naha, and Ryūkyūan students went to China beginning in 1392.[15]

In fact, the Ryūkyū kingdom's central role in brokering exchanges among east Asian states and between east and southeast Asia for nearly three hundred years suggest to some a reversal of prominence between Okinawa and Japan.[16] Yanagita Kunio (1875–1962), a contemporary of Ifa Fuyū and the "father of Japanese folklore studies," posited the idea that the Japanese were migrants from the south through Okinawa from China as indicated by language, rice cultivation, and the cowrie shell monetary system. Like Murayama Shichirō and the archaeologist Kanaseki Takeo, Yanagita believed that the early Ryūkyūan language belonged to the Austronesian family of Taiwan and Oceania, and Kanaseki hypothesized two waves of Melanesian migrations to Okinawa and Japan. Both note the close cultural ties until the seventh century between Okinawa and Taiwan, from whence spread Austronesian languages, and Yanagita, in his *Kaijo no michi* (1961), traces Japanese people and language back to Okinawa and from there to Micronesia. His intention might have been to decouple Japan from a post-colonial Korea and continental Asia, and Yanagita, like others involved in a version of the "noble savage" discourse of the first half of the twentieth century called minzokugaku, might have seen Okinawans as native peoples unpolluted by the contaminants of modernization and linguistic changes that were sweeping Japan.[17] Still, his ideas provided an opening for Okinawa's escape from Japanese domination.

The power of Japan's colonization, nonetheless, rests in the privileges it confers. Thus, for instance, when the Fifth Industrial Exhibition in Osaka opened in 1903 with a display called "The House of Peoples" showing Koreans, Ainu, Taiwanese, and two Okinawan women being supervised by a Japanese man with a whip, some Okinawans expressed outrage because Okinawans, they insisted, were "Japanese."[18] And the "father of Okinawan studies," Ifa, a custodian of the Okinawan Prefectural Library, sought to redress the exclusion of Okinawan history and culture from Japanese discourses by grafting Ryūkyū's islands and peoples onto those of the Yamato trunk. That assimilation, that brand of "Okinawan studies" held, bestowed legitimacy and prestige to a conquered and subject kingdom and people.

In the aftermath of World War I when it acquired some of Germany's holdings in the Marianas, including Palau and the Caroline and Marshall islands, Japan held them as strategic bases for its imperial ambitions. Those "South Sea Islands" gave rise in Japan to sciences of the tropics similar to European and U.S. schools of tropical studies when their empires annexed the tropical band to their temperate homelands.[19] Anthropologists, biologists, medical researchers, and agricultural scientists visited the "South Seas" to study its lands and peoples and to see if Japanese bodies could adapt to the tropical sun, humidity, and heat. From 1914 to World War II, they studied societies and cultures, sexuality and pathology, and saw in their native, islander "other" measurable distinctions. Unlike the Japanese, they concluded, following the trail cut by European discourses and sciences of the tropics, those kanakas were of inferior intelligence, sexually promiscuous, and lazy. Still, even as those South Sea islanders, as its "other," helped to constitute the

9

"Japanese" identity, Okinawans, as so-called "Japan kanaka," formed a link with those natives of the "South Seas," revealing an unbroken line, a continuum along the spectrum of alleged difference between the contrived polarities of "Japanese" and "kanaka."[20]

That problem posed by Okinawans to the simpleminded idea of nation/people is a result of Okinawa's provisional membership in the "Japanese" race predicated upon ethnic assimilation and subjection to the nation-state. And historically and culturally, Okinawans confound the myth of Japonesia because of their southward as well as northward bearings from possible migrations and linguistic and cultural affiliations to commercial and political relations. They reveal the messiness and complexity of nation/people, not as singular in derivation and composition but as multiply layered comprised of human passages from the south and north and of linguistic, religious, economic, and political interactions, exchanges, and impositions. That is the beauty of the Ryūkyūan past.

Moreover, Okinawa's Oceanic compass points to an alternative origin story for the Japanese (Yamato) people. The Jōmon, central figures in the Yamato tradition, suggest descent not from northeast Asian migrants as is supposed by state ideology but from southern China or even southeast Asia. The hunter/gatherer Jōmon, physical anthropology shows, bear Micronesian and Polynesian characteristics, and they all ultimately derive from Malaysian stock. Okinawans, Japanese, and Ainu were a Jōmon people who inhabited those islands for about 10,000 years to 2300 B.C. Beginning around 400 B.C., they were absorbed by the Yayoi, agriculturalists from northeast China who spread into Kyūshū and moved south and north except Hokkaido where the Ainu predominated.[21]

That Jōmon foundation, an archaeologist speculates, was common not only to Hokkaido, Japan, and Okinawa but also Taiwan, east Asia, and the Philippines, and they spread into the Pacific with the migrations of Oceania's peoples, the Micronesians, Melanesians, and Polynesians from their southeast Asian homeland. "Therefore," he concludes, "in both the geographical and biological senses, Japan is an outpost of the Asian continent and, at the same time, an island group in the Oceanic world."[22] That view of Japan's multiple origins reconstituted by successive migrations from diverse sources and peoples is affirmed by linguistic evidence, which shows how shifts in the Japanese language mirror those population changes.[23]

2. Regions

World regions offer discrete units of study for fields within academics in the West. They are justified as coherent geographies of "shared ideas, related lifeways, and long-standing cultural ties,"[24] and, although delineated in disregard of national borders, they are invariably comprised of adjacent countries. The assumption underwriting that spatial design is that landed proximity maps social affinities and groupings of peoples. Hence, we have Okinawa and Japan belonging to the region called East Asia together with China and Korea, and we have other regions such as Southeast Asia, South Asia, and so forth. Those regions justify fields of study called area studies arising in the U.S. especially after

World War II and the onset of the Cold War, despite their resemblance to the ancient and now moribund idea of geographical determinism, which assigned to continents distinctive flora and fauna, including races, and to climates, racial and cultural constitutions.[25] Taxonomy produces coherence, enabling disciplines and explanations. That power to name and classify, of course, produced imperial discourses, which justified expansion, colonies, and the expropriation of land, labor, and culture.

The political nature of world regions and area studies as organized and practiced in the U.S. is shown in the idea of Southeast Asia. The so-called mainland or peninsula encompassing Burma, Thailand, Laos, Vietnam, and Cambodia, along its archipelagic or insular extension involving Singapore, Indonesia, Malaysia, the Philippines, and Brunei, was only grouped and named Southeast Asia during World War II. Previously they were divided into colonies of the British, Dutch, French, and U.S. empires, but in 1942 Japan's military rendered those distinctions irrelevant, especially in light of its ostensible mission of "Asia for Asians" and the dismantling of white supremacy. As a theatre of war along the color line in the midst of the twentieth century, Southeast Asia came into existence.[26] Even as nations, both imagined and real, are human designations of space, regions are "imaginings of what people have wanted the world to be,"[27] and they are conjured in actual struggles and contestations over space and thus possess material and political attributes.

Regions, as bounded spaces, naturalize a social project and construction.[28] The modern nation of Japan, as noted in the previous section of this article, arises from those discursive and material interests to discipline space, and in that, Okinawa is drawn into the rubrics of Japanese and East Asian studies. However, Okinawan studies could just as easily attach itself to Southeast Asian and Oceanic studies as argued by history, physical and cultural anthropology, longstanding economic ties, and contemporary political choices such as coalitions with the Ainu and other Pacific Islanders as indigenous peoples allied against the forces of colonization and assimilation. The field's multiple plantings astride spatial fabrications underscore regionalism's historical and material qualities and interests, and they suggest alternative ways to conceive of our world and its study.

Okinawan studies, it seems to me, is more than a national or regional project; the field, instead, thrives in violations of spatial orders. A good vehicle for transgressing and yet respecting bordered spaces is "local knowledge," as espoused by the anthropologist Clifford Geertz, involving a tack among "incommensurable perspectives on things, dissimilar ways of registering experiences and phrasing lives" and a placement of them "into conceptual proximity such that, though our sense of their distinctiveness is not reduced (normally, it is deepened), they seem somehow less enigmatical than they do when they are looked at apart."[29]

Geertz's proposition, assuredly a longstanding tenet of the comparative method, intrigues nonetheless in the light of imperial area studies or global spaces delineated and named, given coherence, contrasted with their others, and assigned significance by those with the authority. As pointed out by historian and cultural critic Arif Dirlik, there is no

Pacific region, only "a competing set of ideational constructs that project upon a certain location on the globe the imperatives of interest, power, or vision of these historically produced relationships."[30] But the Geertzian search for meaning rather than mechanics or structure and function to make sense of "particular things in particular places" such that they "take particular form and have particular impact" offers a compelling interest for Okinawan studies, which emerges from many local sites to engage the worlds around them.

I am thinking of the numerous islands, along with their distinctive dialects and orientations, all embraced within the compass of Okinawan studies. Consider, for instance, the elasticity of the Ryūkyūs chain and the pulls exerted on its northern islands such as Tokara and Amami by Kyushu and the Yamato and the gravitational forces of Taiwan and the Philippines upon the southern islands of Hateruma and Yonaguni. The middle ground is Okinawa island, which some maintain was peopled by its smaller, nearby neighbor, Kudaka island, where worshippers sit on Ishikibama beach facing southeastward from whence came the first humans, a brother and sister.[31] Farther south on Taketomi island, a brother and sister arrive after a drift voyage, and on Hateruma, plants, foods, and people from Luzon island in the Philippines make landfall.[32] Influences tug from the north and south, and they manifest themselves in local, original knowledges shaped through a process of endemism.

Those peculiar expressions serve to order and bestow meaning upon discrete daily activity, which can implicate simultaneously the local and the global. The kuba palm exemplifies both spatial dimensions. As local knowledge, the kuba is associated with sacred groves, utaki, and on Hatoma, the island's principal deity alights on the kuba leaves, which rustle, and descends to earth along the palm's curved trunk. Those sacred groves of kuba, in the words of a researcher, convey "an impressive sense of peace and quiet [and] communion with Nature."[33] At the same time, the kuba imparts an apprehension of activity and intercourse across local spaces and peoples. Heroic figures, both men and women, paddle their canoes on overnight voyages to the Philippines, and return with the kuba palm in their holds.[34] Whether a gift or a theft from abroad, the kuba palm was transplanted in Ryūkyūan soil and made local, central, and unique to Okinawan subjectivities. Further, the Ryūkyūan home is both the mountain tops along the eastern fringes of the Eurasian plate and the lands of the kuba palm to the south called Pae-Patera or Hae-Hateru(ma).[35] They are not distant oppositions, Okinawa and the Philippines; as sites of origin, they are both local.

3. Landmasses

The world historian Felipe Fernández-Armesto observed that civilizations are commonly considered land based formations, ignoring the fact that they "are grouped around waterways," from the China Sea to the Indian Ocean, the Mediterranean, and the Atlantic and Pacific.[36] This is a reality extended by Barbara Watson Andaya in her 2006 presidential address at the annual meeting of the Association for Asian Studies in San Francisco. In that exhortation to untie Asia from its area studies anchorage, Watson Andaya urges a focus on human interactions between land and sea because by stressing only landed initiatives we miss the interconnections and exchanges taking place upon the ocean's fluid, seemingly borderless space.[37]

What Fernández-Armesto failed to consider and Watson Andaya only gestured at is that continents and islands, the visible land formations upon which they center their contention, bed upon tectonic plates that exceed land's end, extending into ocean depths rarely penetrated by human comprehension. And along the plates' margins, where mass bumps up against mass, molten rock can ooze through the cracks and, given time, solidify and create seamounts, islands, and majestic mountain ranges packed with life's diversity. The totality of those biotic communities and their agencies, including but not limited to humans, should constitute the multiple, if not fluid subject matters of our concern.

In addition, as Watson Andaya noted, oceans are not mere appendages to lands nor are they unadorned waterways around which civilizations are established. As Pacific Islanders long held, the seas were a destination as well as a crossing, watery spaces were marked and named as readily as mountains and valleys, and humans formed relationships, including kinships, with those oceanic places and their resources and populations. Islanders, thus, occupied the water's spaces and thereby rendered them into places of social constitution and production. "Nearly every aspect of life in Micronesia is significantly influenced or controlled by the sea," a study noted. "As compared to the power and moods of the sea, the land is insignificant, humble, dull. The rhythm of life is dictated by the sea."[38]

Moreover, the Western penchant for land over water translates into an assumption that continents are the only landmass that matter. "Oceanic islands," a geologist began, "are small, young, isolated, simple, and subjected to a limited range of environmental factors." Accordingly scientists, famously Charles Darwin on the Galápagos islands and Margaret Mead on Samoa, found them to be ideal research laboratories because of their finite variables and controlled conditions. By contrast, he continued, "consider the continents. They are aggregates of every type of rock produced for billions of years, and most of their history is obscure . . . . The whole is obscured by every type of soil and by plants. Across the continents migrate animals and plants in constant flux. One can have little reason to hope that nature has conducted many controlled experiments on the continents."[39] Those scientific sentiments, those attributions of islands and continents, about simplicity and complexity, stasis and movement, are neither unique nor confined to that branch of human knowledge.

Myths abound in those metageographies or "spatial structures through which people order their knowledge of the world."[40] Widely held to be "tiny spaces" absent significance or moment, islands are commonly represented as feminine—vacant, passive, acted upon, stirred only by outside, manly manipulations.[41] That gendered definition of self or continents, as large, unbroken landmasses has its other, islands, as distant, small bodies of land surrounded by water. Boundedness appears to be an island's natural state, while boundlessness, a continent's. Yet in reality, there are no divides between islands and continents anchored as they both are onto tectonic plates, which form the earth's mantle, albeit of different densities beneath and above the oceans.

Carl Ritter, the most influential human geographer of the nineteenth century, saw continents as the major organizing principle of metageography. "Each continent," he was positive, "is like itself alone . . . each one was so planned and formed as to have its own special function in the progress of human culture." Inevitably, bound to that notion of social evolution and design was Ritter's view that at the apex was Europe, the homeland of white people, followed by Asia, the homeland of yellow people, Africa, of black people, and America, of red.[42] Continents, accordingly, suggested a metageography and hierarchy of civilizations and races.

By the twentieth century, continents were not only assumed to demarcate earth's surface but also to be a "natural" and sometimes divinely ordained state. In the U.S. about mid-century, America was divided into North and South and Antarctica and Australia acquired continental status. The resulting seven continents scheme gained rapid and widespread recognition, despite its glaring defects in the light of zoogeography's demonstration that life forms move relatively freely across continental boundaries, and the geology of tectonic plates that reveal India to be a part of Australia and not Eurasia, and North America's seamless connection to Eurasia under the Bering Sea. Continents not only prove inadequate as a schema of physical geography but of human geography as well insofar as they purport to map cultural and racial differences and their ranks. Still, because they conform to "the basic patterns of land and sea that spring to the eye from a world map," the continental system appears sensible and true.[43]

Likewise visually, islands, with few exceptions, emerge as tiny specks of land especially when seen from the perspective of the Pacific's immensity.[44] "Views of the Pacific from the level of macroeconomics and macropolitics often differ markedly from those from the level of ordinary people," explained Epeli Hau`ofa of his "sea of islands."[45] Accordingly, most versions of world history envision "the Pacific" as its Rim circled by economic and political giants, continental Asia and America. And while seas might serve as fertile breeding grounds for exchanges of goods, peoples, and ideas, they are not ordinarily conceived of as places of generation and production, but as mere watery routes, unlike landed roots, or even barren deserts, a land metaphor, to traverse and endure.[46]

Oceania's smallness is a state of mind, "mental reservations," imposed upon its peoples by European colonizers, Hau`ofa came to understand while driving from Kona to Hilo on the island of Hawai`i. "I saw such scenes of grandeur as I had not seen before: the eerie blackness of regions covered by recent volcanic eruptions; the remote majesty of Maunaloa, long and smooth, the world's largest volcano; the awesome craters of Kīlauea threatening to erupt at any moment; and the lava flow on the coast not far away," he described. "Under the aegis of Pele, and before my very eyes, the Big Island was growing, rising from the depths of a mighty sea. The world of Oceania is not small; it is huge and growing bigger every day."[47]

"Continental men," Hau`ofa continued, in their imperial enactments "drew imaginary lines across the sea, making the colonial boundaries that confined ocean peoples to tiny spaces for the first time." On the contrary, to Oceania's peoples, "their universe comprised not only of land surfaces, but the surrounding ocean as far as they could traverse and exploit it, the underworld with its fire-controlling and earth-shaking denizens, and the heavens above with their hierarchies of powerful gods and named stars and constellations that people could count on to guide their ways across the seas. Their world was anything but tiny."[48]

4. Okinawan Studies

Okinawan studies, accurately conceived, insists upon border crossings of lands and waters, continents and islands, world regions, and nation-states; those enclosures, the field reveals, are paltry human inscriptions and affectations. At the same time, those dominions have real effects on peoples' subjectivities and daily lives and on the mobile social order; they possess discursive and material properties, thereby exemplifying power and its contestation. Implicated within that struggle both as discourse and practice is Okinawan studies in its disruptive and creative senses.

As a subject of islands, Okinawan studies writes against the myth of continents; as an area astride regional divides, the field offers continuities as well as distinctions; and as a periphery of Japan and the U.S., Okinawa renders problematic the national archive and narratives of nation/people and homogeneity. The immensity of those endowments of Okinawan studies to scholarship broadly conceived must not be undervalued or dismissed by thank-you notes for contributions made to the general fund of human knowledge. Okinawan studies, rather, renders dubious those foundational spatial and social categories and ways of apprehending the human condition.

Moreover, knowledge organized around nations, regions, and landmasses constitute discourses involving ideology and language. Their power rests in their ability, conveyed through social apparatuses such schools, churches, policing and prisons, the military and media, and the like, to interpellate subjects as distinguished from their objects and to locate them within those regulatory regimes.[49] Japan and the Japanese, East Asia and East Asians, and continents and their races are examples of those metageographies, discourses, and subjectivities. Multiply and liminally positioned, Okinawa and its peoples expose and contest those imperial estates.

At the same time, Okinawan studies as a discourse can engender the same hegemonic capacities as its opposition. It can essentialize spaces and subjectivities, produce and police ideologies and languages, and interdict agency and travel. Okinawan studies, as we know from its beginnings, has validated governing notions of landmasses, regions, and nations. The problem for Okinawan studies is to free itself from confining ideologies using their language and, at the same time, to visualize imaginative, alternative spaces, understandings, and articulations of self and society.

Such registers arise from the local, the familiar, and their ascent is not burdened by the parceling of lands, regions, civilizations, nations, or peoples, despite their gravities of mass and proximity, kinship and tradition, literatures and archives. Instead, they can confuse certainties, disturb discipline, and energize enigmas while, in Clifford Geertz's words, they "attempt to come to terms with the diversity of the ways human beings construct their lives in the act of leading them."[50] Those interventions ascend from the particular, the local, while retracing their roots and ramifications can launch remarkable voyages across and through lands and seas, radiating and branching in sundry directions.

A case in point is the Shiraho, Ishigaki island creation account of humans who emerge from the amankani (hermit crab) hole. The story appears to validate the land claims of Shiraho's people, but tracing its derivations can complicate and extend considerably its spatial dimensions. Shiraho's origin story might in fact be an import from Hateruma island whose migrants repopulated the town following the devastating 1771 tsunami, which killed about a third of Ishigaki island's population and nearly all of Shiraho's people.[51] Hateruma islanders, as stated earlier, maintain close connections with the Philippines, suggesting a more distant site of origin. Additionally, Ishigaki's people might have come from Taketomi island, which some Ishigaki islanders regard as their ancestral home, whereas Taketomi islanders tell a brother-sister, drift voyage origin story,[52] a creation chronicle of vast Oceania. In just that sense, Shiraho, as a people and place, connects humans with other life forms, islanders with other islanders, and land with sea.

Okinawan studies in motion, like the liquid currents, which define the field's contours and subject matters, reveals how local knowledge or apprehensions of particular things in particular places engages and grapples with ideas and practices in disparate places and times. It can thereby extricate and liberate. And its reach, the influences of this variety of Okinawan studies is only circumscribed by our abilities, energies, and imaginations.

Notes

1) This section, "nations," is a revised, enlarged version originally published as "Preliminary Thoughts on Migration and the Nation/People," in *Proceedings for the International Symposium: Human Migration and the 21st Century Global Society—Immigration, Language, and Literature*, edited by Nakahodo Masanori, Yamazato Katsunori, and Ishihara Masahide (University of the Ryūkyūs, March 2009), 79–84.
2) This problem is of course the reason for the "imagined community" of the nation as described by Benedict Anderson in his *Imagined Communities: Reflections on the Origin and Spread of Nationalism* (London: Verso, 1983).
3) As quoted in John W. Dower, *War Without Mercy: Race and Power in the Pacific War* (New York: Pantheon Books, 1986), 222.
4) Tessa Morris-Suzuki, "A Descent into the Past: The Frontier in the Construction of Japanese Identity," in *Multicultural Japan: Paleolithic to Postmodern*, eds. Donald Denoon et al. (Cambridge, England: Cambridge University Press, 1996), 82–88.
5) Morris-Suzuki, "Descent," 83, 85–86.
6) Hokama Shūzen, "Okinawa in the Matrix of Pacific Ocean Culture," in *Okinawan Diaspora*, ed. Ronald Y. Nakasone (Honolulu: University of Hawai'i Press, 2002), 49.
7) See Yōichi Higuchi, "When Society Itself Is the Tyrant," *Japan Quarterly* 35:4 (October-December

1988): 350–56.
8) See, e.g., Hanazaki Kohei, "Ainu Moshir and Yaponesia: Ainu and Okinawan Identities in Contemporary Japan," in Denoon, *Multicultural Japan*, 117–31; and Katarina Sjöberg, "Positioning Oneself in the Japanese Nation State: The Hokkaido Ainu Case," in *Transcultural Japan: At the Borderlands of Race, Gender, and Identity*, eds. David Blake Willis and Stephen Murphy-Shigematsu (London: Routledge, 2008), 197–216.
9) Ronald Y. Nakasone, "An Impossible Possibility," in Nakasone, *Okinawan Diaspora*, 20–21.
10) Hokama, "Okinawa," 49.
11) Toichi Mabuchi, "Tales Concerning the Origin of Grains in the Insular Areas of Eastern and Southeastern Asia," *Asian Folklore Studies* 23:1 (1964): 6–18; Ronald Y. Nakasone, "Agari-umaai: An Okinawan Pilgrimage," in Nakasone, *Okinawan Diaspora*, 144, 147–48; and Mitsugu Sakihara, "History of Okinawa," in *Uchinanchu: A History of Okinawans in Hawaii* (Honolulu: Ethnic Studies Oral History Project, University of Hawaii at Manoa, 1981), 7–8.
12) As cited in Hokama, "Okinawa," 46. For other origin stories of the Oceania type, see G. H. Kerr, "The Eastern Islands," T1-2, Y1-2, unpubl. manuscript, GHK1J04003, G. H. Kerr Papers, Okinawa Prefectural Archives. And on the sister-kami figure as an Oceania type, see Toichi Mabuchi, "Spiritual Predominance of the Sister," in *Ryukyuan Culture and Society: A Survey*, ed. Allan H. Smith (Honolulu: University of Hawaii Press, 1964), 79–91.
13) Hokama, "Okinawa," 46, 50–52.
14) On the Southeast Asian trade, see Shunzo Sakamaki, "Ryukyu and Southeast Asia," *Journal of Asian Studies* 23:3 (May 1964): 383–89; and Sakihara, "History," 7. See Robert K. Sakai, "The Satsuma-Ryukyu Trade and the Tokugawa Seclusion Policy," *Journal of Asian Studies* 23:3 (May 1964): 391–403, for the trade with Japan.
15) Mitsugu Matsuda, "The Ryukyuan Government Scholarship Students to China, 1392–1868," *Monumenta Nipponica* 21:3/4 (1966): 273–304.
16) See, e.g., Josef Kreiner, "Notes on the History of European-Ryūkyūan Contacts," in *Sources of Ryūkyūan History and Culture in European Collections*, Monograph No. 13, ed. Josef Kreiner (Tokyo: German Institute of Japanese Studies, 1996), 15–41; and Josef Kreiner, "Ryūkyūan History in Comparative Perspective," in *Ryûkyû in World History*, ed. Josef Kreiner (Bonn, Germany: Bier'sche Verlagsanstalt, 2001), 1–39.
17) Hokama, "Okinawa," 48–49; Sakihara, "History," 4; and Alan S. Christy, "The Making of Imperial Subjects in Okinawa," *positions* 1:3 (Winter 1993): 623, 625–27, fn. 49, p. 637.
18) Christy, "Making," 607–08.
19) See e.g., my *Pineapple Culture: A History of the Tropical and Temperate Zones* (Berkeley: University of California Press, 2009).
20) Tomiyama Ichirō, "Colonialism and the Sciences of the Tropical Zone: The Academic Analysis of Difference in 'the Island Peoples'," *positions* 3:2 (Fall 1995): 367–91.
21) On the commonalities but also divergences of Jōmon culture in Japan and Okinawa, see Richard Pearson, "The Place of Okinawa in Japanese Historical Identity," in Denoon, *Multicultural Japan*, 95–116.
22) Katayama Kazumichi, "The Japanese as an Asia-Pacific Population," in Denoon, *Multicultural Japan*, 24–27, 28.
23) John C. Maher, "North Kyushu Creole: A Language-Contact Model for the Origins of Japanese," in Denoon, *Multicultural Japan*, 31–45.
24) Martin W. Lewis and Kären E. Wigen, *The Myth of Continents: A Critique of Metageography* (Berkeley: University of California Press, 1997), 158.
25) See, e.g., my *Pineapple Culture*, 5–25.
26) Lewis and Wigen, *Myth of Continents*, 170–73; and Matthew H. Edney, "Mapping Parts of the World," in *Maps: Finding Our Place in the World*, eds. James R. Akerman and Robert W. Karnow, Jr. (Chicago: University of Chicago Press, 2007), 139.
27) Edney, "Mapping," 139.
28) See, e.g., the process by which scholars assigned coherence to the region, Southeast Asia, in Lewis and

Wigen, *Myth of Continents*, 173–76.
29) Clifford Geertz, *Local Knowledge: Further Essays in Interpretive Anthropology* (New York: Basic Books, 1983), 15, 233.
30) Arif Dirlik, "The Asia-Pacific Idea: Reality and Representation in the Invention of a Regional Structure," *Journal of World History* 3:1 (Spring 1992): 56.
31) From a tour of Kudaka island led by Akamine Masanobu, July 4, 2009.
32) G. H. Kerr, [untitled manuscript], 46–61, 138, 160–61, 171, 178, GHK1J04004, G. H. Kerr Papers, Okinawa Prefectural Archives.
33) G. H. Kerr, "Far Eastern Islands," 142, GHK1J04002, G. H. Kerr Papers, Okinawa Prefectural Archives.
34) Ibid., 153; and Kerr, "Eastern Sea Islands," 17.
35) Kerr, "Eastern Sea Islands," 17.
36) Felipe Fernández-Armesto, *Millennium: A History of the Last Thousand Years* (New York: Charles Scribner's Sons, 1995), 20. See also, Sugata Bose, *A Hundred Horizons: The Indian Ocean in the Age of Global Empire* (Cambridge, Massachusetts: Harvard University Press, 2006).
37) Barbara Watson Andaya, "Oceans Unbounded: Traversing Asia across 'Area Studies'," *Journal of Asian Studies* 65:4 (November 2006): 669–90.
38) As quoted in Philip E. Steinberg, *The Social Construction of the Ocean* (Cambridge, England: Cambridge University Press, 2001), 53, 55. See also, Paul D'Arcy, *The People of the Sea: Environment, Identity, and History in Oceania* (Honolulu: University of Hawai`i Press, 2006) on the sea as a home, site of production, and a source of belief systems.
39) H. W. Menard, *Islands* (New York: Scientific American Books, 1986), 1. On islands as scientific laboratories, see Menard, *Islands*; Robert H. MacArthur and Edward O. Wilson, *The Theory of Island Biogeography* (Princeton, New Jersey: Princeton University Press, 1967); and Edward J. Larson, *Evolution's Workshop: God and Science in the Galapagos Islands* (New York: Basic Books, 2001).
40) Lewis and Wigen, *Myth of Continents*, ix.
41) See e.g., Judith Williamson, "Woman Is an Island: Femininity and Colonization," in *Studies in Entertainment: Critical Approaches to Mass Culture*, ed. Tania Modleski (Bloomington: Indiana University Press, 1986), 99–118.
42) Lewis and Wigen, *Myth of Continents*, ix, 30.
43) Lewis and Wigen, *Myth of Continents*, 31–35.
44) For evolving European views of islands, see especially John Gillis, *Islands of the Mind: How the Human Imagination Created the Atlantic World* (New York: Palgrave Macmillan, 2004); Rod Edmond and Vanessa Smith (eds.), *Islands in History and Representation* (London: Routledge, 2003); and John Fowles, *Islands* (Boston: Little, Brown, 1978). On Pacific islands, see Bernard Smith, *European Vision and the South Pacific* (New Haven, Connecticut: Yale University Press, 1960); Greg Dening, *Islands and Beaches: Discourse on a Silent Land, Marquesas 1774–1880* (Honolulu: University Press of Hawaii, 1980); Rod Edmond, *Representing the South Pacific: Colonial Discourse from Cook to Gauguin* (Cambridge, England: Cambridge University Press, 1997); Nicholas Thomas, *In Oceania: Visions, Artifacts, Histories* (Durham, North Carolina: Duke University Press, 1997); and K. R. Howe, *Nature, Culture, and History: The "Knowing" of Oceania* (Honolulu: University of Hawai`i Press, 2000).
45) Epeli Hau`ofa, "Our Sea of Islands," *Contemporary Pacific* 6:1 (Spring 1994): 148–61. For an earlier version of Hau`ofa's "Our Sea," and responses to it, see Eric Waddell, Vijay Naidu, and Epeli Hau`ofa (eds.), *A New Oceania: Rediscovering Our Sea of Islands* (Suva, Fiji: University of the South Pacific, 1993).
46) For a study of the social construction of oceanic space, its uses, regulations, and representations, see Steinberg, *Social Construction*.
47) Hau`ofa, "Our Sea," 151, 152.
48) Ibid., 152, 153. See also, Steinberg, *Social Construction*, 39–67 for a comparative view, including a Micronesian perspective, of the ocean.
49) See, e.g., Louis Althusser, *Essays on Ideology* (London: Verso, 1984).

50) Geertz, *Local Knowledge*, 16.
51) Oral history, Ishigaki Shigeru, Ishigaki City, July 24, 2009, conducted by Wesley Ueunten.
52) G. H. Kerr, [untitled manuscript], 132, 136,138.

References

Althusser, L. (1984). *Essays on ideology*. London: Verso.
Andaya, B. W. (2006, November). Oceans unbounded: Traversing Asia across "area studies." *Journal of Asian Studies*, 65(4), 669–90.
Bose, S. (2006). *A hundred horizons: The Indian Ocean in the age of global empire*. Cambridge, Massachusetts: Harvard University Press.
Christy, A. S. (1993, Winter). The making of imperial subjects in Okinawa. *positions*, 1:3, 623, 625–27, fn. 49, 637.
D'Arcy, P. (2006). *The People of the sea: Environment, identity, and history in Oceania*. Honolulu: University of Hawai'i Press.
Dening, G. (1980). *Islands and beaches: Discourse on a silent land, Marquesas 1774–1880*. Honolulu: University Press of Hawaii.
Dirlik, A. (1992, Spring). The Asia-Pacific idea: Reality and representation in the invention of a regional structure. *Journal of World History*, 3:1, 56.
Dower, J. W. (1986). *War Without Mercy: Race and Power in the Pacific War*. New York: Pantheon Books.
Edmond, R. & Smith,V. (Eds.) (2003). *Islands in History and Representation*. London: Routledge, 2003.
Edney, M. H. (2007). Mapping parts of the world. In J. R. Akerman & R. W. Karnow, Jr. (Eds.), *Maps: Finding Our Place in the World* (p. 139), Chicago: University of Chicago Press.
Edmond, R. (1997). *Representing the South Pacific: Colonial discourse from Cook to Gauguin*. Cambridge, England: Cambridge University Press.
Fernández-Armesto, F. (1995). *Millennium: A history of the last thousand years*. New York: Charles Scribner's Sons.
Fowles, J. (1978). *Islands*. Boston: Little, Brown.
Geertz, C. (1983). *Local knowledge: Further essays in interpretive anthropology*. New York: Basic Books.
Gillis, J. (2004). *Islands of the mind: How the human imagination created the Atlantic world*. New York: Palgrave Macmillan.
Hanazaki, K. (1996). Ainu moshir and yaponesia: Ainu and Okinawan identities in contemporary Japan. In D. Denoon, et al. (Eds.), *Multicultural Japan: Paleolithic to postmodern* (pp. 117–31). Cambridge, England: Cambridge University Press.
Hau'ofa, E. (1994, Spring). Our sea of islands. *Contemporary Pacific*, 6(1), 148–61.
Higuchi,Y. (1988, October-December). When society itself is the tyrant. *Japan Quarterly*, 35(4), 350–56.
Hokama, S. (2002). Okinawa in the matrix of pacific ocean culture. In R. Y. Nakasone (Ed.), *Okinawan Diaspora*. Honolulu: University of Hawai'i Press.
Howe, K. R. (2000). *Nature, culture, and history: The "knowing" of Oceania*. Honolulu: University of Hawai'i Press.
Ishigaki, S. (2009, July 24). Oral history. Conducted by Wesley Ueunten. Ishigaki City.
Katayama, K. (1996). "The Japanese as an Asia-Pacific Population," In D. Denoon, et al., (Eds.), *Multicultural Japan: Paleolithic to postmodern* (pp. 24–27, 28). Cambridge, England: Cambridge University Press.
Kerr, G. H. [untitled manuscript], 46–61, 138, 160–61, 171, 178, GHK1J04004, G. H. Kerr Papers, Okinawa Prefectural Archives.
Kerr, G. H. "Far Eastern Islands," 142, GHK1J04002, G. H. Kerr Papers, Okinawa Prefectural Archives.
Kerr, G. H. "The Eastern Islands," T1-2, Y1-2, unpubl. manuscript, GHK1J04003, G. H. Kerr Papers, Okinawa Prefectural Archives.
Kreiner, J. (1996). Notes on the history of European-Ryūkyūan contacts. In J. Kreiner. (Ed.), *Sources of Ryūkyūan history and culture in European collections*, Monograph No. 13, (pp. 15–41), Tokyo: German

Institute of Japanese Studies.

Kreiner, J. (2001). Ryūkyūan history in comparative perspective. In J. Kreiner. (Ed.), *Ryûkyû in World History*. (pp. 1–39), Bonn, Germany: Bier'sche Verlagsanstalt.

Larson, E. J. (2001). *Evolution's workshop: God and science in the Galapagos Islands*. New York: Basic Books.

Lewis, M. W. & Wigen, K. E. (1997). *The myth of continents: A critique of metageography*. Berkeley: University of California Press.

Mabuchi, T. (1964). Spiritual predominance of the sister. In A. H. Smith (Ed.), *Ryukyuan Culture and Society: A Survey* (pp. 79–91), Honolulu: University of Hawaii Press.

MacArthur, R. H. & Wilson, E. O. (1967). *The theory of island biogeography*. Princeton, New Jersey: Princeton University Press.

Maher, J. C. (1996). North Kyushu creole: A language-contact model for the origins of Japanese. In D. Denoon, et al., (Eds.), *Multicultural Japan: Paleolithic to postmodern*. (pp. 31–45). Cambridge, England: Cambridge University Press.

Matsuda,M. (1966). The Ryukyuan government scholarship students to China, 1392–1868. *Monumenta Nipponica*, 21:3/4, 273–304.

Menard, H. W. (1986). *Islands*. New York: Scientific American Books.

Morris-Suzuki, T. (1996). A descent into the past: the frontier in the construction of Japanese identity. In Denoon, D., et al. (Eds.), *Multicultural Japan: Paleolithic to Postmodern* (pp. 82–88). Cambridge, England: Cambridge University Press.

Nakasone, R. Y. (2002). An impossible possibility. In R. Y. Nakasone (Ed.), *Okinawan diaspora* (pp. 20–21). Honolulu: University of Hawai'i Press.

Nakasone, R. Y. (2002). Agari-umaai: An Okinawan pilgrimage. In R. Y. Nakasone. (Ed.), *Okinawan diaspora* (pp. 144, 147–48). Honolulu: University of Hawai'i Press.

Okihiro, G. Y. (2009, March). Preliminary thoughts on migration and the nation/people." In M. Ishihara (Ed.), *Proceedings for the International Symposium: Human Migration and the 21st Century Global Society— Immigration, Language, and Literature* (pp. 79–84), University of the Ryukyus, Okinawa, Japan.

Okihiro, G. Y. (2009). *Pineapple culture: A history of the tropical and temperate zones*. Berkeley: University of California Press.

Pearson, R. (1996). The place of Okinawa in Japanese historical identity. In D. Denoon, et al., (Eds.), *Multicultural Japan: Paleolithic to postmodern* (pp. 95–116). Cambridge, England: Cambridge University Pres.

Sakamaki, S. (1964, May). Ryukyu and Southeast Asia. *Journal of Asian Studies*, 23:3, 383–89.

Sakai, R. K. (1964, May). The Satsuma-Ryukyu trade and the Tokugawa seclusion policy. *Journal of Asian Studies* 23(3), 391–403.

Sakihara, M. (1981). History of Okinawa. In *Uchinanchu: A History of Okinawans in Hawaii*. Honolulu: Ethnic Studies Oral History Project (pp. 7–8). University of Hawaii at Manoa.

Sjöberg, K. (2008). Positioning oneself in the Japanese nation state: the Hokkaido Ainu case. In D. B. Willis & S. Murphy-Shigematsu (Eds.), *Transcultural Japan: At the borderlands of race, gender, and identity* (pp. 197–216). London: Routledge, 2008.

Smith, B. (1960). *European vision and the South Pacific*. New Haven, Connecticut: Yale University Press.

Steinberg, P. E. (2001). *The Social construction of the Ocean*. Cambridge, England: Cambridge University Press.

Thomas, N. (1997). *In Oceania: Visions, artifacts, histories*. Durham, North Carolina: Duke University Press.

Tomiyama, I. (1995, Fall), Colonialism and the sciences of the tropical zone: The academic analysis of difference in "the Island peoples." *positions*, 3:2, 367–91.

Waddell, E., Naidu V., & Epeli Hau'ofa, (Eds.). (1993). *A new Oceania: Rediscovering our sea of islands*. Suva, Fiji: University of the South Pacific.

Williamson, J. (1986). Woman is an island: Femininity and colonization. In Modleski, T. (Ed.), *Studies in Entertainment: Critical Approaches to Mass Culture*. (pp. 99–118), Bloomington: Indiana University Press.

明清交替期の中琉日関係再考
──琉球国王の册封問題を中心に──

西 里 喜 行*

The Problem of Royal Investiture in the Ryukyu Kingdom in the Ming-Qing Transition Period

NISHIZATO Kikou

Shoken（尚賢、a Ryukyu King）chose a path that strengthened the ties between his and the Nan（Southern）Ming（南明）administration in China at the expense of the Ryukyu Kingdom's relationship with the Qing Dynasty（清朝）. One reason was the longstanding affiliation between Ryukyu and the Ming Dynasty（明朝）over the course of 250 years. Another more important reason was that the Nan Ming accepted Ryukyu's request to restart the raw silk trade. The Southern Ming authorities made an effort to obtain the loyalty of Shoken, but militarily, at least, they could not invest him as the Ryukyu king. Japanese authorities（Satsuma 薩摩 and Edobakufu 江戸幕府）considered the Qing Dynasty a threat to Japan and admitted tacitly that Shoken chose the Southern Ming. After Shoken died, Shositsu（尚質）inherited the throne and adopted an ambiguous diplomatic policy toward the Southern Ming and the Qing Dynasty for reasons of economic pragmatism. Therefore, he did not wish for that the Qing ambassador to come to the Ryukyus and requested instead that the Ryukyu delegation bring back a signature stamp and an Imperial edict. The Qing emperor（Shunzhi 順治）declared that an ambassador would be dispatched to Ryukyu to clarify the authority of the Qing Dynasty, but after several years, it canceled the mission to Ryukyu because of the risks involved in marine transit.

The Kangxi（康熙）emperor reverted to the policy of the Shunzhi emperor, positively promoted the policy of investiture of Shositsu, and ordered the Qing ambassador to travel to Ryukyu. Simultaneously, the Kangxi emperor sent an Imperial edict to Shositsu and indicated that the investiture of Shositsu had been delayed due to neglect of duty by the ambassador. Furthermore, Kangxi indicated that the crime of neglect of duty by the Qing ambassador had been punished and that representatives had been ordered to sail to Ryukyu to invest Shositsu. Satsuma and Bakufu feared that the Qing ambassador would force his own manners and customs on the Ryukyus but finally tacitly accepted the investiture of Shositsu as the Ryukyu king by the Kangxi emperor.

---

* 沖縄大学教授　Professor, Okinawa University

はじめに

　近代以前の東アジアにおいては、中国王朝が国際秩序の中心に位置していた。中国王朝の皇帝が周辺諸国（藩属国）の首長を国王として認知することを冊封という。冊封には二つの方法があった。一つは、皇帝の使者（天使＝冊封使）を派遣して、勅書（冊封詔書）を直接国王に交付する方法、即ち頒封である。もう一つは、冊封使を派遣せず、冊封詔書を藩属国の使節に交付して持ち帰らせる方法、即ち領封である[1]。琉球国王の場合は、いずれも頒封方式で冊封されている。頒封方式による冊封に当たっては、次のような外交的手続き（手順）を経ることが必要とされた。即ち、①前国王の訃報（告訃）→②王位継承者（国王世子）の冊封要請（請封）→③中国王朝の冊封決定通知→④冊封使迎接の使者（迎接使＝接封使）派遣→⑤冊封使の来琉→首里城における冊封式典、⑥冊封に感謝する謝恩使の派遣、という外交プロセスである。

　冊封前後のプロセスにおいて、前国王の死去を報告する時期や新国王の冊封を要請する時期の決定は、琉球国内の王位継承者の判断に委ねられていた[2]。王位継承から冊封までの期間、即ち王位継承者が自らを国王世子と称する期間は、通常数年以内である。通常とは異なり、王位継承から冊封までに、長期の時間を必要としたのは尚泰（18年）、尚寧（17年）、尚質（15年）、尚貞（14年）、尚豊（12年）の場合である。また、請封したにもかかわらず冊封されなかったのは尚賢の場合である。以上の六名の王位継承者はいずれも琉球王国が対外的危機に直面していた時期の国王（世子）であることに注目すべきであろう。とりわけ中国大陸における明清交替の歴史的転換期に、琉球王国で王位を継承した尚賢・尚質・尚貞の三名は、中国王朝の皇帝から冊封を受けるに当たって、大きな困難に直面せざるを得なかったことに注目したい。

　本稿の課題は、明清交替期における琉球国王の冊封をめぐる問題を、中国・琉球・日本の相互関係（中琉日関係）の中に位置づけて再検討することである。ただ、ここでいう明清交替期とは、清朝の中国支配の開始（1644年）から三藩の乱を経て台湾の鄭氏政権の崩壊（1683年）に至る40年間の歴史的転換期全体を包括する概念であるが、本稿では、その前半期における尚賢・尚質の冊封問題を中心に据えて、先行研究を踏まえながら[3]、主として琉球側がどのような選択肢を模索し追求したのかという視点から、この時期の中琉日関係の諸相を再検討・再考察してみたい。

1. 尚賢の請封前後の中琉日関係の諸相

1-1　明末の中琉日関係における諸問題

　薩摩島津軍の琉球侵攻（1609年）から明清交替の開始（1644年）に至る17世紀の前半、明朝と琉球王国の間には次のような困難な問題が生じていた。

　第一に貢期改定問題。萬暦40（1612）年、明朝皇帝は琉球が薩摩島津軍の侵攻を蒙って疲弊しているという理由で、十年後に進貢するよう命じた。その結果、進貢貿易の機

会を大幅に制限され、経済的に大打撃を蒙ることになった琉球は、従来の貢期（二年一貢）の回復を繰り返し要請し、十年後の天啓3（1623）年には五年一貢へ、さらに十一年後の崇禎7（1634）年には旧来の二年一貢に復し、貢期改定問題はようやく解決する[4]。

第二に尚豊の冊封問題。薩摩島津軍の侵攻を蒙った後も、薩摩藩に面従腹背の抵抗を続けていた尚寧王は泰昌1（1620）年に死去した。王位を継承した尚豊は、尚寧王の死去を明朝へ報告するとともに、冊封を要請する使節（請封使）を、天啓2（1622）年・5（1625）年・6（1626）年・7（1627）年・崇禎3（1630）年と繰り返し派遣した。請封使の派遣が繰り返されたのは五年一貢の貢期を実質的に短縮するための措置でもあったと思われる。尚豊の冊封が異常に遅延したのは、薩摩支配下の琉球に疑惑の目を向けていた明朝側が薩摩の進貢貿易への介入を警戒したからである。琉球側の度重なる請封の熱意を受け止めて、崇禎6（1633）年、明朝は冊封使（杜三策・楊掄）を琉球へ派遣し、尚豊を冊封した[5]。

第三に白糸貿易をめぐる王銀詐取事件（琉球使節の密貿易摘発事件）。尚豊冊封の翌年（1634年）、薩摩藩は琉球の進貢貿易に介入し大量の資金を投入した。福建へ派遣された琉球使節は明朝の白糸貿易取り締まりが厳しいことを知りながらも、薩摩側の要求（圧力）を回避できず、福建で牙行（仲介商人）や通訳らの協力を得て大量の白糸を購入した。福建当局は琉球人が購入した白糸を密貿易品として摘発・没収した。同様の密貿易摘発事件は二年後の崇禎9（1636）年にも繰り返された。明朝は翌年（1637年）以降、琉球の白糸貿易を厳禁した。以後、琉球側にとっては、白糸貿易の再開・許可をかちとることが大きな課題となる[6]。

第四に白糸貿易再開問題と尚賢の冊封問題。薩摩の期待に反して白糸貿易に失敗した尚豊王は、薩摩当局から拝領した抹茶を飲んで即死した[7]。崇禎14（1641）年、尚賢が王位を継承すると、翌15（1642）年の進貢の年に、進貢使（蔡錦ら）を派遣して尚豊王の死去を報告し、併せて尚賢の冊封を要請した[8]。しかし、明朝から冊封決定の通知がなく、尚賢は崇禎17（1644）年にも、再度尚豊王死去の報告と冊封要請のための使節（請封使）を派遣し、福建布政使司と礼部あてに正式に請封の咨文（公文書）を提出することにした[9]。請封使の金応元は尚賢の冊封要請の件だけでなく、白糸貿易の許可・再開を要請する任務をも帯びていた[10]。

1-2　南明政権と琉球王国と薩摩藩（江戸幕府）

進貢使兼請封使の金応元らが福州へ到着した頃、明朝は滅亡して清軍が北京へ入城し、清朝の中国支配が始まっていた。以後、約40年間、明朝復活の目標を掲げた福王・唐王・魯王・永明王や鄭成功らの南明政権が各地に相次いで樹立され、清朝の中国支配に抵抗したため、明清交替の動乱が続くことになる[11]。

明朝滅亡の直後、南京では福王（弘光帝）が即位して弘光政権を樹立した。福州でこの情報に接した金応元らは、自らの判断にもとづいて崇禎17（1644）年10月〜11月頃南京へ赴き、弘光政権へ進貢・請封すると同時に、白糸貿易の許可を要請したところ、弘光

政権は金応元らの要請をほぼ全面的に承認し[12]、冊封使の派遣についても計画はされたものの実行されず[13]、福州左衛指揮の花煾を招撫使として派遣しただけであった。花煾は弘光元（1645）年2月琉球へ到着、首里城で弘光帝の詔書を宣読した[14]。

琉球側は花煾の来琉についての情報を直ちに薩摩藩へも伝達したが、薩摩藩は花煾が招撫使として来琉したことに大きな関心を示しつつも、琉球側に特別の指示を与えているわけではない[15]。弘光政権が冊封使を派遣するのに先だってまず招撫使を派遣したのは、明朝と琉球の関係を自動的に継承するのではなく、琉球との新たな関係を構築する必要があると判断したからであろう[16]。琉球側は花煾の招撫に応じて弘光政権の正統性を認め、宗主国として清朝ではなく南明を選択したわけであるが、南明に対して改めて尚賢の冊封を要請（請封）したのかどうか明らかではない。

尚賢は弘光元（1645）年4月崇禎帝毅宗への進香使として毛大用らを、招撫使花煾の帰国案内役として鄭子廉らを福州へ派遣している[17]。しかし、毛大用らの福州到着前後に、南京の弘光政権は清軍の攻撃を受けて崩壊した。その直後の隆武元（1645）年9月、唐王（隆武帝）が福建で即位し、隆武政権を樹立した。南京から福州へ戻っていた進貢使兼請封使の金応元らは直ちに隆武帝へ謁見し、白糸貿易の許可を要請した。隆武帝は金応元らの要請を受け容れ、招撫使を琉球へ派遣することにした。招撫使の閔邦基は翌年（隆武2年＝1646年）1月、琉球へ到着するや、首里城へ赴き隆武帝の詔勅を宣読している。これに応えて、尚賢は同年4月、隆武帝の即位を慶賀する使者（毛泰久・金正春）を閔邦基に同行させて福州へ派遣した[18]。

同時期に、福州においては崇禎帝毅宗への進香使として派遣された毛大用らが隆武政権へ進香品を納め、まもなく進貢使兼請封使の金応元らとともに福州を離れ、同年7月帰国した[19]。その一ヶ月後の同年8月、隆武帝の使者（黄徴明）が日本の長崎に到り、鄭芝竜の援軍要請の書翰を提出している[20]。この時、薩摩藩（島津氏）は援軍派遣の場合には先陣を承りたいと申し出て、南明側への加担に積極的な態度を見せていることに注目すべきであろう[21]。

毛大用・金応元らと入れ替わりに福州へ到着した慶賀使節の毛泰久・金正春らも隆武帝へ拝謁し、無事慶賀の任務を果たし終え、同年の夏には福州を離れた。ところが、帰国の途中、毛泰久らは閩安鎮外の琅岐地方で海賊と遭遇し、船隻・積荷をすべて掠奪され、九死に一生を得て福州琉球館へたどり着いた。この時、隆武政権はすでに崩壊し、福州は清軍の支配下に入っていた[22]。

清軍による福州奪回の情報は同年10月には長崎から江戸幕府のもとへ伝達されたため、幕府は最終的に援軍派遣を中止する方針を決定している[23]。と同時に、海外情報による韃靼脅威論を背景に、幕府は清軍の日本侵略の可能性を考慮し、薩摩藩を通じて琉球諸島の海防強化を命じていることに注目すべきであろう[24]。

1-3 琉球使節と清国当局の遭遇・接触

隆武政権の崩壊によって中琉関係は断絶の危機に直面した。中琉関係を継続するには、

琉球と清朝との外交関係を形成する契機が必要であった。毛泰久らは土通事（中国人の琉球語通訳）謝必振の忠告に従い、王府当局や薩摩藩の指示を待つことなく、自らの判断で清国側へ帰順する方針を選択した。とは言え、清朝の辮髪令に従うことには躊躇せざるを得なかった。そこで、毛泰久らは明国風の髪型を琉球風の結髪に変えただけで、順治3（1646）年10月7日福州城内の清国将軍へ帰順を表明した。清国将軍の貝勒博洛は土通事の謝必振に対して、毛泰久・金正春・王明佐らを北京へ連行し順治帝へ拝謁させよと命じた[25]。

毛泰久らは同年12月8日謝必振に随行して福州を出発、北京へ向かう途中、福州人で南京駐在中の経略洪承疇に投誠の意思を表明し、翌順治4（1647）年4月北京に入った。毛泰久らの清朝への帰順表明に対して、清朝礼部は明朝から賜給された詔勅・印鑑の引き渡しを待って冊封すべしと上奏し、順治帝の了承を得た。順治帝は謝必振に対して琉球へ渡航し尚賢を招撫するよう命じた[26]。

謝必振は同年6月、毛泰久らを引き連れて北京を出発し、9月には福建の浦城に到った。山賊横行のため浦城に留まること十カ月、順治5（1648）年4月、延平府へたどり着いた。折しも魯監国軍を率いる鄭彩らの福州攻撃のため、延平府に留まること二ヶ月、この間に毛泰久は病死した。同年6月、謝必振・金正春らはようやく福州へ到着したが、魯監国軍の海上活動に妨げられて琉球へ渡航することができず、一年間も福州に滞留することとなる[27]。

この間、琉球側には毛泰久・金正春らの動向は伝えられていなかった。尚賢は隆武政権の存在を前提として、毛泰久らの消息と情報収集のため、探問使者の蔡祚隆を福州へ派遣したが、蔡祚隆らの探問船は温州へ漂着して海賊に襲撃され、順治4（1647）年10月には琉球へ逃げ帰ったと言われる。その直前の9月22日、尚賢は冊封を受けることなく死去し、弟の尚質が王位を継承した[28]。

2. 尚質の冊封をめぐる中琉日関係の諸問題

2-1 招撫使謝必振の第一次来琉と琉球側の等距離外交

清朝の順治帝から招撫使に任ぜられた謝必振は、福州に滞留していた金正春らの琉球人50名を引き連れ、順治6（1649）年6月福州を出港したが、途中暴風に遭い薩摩の山川港に漂着、長崎へ回航されて取り調べを受け、那覇港へ到着したのは同年9月のことである。金正春にとっては、三年半ぶりの帰国であった[29]。

尚質の帰順を促すため首里城に乗り込んだ謝必振は、尚質に向かって順治帝の詔書を宣読し、明朝賜給の詔勅・印鑑を引き渡すよう要求した。尚質は謝必振の勧告に応じ、同年11月、梁廷翰・周国盛らに投誠の表文を持参させることを決定したが、明朝賜給の勅印引き渡し要求には応じることなく、来年に派遣する予定の慶賀使に持参させると約束しただけであった[30]。

その背景には、南明側からも琉球に対する積極的なアプローチが続いているという事

情が存在した。謝必振の来琉より二ヶ月前（49年4月6日）、福州へ派遣された探問船の蔡祚隆が閩江河口の定海で魯監国軍と遭遇し、同年6月監国魯王の勅書と建国公鄭彩の書簡等四通を持ち帰っていた[31]。監国魯王の尚質あての「勅諭」によれば、「私、魯王は明を建国した洪武帝の九世の孫である。…残念なことに、満虜（満州人）が勝手に中国に盤踞し、わが社稷（国家）を踏みにじったので、私はついに両浙に正義の旗を建て、福建に軍隊を派遣し、今日までの四年間、苦労を重ねて勢力拡張を図っている。…惟うに、そなたの国（琉球国）は明朝皇室に忠誠を尽くし、恭順の意思を固くしている。使者の蔡祚隆等は進貢のため山川を跋渉してきた。その労苦は甚だしい。そこで、私、魯王の署名入りの書翰を送り、そなたの国を慰労する。…旧来の臣下としての徳を称え、新封（新たな冊封詔書？）を与える。云々」[32]とあり、琉球の明朝及び南明への入貢を忠誠心の表明として高く評価している。尚質にとっては、清朝側の謝必振の勧告に応じて従来の忠誠の対象を公然と転換するわけにはいかない事情があったのである。尚質が南明政権と清朝政権の間で去就に迷わざるを得なかったのも当然であった。

　謝必振は尚質の曖昧な対応に不満を抱きながらも、来年の慶賀使派遣の約束に期待して、ひとまず梁廷翰・周国盛らを伴って福州へ帰還した後、さらに復命のため周国盛を率いて北京へ赴くこととし、翌順治7（1650）年2月福州を出発した[33]。その後、尚質は謝必振に約束したとおり、順治7（1650）年10月順治帝即位の慶賀使を派遣したものの、慶賀使の阿榜琨・蔡錦には明朝賜給の印勅を持参させず、しかも阿榜琨・蔡錦らを乗せた船は海上で遭難し、音信不通となったと弁明している[34]。どうやら尚質には明朝賜給の勅印を清朝へ引き渡す意思はなかったようである。蓋し、順治9（1652）年春に福州へ派遣された探問船の蔡時春らにも明朝の印勅を持参させておらず[35]、他方で、琉球当局の意向を斟酌した薩摩藩当局からも、慶安4（1651）年9月18日付の書簡で、来春福州へ派遣される予定の琉球の「左右聞船」（探問船）に清朝宛と南明宛の文書を持参させるようにと指示されていたことから[36]、蔡時春らは宛先の異なる二通の文書を持参していたものと思われる。かくて、この時点では、琉球側も薩摩藩側も南明政権と清朝政権に対して、等距離（両面）外交の方針を堅持していたと見るべきあろう。

　清朝側では、琉球の慶賀使が約束通り北京に到着しないことに不信感を強めていた。北京へ赴いて投誠の表文を提出した周国盛は、招撫使の謝必振とともに長期にわたって北京に留置され、慶賀使の到着を一日千秋の思いで待ち続けた。周国盛は事実上、人質の役割を担わされていたと見るべきであろう[37]。

2-2　招撫使謝必振の第二次来琉と尚質の慶賀使派遣

　順治8（1651）年9月、慶賀使の到着を待ちかねた順治帝は謝必振に対して、再度の琉球渡航を命じた。謝必振は周国盛を引き連れて北京を出発、同年11月初旬には福州へ到着した。福建当局は謝必振に対して直ちに琉球へ出発するよう要請した。謝必振は直ちに要請に応じることなく、約半年間、琉球船が明朝の印勅を持参して来るのを待った。予想通り、順治9（1652）年春琉球の探問船は福州へ入港したが、探問使者（蔡時春）は

明朝の印勅を持参していなかった。琉球の使者が印勅を持参して来れば、再度琉球へ渡航する必要はなく、清国側にとっても琉球側にとっても、リスクとコストが軽減されるはずだという謝必振の期待は裏切られた。琉球の探問船に猜疑の念を抱いた福建当局は乗船者と船舶を勾留して尋問した。謝必振の奔走・斡旋によって福建当局の猜疑心はひとまず解消された[38]。

　清朝に対する琉球の忠誠を確定するために、謝必振はついに再度の琉球渡航を決意し、周国盛らを伴って福州を出港、同年7月那覇港へ到着した。上陸に先だって、謝必振は琉球の外交担当者（長史司）に対し、慶賀使の派遣と明朝賜給の印勅の引き渡しを催促する「咨文」（書簡）を提出し、前回第一次の来琉から今回第二次の来琉に至った経緯とその背景を、次のように指摘している。

　「ご承知のように、私（謝必振）は数年前に清朝皇帝の命令を受けて、（中略）清朝への帰順を促すために、初めて貴国を訪問した。その時、貴国は進貢品を準備することが困難だとして、使節の周国盛に忠誠の表文だけを持参させることとした。（中略）順治七年の二月中に、私は周国盛を伴って北京へ赴き、周国盛から忠誠の表文を提出したところ、清朝皇帝は大いに喜んで受け容れ、私たちに賞賜品を下された。（中略）ところが、残念なことに、貴国の表文には明朝から賜給された印鑑と詔勅は返還しないとの意味が込められていた。その文中から判断すれば、貴国が清朝への忠誠をためらい二心を懐いているのではないかという疑惑が生じないわけではない。（中略）その後、貴国の慶賀使節が北京へ到着したという知らせもなく、私と周国盛は一年半余の間、郷里を遠く離れて北京に逗留し続けることになった。（中略）わが皇帝の大いなる思いやりを蒙り、周国盛の忠誠心を信頼し、心を一つにして力をあわせ、私たちはなんとか困難な問題を処理して帰り着くことができたのである。この事実は、貴国が清朝の信用を失うような挙動を示したものの、清朝は貴国を忘恩の徒にしないように配慮したことを意味している。そうであるからこそ、皇帝はまた勅書一通を下し、私を再び貴国へ派遣して頒布させることにしたのである。云々」[39]と。

　要するに、琉球当局は約束通りに明の印勅を引き渡さず、清朝当局の信頼を失ってしまったにもかかわらず、順治帝はなお琉球の罪を咎めず、招撫のため謝必振に再び琉球渡航を命じたことを強調しながら、他方で謝必振自らが琉球の国益のために如何に心血を注ぎ苦心惨憺してきたかという個人的事情をも強調していることに注目すべきであろう。

　謝必振が自ら直接三司官や国王世子へ要請せず、長史司あてに咨文（書簡）を提出したのは、招撫通事官が長史司と同等の地位にあるとみなされていたからであろうか。ともあれ、謝必振の書簡の中の「貴国は尚お信を天朝に失うも、天朝は未だ貴国を恩に辜くとせざるなり」という一句は、順治帝の勅命を背景としているだけに琉球当局には大きなプレッシャーとなったであろう。加えてまた、謝必振が琉球使節を伴って福州と北京の間を二度も往復し、琉球招撫のために二度も来琉したという事情を、琉球当局は重く受け止めないわけにはいかなかったと思われる。

かくて、尚質は謝必振を首里城に迎えて恭順の意を示し、慶賀使の派遣と明朝の印勅の引き渡しを約束、印勅を持参した慶賀使を謝必振に同行させることにした。但し、返還される勅は、尚寧・尚豊宛の勅に限られ、慶賀使が請封使を兼任したわけでもないことに留意すべきであろう。順治10（1653）年2月、謝必振は慶賀使の馬宗毅・蔡祚隆を伴い那覇港から福州へ帰還、さらに福州を出発して北京へ到着したのは翌順治11（1654）年3月のことであった[40]。

2-3　尚質の冊封をめぐる琉球と清朝と薩摩／幕府の思惑

　馬宗毅らの任務は明朝賜給の印勅を清朝へ提出し、併せて順治帝の即位を慶賀することであった。請封の任務も与えられていたのかどうかは明かでなく、一つの検討すべき課題である。福建巡撫佟国器の上奏文（順治10年9月2日付）の中では、「琉球国中山王世子の尚質は天朝（清朝）を慕って臣服し、これまでにすでに表文を提出して忠誠を表明し、（中略）慎んで新綸（新たな勅書）に遵い、王舅馬宗毅・正議大夫蔡祚隆等を派遣して進貢品を献上し、皇帝陛下の即位を衷心から慶賀し、また滅びた明朝の勅印を返納し、新たな清朝の符命（印勅）を求め、同時に清朝の徳威を永久に蒙ることを願っています」と報告されている[41]。つまり、明清交替という維新変革に当たって、尚質は明朝賜給の勅印を引き渡し、代わりに清朝の符命（勅印）を頂きたいと申し出ているだけであって、清朝に対して明確な請封の意思を表明しているわけではない。

　馬宗毅が持参した尚質の上奏文にも次のように言う。──「琉球国中山王世子の尚質から謹んで上奏します。（中略）いま、私の重臣を遣わし、明朝の勅書二通・印信一個を持参させて返納します。ところで考えてみますと、本国（琉球）は三十六の島々からなり、一切の行政事務には必ず印信を必要としますので、長い間印信のないまま過ごすわけにはいきません。どうか、皇帝陛下から命令を出して印鑑を鋳造させ、私が派遣した慶賀使節で王舅の馬宗毅に与えて持ち帰らせ、異国の琉球にも天朝の尊厳を知らしめ、永久に讃えさせて頂きますようお願いします」[42]と。清朝礼部の上奏文の中でも、「世子尚質の上奏文の中で、どうか、勅印は私が派遣した王舅の馬宗毅に与えて持ち帰らせて頂きたい、と言っています」[43]と指摘されているように、尚質は清朝に対して明確な請封の意思表示をしていないだけでなく、言外に清朝使臣の来琉を回避したいという意思を表明していることに注目すべきであろう。

　尚質が明確に請封の意思表示をせず、むしろ清朝使臣の来琉を回避しようとしたのは何故であろうか。この時点で、琉球側は南明政権との関係を断ち切り、明確に清朝を宗主国として選択したわけではなく、依然として南明・清朝との等距離外交を維持する方針を変えていなかったからであろうと思われる[44]。

　尚質の真意を見抜いた清朝礼部の胡世安は、意図的に尚質の印勅賜給要請を請封の意思表示と読み替え、「尚質は清朝皇帝の印勅を馬宗毅に与えて持ち帰らせて欲しいと要請しているが、今回は初めて帰順した遠国に対する清朝最初の冊封なので、冊封使を琉球へ派遣して天朝の徳威を明示し、且つ柔遠の意思を示すべきである」と提案し[45]、名分

論の視点から「頒封」方式の冊封を選択していることに留意しておきたい。順治帝は礼部尚書の胡世安の提案を承認し、順治11（1654）年7月1日、冊封使の琉球派遣による冊封（頒封）を決定、冊封正副使の張学礼・王垓に琉球渡航を命じた。張学礼らは土通事の謝必振と慶賀使の馬宗毅らを伴って北京を出発、翌順治12（1655）年3月福州へ到着する。しかし、福州では琉球渡航のための冊封使船が用意できず、海上における鄭成功らの反清活動にも阻まれ、張学礼らは長期間福州に留まらざるを得なくなる[46]。

この時期、日本側（薩摩藩/江戸幕府）にも福州では冊封使派遣の準備が進んでいるという情報が伝えられていた。薩摩藩は冊封使が尚質に韃靼（清朝）の衣冠を賜給したり、琉球人に韃靼風の辮髪を強制することを恐れ、明暦元（1655）年7月、「万一、韃靼人之為体ニ申越候ハバ、罷成候間敷、達て申断、冠船（冊封使船）をも追返候歟、又ハ彼使者無合点追返候儀も不罷成、還て彼方より事をも仕出候ハバ、討果申体ニも可有之哉、是ハ急々御内談肝要之儀ニ候」と、冊封使が辮髪を強制した場合の対応措置として、冊封使の追放か殺害かという強硬な選択肢を提起し、さらに「琉球国ハ、唐へ通融無之候ては不叶由候へども、御外聞旁、日本之瑕ニ罷成候ハバ、琉球之不自由成分ハ、堪忍被仕候様ニ可被仰付候」と、実益論の視点から琉球の「通融」を配慮するよりも名分論の視点から「日本之瑕」を回避すべしとの藩論をとりまとめ、江戸幕府へ上申している[47]。ところが、幕府は「若使者琉球国江相渡候而、髪を剃、衣裳等遣候ハヽ、彼方之申通ニ可仕候」[48]と回答し、冊封使が琉球に韃靼の衣冠・辮髪を強制するのであれば、そのまま受け容れるようにと指示していることに注目すべきであろう。

要するに、幕府は名分論の視点から対清戦争のリスクを覚悟して冊封使の要求を拒否するよりも、実益論（実利主義）の視点から清国と琉球の冊封進貢関係を継続させる方針を選択したのである。もっとも、清朝側の冊封使が来琉して尚質を冊封することについては、薩摩藩にせよ江戸幕府にせよ、いずれも大きなリスクとして受け止め、できるだけ回避したいというのが本音であったことに留意しておきたい。

2-4　清朝内部における方針転換と琉球の対応

張学礼らは琉球渡航の条件が調わないことを理由に、礼部に対して琉球冊封の中止、冊封使の北京への引き揚げを要請した。張学礼等の要請を受けて、礼部尚書の王崇簡は順治15（1658）年7月の上奏文で、「海上のリスクを考慮して冊封使の琉球派遣を中止し、冊封正副使を北京へ呼び戻すこと、琉球の慶賀使は福州に留置すること」を提案し、順治帝の了承を得た[49]。召還命令を受けた冊封正副使の張学礼・王垓らは翌順治16（1659）年閏3月北京へ戻った。冊封使の任務を解かれた張学礼は、まもなく江南道監察御史兼巡塩御史として任地へ赴任した[50]。

冊封使節の解任により尚質の冊封は無期延期となった。冊封使船の調達などのコストや海上のリスクを強調する官僚層の動向を、順治帝も無視できなかったからであろう。換言すれば、清朝の官僚層内部で冊封使の派遣賛成派と派遣反対派の論争が繰り返され、とりあえず後者が勝利したことを暗示している。琉球側の世子尚質や慶賀使の馬宗毅ら

が明確に請封の意思表示をせず、むしろ冊封使の琉球来航を回避したいという意向を示していたことも、清朝官僚層のなかの冊封使派遣反対派の勢力を増大させたものと思われる。順治12（1655）年以来、事実上人質として福州に留置された慶賀使の馬宗毅は、四年後の順治16（1659）年6月22日、帰国の希望もかなわず病没した[51]。

この間、福建に留まって帰国しない慶賀使の消息を探問するために、尚質は都通事・使者の田時盛・馬知記らを、順治11（1654）年3月と翌年2月に福州へ派遣したが、田時盛らはその都度海賊に阻まれて逃げ返ったと言われる。にもかかわらず、尚質は順治13（1656）年にもまた林士奇・英俊らを福州へ派遣している[52]。ところが、林士奇らも慶賀使の馬宗毅らを引き取って帰国することはできなかったのである。

しかし、1660年代に入り、東アジアの政治情勢に今一度変化の兆しが現れた。順治18（1661）年1月順治帝が死去し、康熙帝が即位した。同年、南明の永暦帝が清軍によって捕縛され、永明政権は崩壊した。他方で、鄭成功が台湾のオランダ人を制圧し、鄭氏政権の根拠地を台湾へ移したのも、同年のことであった。翌年、鄭成功は病死し、鄭経がその後を継承した[53]。

順治帝の後を継いだ康熙帝は方針を再転換して、尚質の冊封を積極的に推進し、康熙元（1662）年張学礼らに琉球渡航を命ずるとともに、尚質あての勅書において、冊封が遅延した理由を次のように弁明している。――「世祖章皇帝（順治帝）は（中略）正使兵科副理官の張学礼と副使行人司行人の王垓に命じて勅印を持参して琉球へ赴き、爾（尚質）を琉球国中山王に冊封させようとした。ところが、琉球への海上航路が通ぜず、長い間福州に滞在することとなり、爾の使者の中にも物故してしまう者が甚だ多い状態となった。張学礼等は命令を受けて北京へ帰った後も、そのような実情を上奏して報告せず、福建の地方官たちもまた上奏して指示を受けようとはしなかった。朕は何回も詰問してはじめて、このような実情を知った次第である。朕が思うには、爾の国は心を傾けて進貢しているので、当然優待されるべきである。然るに冊封使や地方官は福州に留まったまま出航の時期を遅らせた。このことは実に朕が遠国の人々を思い遣る気持ちに沿うものではない。今、すでに正副使・督撫等の官員を個別に処分し、琉球の使臣には従来にも増して恩賞を与えた。以上の事情により、正使の張学礼と副使の王垓に対して、自らの前罪を贖うため、暫くの間、元の冊封使の職に戻り、速やかに琉球の使者を伴って渡航するよう命じた次第である」[54]と。

要するに、かくも長い間冊封が遅延したのは冊封使の張学礼・王垓や地方督撫らの職務怠慢のためであると強調し、その罪を詰責して責任を果たさせることにした旨、弁明していることに注目すべきであろう。

琉球渡航を命ぜられた張学礼らは康熙2（1663）年4月福州へ到着、土通事の謝必振らとともに渡航準備に当たり、同年5月12日福州出発、6月25日那覇港へ到着した。謝必振にとっては第三次の渡航であり、蔡祚隆にとっては実に10年ぶりの帰国であった[55]。

ところが、尚質は突然の冊封使船の来航に当惑した。というのも、従来、冊封使来航の前年に迎接使（接封使）を派遣する慣例であったが、冊封使の張学礼からは事前に何の

連絡もなく、加えてまた首里城が三年前の順治17（1660）年に焼失し、まだ再建されていないという事情があったからである[56]。請封の明確な意思表示をしていなかった尚質にとっては、冊封使の来航は全く予想外の事態であったが、土通事謝必振等の適切な仲介・斡旋を経て、康熙2（1663）年7月17日冊封の式典を済ませ、ひとまず清朝と琉球の宗属関係を軌道に載せることができたことに注目したい[57]。

おわりに

　以上、明清交替期の前半における中琉日関係の諸相を、琉球王国の王位継承者の冊封問題を中心に据えて検討し考察した。最後に、清朝と南明と薩摩/幕府の狭間で琉球はどのような選択肢を追求したのかという視点から、尚賢・尚質の冊封問題を整理すれば、次の通りである。

　尚賢の場合、明朝への200年余の進貢と二度にわたる請封という事実（名分論）を踏まえ、他方で白糸貿易の再開という経済的メリット（実益論）の視点から、南明政権を忠誠の対象として選択し、薩摩藩や江戸幕府も韃靼（清朝）脅威論を背景に、華夷秩序の理念（名分論）から南明政権へのシンパシーを示し、尚賢の選択肢を追認（容認）した。南明政権は清朝政権との正当性を争うためにも、名分論の視点から琉球の忠誠を必要として招撫使を派遣しただけでなく、白糸貿易の再開要請にも応じたが、政治的軍事的情勢に規制されて尚賢を冊封することはできなかった。

　尚質の場合、政権の正当性を争う清朝と南明の双方から積極的にアプローチされて等距離（両面）外交方針を採らざるを得ず、他方でリスクとコストを考慮して、清朝に対しては冊封使の来琉を回避するために「領封」方式の冊封を要請した。ところが、清朝は政権の正当性を明示するという名分論の視点から、冊封使を派遣する「頒封」方式を選択したものの、まもなくリスクとコストの視点から「頒封」中止を決定し、康熙帝即位後に方針を再転換して「頒封」方式の冊封を断行した。清朝政権の琉球への積極的アプローチに対して、韃靼風俗（辮髪）の強制を恐れた薩摩藩や江戸幕府は警戒しながら消極的に対応したものの、冊封使を受け容れた琉球側の選択を容認せざるを得なかったことに注目すべきであろう。

注

1) 金城正篤（1996）、参照。
2) なお、尚清王の請封の際に琉球側から結状［世子の出自・身元保証書］を提出して以来、請封には結状を添付することが慣例となったことについては、原田禹雄（2003: pp. 38-39）、参照。また、琉球王国が薩摩藩の従属下に置かれて以後、王位継承者はまず薩摩藩主及び徳川将軍の承認を得た上で、中国王朝に対して請封するという手続きが必要となったが、薩摩藩主や徳川将軍が王位継承者の申請を承認しなかった事例はなく、王位継承の実質的主導権は琉球当局の側にあったことについては、豊見山和行（2000）、参照。また、属国としての琉球外交の「自由」と限界については、張存武（1991）、参照。

3) 明清交替期の中琉日関係に関わる問題を論及した主な先行研究は、参考文献を参照のこと。
4) 『神宗実録』萬暦40.11乙巳。『熹宗実録』天啓3.3丁巳。『球陽』原文編p.2。
5) 『中山世譜』巻8、『琉球史料叢書』4、pp.111–115。『球陽』原文編p.208、p.212、p.214。『歴代宝案』第一集第十八巻八号文書（以下、1–18–08のように表記する）、1–18–09、1–18–10、1–18–13、1–18–16、1–18–18、1–18–21、1–18–23〜1–18–25、1–19–05、1–19–09、1–19–12、1–32–24。
6) 土肥祐子（1994）。西里喜行（1997）、参照。
7) 島尻勝太郎（1980）p.108、原田禹雄（2003: pp.56–57）。
8) 『歴代宝案』1–20–18。
9) 『歴代宝案』1–20–21。
10) 『歴代宝案』1–20–22。
11) 陳捷先『明清史』（三民書局、中華民国79年）。
12) 『歴代宝案』1–36–01、1–36–02、1–36–03。
13) 呉元豊（2002）において、氏は『偏安排日事跡』第14巻に依拠して、弘光帝は弘光元年（1645）3月の時点で、「陳燕翼・韓元勛を冊封使として琉球国へ派遣し、冊封の礼を行う予定であった」と指摘されている。しかし、招撫使の花煜が琉球から福州へ帰還したのは冊封使が決定された後のことであり、琉球側からは弘光帝の即位慶賀と崇禎帝への進香を兼ねた使節が派遣されただけで、冊封要請（請封）の使節は派遣されていない。なお、『偏安排日事跡』14巻の記事については、未見。
14) 『大宗毛氏家譜』毛泰久の条。田名真之（2000）、参照。
15) 『中山世譜』附巻一によれば、「本年（弘光元、順治2）、花煜指揮の来臨を捷報し、兼ねて金銀を諸借するの為に、紅氏我謝筑殿正安を遣わし、薩州に到らしむ。五月回国す」とある（『琉球史料叢書』五、p.14）。大坂や江戸の薩摩藩邸でも花煜来琉の情報には大きな関心が向けられようで、「大明国一両年以来乱入候様」についても琉球から情報伝達があり次第、詳細に報告するようにと国元へ指示しているものの、花煜に対する琉球側の対応には特にコメントしていないことに注目すべきであろう（『鹿児島県史料　旧記雑録追録一』25号文書、p.19）。この時期、江戸幕府の側も韃靼（清朝）脅威論の見地から、海防強化の方針のもとに琉球諸島の防衛体制を強化するとともに、他方で、琉球の対明貿易を続行させる方針を採ったことから（『鹿児島県史料　旧記雑録追録一』80号、p.45）、南明側の使者（花煜）に対する琉球側の対応にクレームをつけることはなかった。
16) 花煜が宣読した詔書が明朝皇帝の冊封詔書であるのか、南明の弘光帝の即位の詔書であるのか、等の問題については、徐玉虎（1982）と呉元豊（2002）の議論がある。
17) 島尻勝太郎（1980）、田名真之（2000）、参照。『歴代宝案』1–36–06等参照。
18) 『那覇市史』資料篇第1巻6、pp.940–941。
19) 『歴代宝案』1–37–05。『中山世譜』巻8、『琉球史料叢書』四、p.117。『那覇市史』資料篇第1巻8、p.408。
20) 黄徴明が長崎奉行へ提出した鄭芝竜書翰は江戸幕府へ伝達され、江戸幕府内部でも援軍派遣の是非について検討された（『華夷変態』巻一、東洋文庫刊『華夷変態』上冊、pp.15–22）。
21) 『鹿児島県史料　旧記雑録追録一』87号文書（pp.49–50）、94号文書（p.53）。
22) 『那覇市史』資料篇第1巻6、p.942。『球陽』原文編p.217。
23) 『華夷変態』巻一（『華夷変態』上冊、p.24）。
24) 村上直次郎訳『長崎オランダ商館の日記』第二輯（岩波書店、1957: p.121）。紙屋敦之（1990: p.95）。真栄平房昭（1985）、参照。
25) 西里喜行（2002）、田名真之（2000）、参照。
26) 『中山世譜』巻八（『琉球史料叢書』四、p.117）。『歴代宝案』1–03–02、1–09–01。『清史稿』巻526「属国」一。
27) 『那覇市史』資料篇第1巻6、pp.942–943。

28) 『歴代宝案』1-37-19。『中山世譜』巻8（『琉球史料叢書』四、p. 117）。
29) 『那覇市史』資料篇第1巻6, pp. 942–943。
30) 『歴代宝案』1-21-03。
31) 『華夷変態』巻一（『華夷変態』上冊、pp. 35–44）。
32) 『華夷変態』巻一（『華夷変態』上冊、pp. 35–36）。
33) 『中山世譜』巻8（『琉球史料叢書』四、p. 119）。『那覇市史』資料篇第1巻6, p. 380。
34) 『歴代宝案』1-21-05。『中山世譜』巻8（『琉球史料叢書』四、p. 119）。『那覇市史』資料篇第1巻7, pp. 4–5。なお、この時、阿榜琨は遭難して死亡したわけではなく、琉球側の弁明は虚偽の可能性が高いことについては、高瀬恭子（1978）、参照。
35) 『歴代宝案』1-09-04。
36) 『鹿児島県史料　旧記雑録追録一』396号、p. 204。
37) 周国盛の家譜に「国盛、独り謝必振と同に上京し、京都に寓留すること殆ど一載に及ぶ。此の時に当たり、厳に陟るの懐、言いて喩うる能わず」とある（『那覇市史』資料篇第1巻6、p. 380）。
38) 『歴代宝案』1-09-04。『中山世譜』巻8（『琉球史料叢書』四、p. 119）。なお、この間の経緯については、謝必振の琉球国長史司あて咨文に次のように指摘されている。――「［順治］八年十一月に至りて閩に到る。撫院は諭するに、王命森厳なれば促即に啓行すべきを以てす。本使又辞して、勅書は重大なれども風汛は時に非ざれば稍らく来年を待たんとす。実は今春、賀船の自ら至るを候ち、一は以て往返の航海の艱を免れ、二は以て貴国の供応の費を省かんと欲するなり。想わざりき、今春の来船は只だ探聴を以て名と為すのみとは。故閩の印勅は又申ねて説う無ければ、遂に院・司の猜疑を起こし、人船を拘繋し、題して定奪を候たんとす。本使、百計もて図維し、権に従りて酌処し、姑らく大夫の蔡時春を以て存留と為し、以て口実を塞ぎ、以て疑隙を消し、瓦全して事を終えたるは、亦た貴国の福なり」と（『歴代宝案』1-09-04、校訂本第一冊、pp. 295–296）。
39) 『歴代宝案』1-09-04（校訂本第一冊、pp. 295–296）。『世祖実録』巻60、順治8年9月壬午の条。
40) 『歴代宝案』1-09-05。『中山世譜』巻8（『琉球史料叢書』四、p. 119）。『世祖実録』巻82、順治11年3月丁酉の条。
41) 「内閣礼科史書」第13冊、呉元豊（1996）、参照。
42) 『歴代宝案』1-14-03（校訂本第一冊、p. 454）。
43) 『歴代宝案』1-05-02（校訂本第一冊、p. 156）。
44) 川勝守（1996）、参照。
45) 『歴代宝案』1-05-02（校訂本第一冊、p. 156）。
46) 『世祖実録』巻85、順治11年7月戊子朔。『那覇市史』資料篇第1巻6, pp. 298–299, p. 943。張学礼著・原田禹雄訳注『使琉球記・中山紀略』（榕樹書林、1998年）参照。
47) 『島津家列朝制度』巻之二十一、1228号文書、藩法研究会編『藩法集8　鹿児島藩上』（創文社、1969: pp. 645–647）。
48) 伊地知季安『琉球御掛衆愚按之覚』（東京大学史料編纂所所蔵）。紙屋敦之（1990: p. 225）参照。
49) 「内閣満文礼科史書」第53冊、呉元豊（1996）、参照。
50) 張学礼「使琉球紀」p. 2（前掲・原田訳注本所収）、参照。
51) 「内閣満文礼科史書」第76冊。呉元豊（1996）、参照。
52) 『歴代宝案』1-21-06。
53) 『対外関係史総合年表』（吉川弘文館、1999年）、参照。
54) 『歴代宝案』1-03-08（『歴代宝案』校訂本第一冊、p. 114）。
55) 『中山世譜』巻8（『琉球史料叢書』四、p. 120）。『球陽』原文編、p. 222。張学礼著・原田訳注『使琉球紀・中山紀略』（榕樹書林、1998年）、参照。
56) 『球陽』原文編、p. 221。

57）『球陽』原文編、p.222。張学礼著・原田訳注『使琉球紀・中山紀略』（榕樹書林、1998年）参照。

参考文献

石原道博（1945）『明末清初日本乞師の研究』富山房、東京。
上原兼善（1981）『鎖国と藩貿易』第二章、八重岳書房、東京。
紙屋敦之（1985）「七島郡司考――明清交替と琉球支配――」『南島史学』第25・26合併号、東京。
紙屋敦之（1990）『幕藩制国家の琉球支配』校倉書房、東京。
川勝守（1996）「《華夷変態》与清、琉球册封関係的形成」『第五届中琉歴史関係学術会議論文集』中琉文化経済協会、台北。
川勝守（2000）『日本近世と東アジア世界』吉川弘文館、東京。
金城正篤（1996）「頒封論・領封論」『第三回琉球・中国交渉史に関するシンポジウム論文集』沖縄県教育委員会、沖縄。
呉元豊（1996）「清初册封琉球国王尚質始末」『第三届琉球・中国交渉史研討会論文集』沖縄県教育委員会、沖縄。
呉元豊（2002）「南明時期の中琉関係について」『第六回琉球・中国交渉史に関するシンポジウム論文集』沖縄県教育委員会、沖縄。
島尻勝太郎（1980）「明末清初の内戦と琉球――空道と二葉の文書――」「薩摩侵寇後の琉球――張学礼『使琉球記』を中心に――」『近世沖縄の社会と宗教』三一書房、東京。
徐玉虎（1982）『明代琉球王国対外関係之研究』台湾学生書局、台北。
高瀬恭子（1978）「明清交替時の琉球国の対中国姿勢」『お茶の水史学』22号、東京。
田名真之（2000）「明清交代期の琉球」『第六届中琉歴史関係学術研討会論文集』中国第一歴史檔案館、北京。
張啓雄（2001）「琉球棄明投清的認同転換」『琉球認同與帰属論争』中央研究院東北亜区域研究、台北。
張存武（1991）「対於明琉関係的幾点認識」『第三届中琉歴史関係国際学術会議論文集』中琉文化経済協会、台北。
陳捷先（2000）「康熙皇帝対中琉関係延続与加強的貢献」『第六届中琉歴史関係学術研討会論文集』中国第一歴史檔案館、北京。
鄭梁生（1993）「琉球在清代册封体制中的定位試探――以順治・康熙・雍正三朝爲例――」『第四回琉中歴史関係国際学術会議琉中歴史関係論文集』琉球中国関係国際学術会議、沖縄。
土肥祐子（1994）「中琉貿易における王銀詐取事件」『史艸』35号、東京。
豊見山和行（1988）「近世琉球の外交と社会――册封関係との関連から――」『歴史学研究』第586号、東京。
豊見山和行（2000）「複合支配と地域――従属的二重朝貢国・琉球の場合」『支配の地域史』山川出版社、東京。
西里喜行（1997）「中琉交渉史における土通事と牙行（球商）」『琉球大学教育学部紀要』第50集、沖縄。
西里喜行（2002）「土通事・謝必振とその後裔たち――中琉交渉史の一側面――」『琉球大学教育学部紀要』第60集、沖縄。
原田禹雄（2003）『琉球と中国――忘れられた册封使』吉川弘文館、東京。
真栄平房昭（1985）「近世琉球の対中国外交――明清動乱期を中心に――」『地方史研究』第197号、第35巻5号、東京。
頼正維（2004）『康熙時期的中琉関係』海洋出版社、福建。
楊彦杰（1996）「明清之際的中琉関係――以琉使入貢為中心――」『第五届中琉歴史関係学術会議論文集』福建教育出版社、福建。

琉球祭祀にみる虚構と現実

伊　従　　　勉*

Reality and Illusion in Ritual Performance in Ryukyu

IYORI Tsutomu

Until the year 1673, the king and supreme priestess of the ancient Ryukyu Dynasty had conducted a pilgrimage every two years to the eastern island of Kudaka via state sanctuaries in the East. The ritual sequences along the route were recorded in ritual songs edited into a Corpus of State Ritual Songs *Omoro-Soushi*. After 1673, the itinerary to Kudaka Island was replaced by a distant prayer ritual from the sanctuary Seifa located on the other side of the channel commanding a view of the island. The original route songs, although in a shorter version, were sung there and recorded as if they had really performed the pilgrimage to Kudaka. That was the case with the enthronement rite (*O-ara-ori*) of the supreme priestess, which was conducted in Seifa Sanctuary ten times between 1677 and 1875. There was another sort of illusional performance in the state rituals in the Shuri royal castle. The 22nd volume of *Omoro-Soushi* recorded a series of rituals where the royal lady-priestesses were richly described in the songs, while in reality none of the priestesses was present but recollected simply by the singing of old ritual songs in the palace court. The reality of the royal rituals of the Ryukyu Dynasty in the 18th century lies in the disappearance of royal lady-priestesses from festive scenes; however, the absence was camouflaged by illusionary performances of old ritual songs, composing an ambivalent remaining authenticity of lost old state rituals.

はじめに

　琉球王府時代以来現在まで継承されている沖縄各地のカミ祭祀には、時に祭祀現場の状況に対応しない仮想の行為を歌謡の吟唱で代理する場面が見られる。本稿[1]では、仮想行為を含む祭祀の事例を二グループに分けて、その儀礼が表現する祭祀空間の特性を考察してみることにする。

　ひとつは、琉球祭祀の空間原則のひとつである「お通し」の表現として、聖地巡拝を代理する儀礼である。すなわち本来参拝すべき聖地への巡礼を行わずに、それを望みう

---

* 京都大学教授　Professor, Kyoto University

る場所からの遙拝で代替するか、もしくは実際には行わない巡礼の道行きを歌謡により補完する方法である。

　この代用行為には、聖地巡礼祭祀がかつて行われていた前提、もしくは、他の祭祀状況においては聖地巡拝が依然として行われているが、何らかの理由によって巡拝を行うことができないという前提条件が必要である。本稿では、このような事例として、王府東方祭祀と首里城祭祀を中心に巡拝代理幻視祭祀の事例を取り上げてみる。

　王府祭祀では、聞得大君が国王を伴って久高島に渡島し聖地で太陽霊を国王に授ける儀礼を行っていた痕跡が、『おもろさうし』所収の久高往還の航海オモロと久高島の聖地での憑霊儀礼のオモロ、そして1978年まで行われていた久高島でのイザイホー祭祀にも痕跡が確認できる。この行幸は、旧暦二月の麦のシキョマにおける国王と聞得大君による久高島渡島祭祀とは別のもので、正史や史書にははっきりとした記録がないものである。

　1673年以降、この行幸の慣行が代理官の派遣に代替され、1677年以降斎場御嶽で執行されるようになる聞得大君の就任儀礼「御新下り」のなかでも、実際に執行されなくなった久高島往還の過程が、航海の歌謡の吟唱により代理されるようになったと考えられる。

　そのような代替の痕跡は、早くは『おもろさうし』巻22「知念久高行幸之御時おもろ」の採録オモロの並べ方に観察できる。その順序は、現実に行われた巡礼ルートを謡う部分と、明らかに仮想の久高往還部分（斎場御嶽からの御通しに相当する）とから成り立っており、全体としては仮想の東御廻りルートを構成している。

　聖地巡拝祭祀の代替行為は、王府祭祀にだけみられる特有のものではない。今日の民間年中祭祀のなかにも、その痕跡を確認することができる。例えば、久米島儀間・嘉手苅集落の旧暦六月稲大祭の朝神・夕神の伊敷索グスク上りの過程は、夕神については省略され嘉手苅集落の外れの祭場からの遙拝祭祀となっており、その際に謡われる祭祀歌謡タカビラコンナ（クェーナ）［仲原1998］には、島の最高神女君南風が首里城に登城したルートが断片化して謡われ、現実のグスク（伊敷索城跡）上りとかつての首里城上りの幻想とが掛け合わされている［伊從2005a］。これも、聞得大君の行幸航海と同様、かつて君南風が祝儀の度に首里城に登っていた慣行[2]の記憶が、民間祭祀に刻印されている事例と考えられる。

　さらには、『琉球国由来記』（以下『由来記』）に記録されている諸間切の稲祭祀歌謡の中には、幻想の聖地である御嶽・オボツ山参拝を「お通し」で代替祭祀している事例[3]が散見する。王府時代のみか、近代に記録された各地の祭祀歌謡の中にも、そして現代の祭祀にもこのような代替事例が指摘でき、琉球一円に流布している祭祀の簡略方法である。

　二番目の種類の代替幻視祭祀とは、次のようなものである。祭祀状況の異なる幾編もの本歌を、祭祀文脈を外して、歌に登場する祭場や神女などの項目を手掛かりにつなぎあわせ、全く別の仮想の祭祀状況を出現させる代理儀礼である。典型事例としては、首里城正殿を祭場とした稲穂・稲大祭の国王出御の「美御前揃之御規式」（行政儀礼）があ

る。聖域に登場する神女が謡われていながら、神女は現実の祭場には不在であり、祭場も王城の聖地ではなく正殿の一階下庫理である。近世の首里城特有の祭祀状況が見て取れる。

　琉球祭祀における歌謡の吟詠のかたちをとった幻視（代理）祭祀と現実の祭場の違和状況については、祭祀文学研究においても従来十分検討されてきていない問題である。祭祀の解読に重要な鍵をにぎるオモロの研究としては、オモロに表記される祭祀のモチーフ分類についての詳しい研究[4]や、重複オモロの詩形上の異同について詳細な分類検討を行った研究[5]が存在するが、祭祀自体が仮想であった可能性の検討や、他の祭祀状況で記録されたオモロを別の祭祀に転用して生じたと思われる重複歌や類型歌の祭祀状況の検討については、未だ研究が十分に行われていないと思われる[6]。祭祀現場の空間論的な類型分析の立場からその課題の一端に挑んでみようとするのが本稿の狙いである。

1. 国王と聞得大君の久高島渡島行幸儀礼とその代替祭祀

1-1　現実の渡島祭祀

　沖縄島南部東方（大里・佐敷・知念・玉城間切）を舞台にする琉球王国祭祀のうち、久高島に国王と最高神女聞得大君が揃って行幸祭祀していたことは、いくつかの史書や伝記[7]に明記されており、王国の祭祀歌謡集である『おもろさうし』にも実際の経路や航路途上で謡われたと推測されるオモロ（後述）が採録されていることからも、第一尚王朝期から行われていた国家的祭祀であったことが確認できる。

　行幸の時節としては、前記史料に挙げられている二月麦と四月稲のシキョマが定期的な行幸と確認できるほか、王族神女の就任時に、国王を伴った久高行幸が不定期で行われた可能性が考えられる。それは、オモロ854に謡われる尚真王に神女が長寿霊を授ける儀礼に相当する。1677年以降斎場御嶽で行われるようになる聞得大君の就任儀礼「御新下り」において、久高島往還の過程を歌謡で叙述する過程が挿入されている事実［玉城1975］からも、国王と大君の久高行幸の前史がうかがえる。

　また、史書や伝記が伝える大君の漂流伝説[8]に大君の帰還ルートが示されており、それが久高島イザイホー神事のアリクヤーと柄杓取りのティルルで謡われる神の来訪ルートが久高島から対岸の斎場御嶽に渡り、佐敷与那原を経て首里城そして聞得大君御殿にまで及んでいること［畠山1991: p.40］と同一なのである。これらによって実際の航海の経路を復元してみると、次のように想定できることは拙稿［伊從(1993) 2005b: p.395］で詳しく考察した。すなわち、

　　聞得大君御殿 → 首里城 → 与那原（与那原古浜御殿、出航）→ 馬天浜（佐敷）→ 斎場御嶽（下船および斎場御嶽聖域巡拝）→ 久高渡島 → フボー御嶽 → 久高祭庭 → 久高君泊（出航）→ 斎場御嶽 → 馬天浜 → 与那原（下船）→ 首里城 → 聞得大君御殿

　これは、首里城から斎場御嶽に向かう近世の御新下り日記に記述される陸路[9]とは違い、与那原から出航し、途中、馬天と斎場御嶽で停船して順次聖地拝礼を行い、久高渡

中に乗り出すかつての行幸航路と考えられる。王府末期の史料『聞得大君御殿幷御城御規式之御次第』(1875年編)に記載されている五月の久高行幸のように[10]、この行幸には首里三平等の大あむしられが三人とも同行し、久高までは首里の大あむしられ（なよかさ）と首里根神（みよちよのの袖清ら）[オモロ、通番号838番]が同行したものと考えられる。他の二人の大あむしられは、斎場御嶽三庫理から久高渡中を横断する聞得大君らの無事を祈ったものと推測できる[伊從2005b: p.530]。斎場御嶽の三庫理とは、首里城の聖域京の内に設定された「三庫理」[同前: p.280、p.511]と同様、首里三平等の三人の大あむしられが礼拝する聖地と考えられるのである[同前: p.529]。

このルートに沿って行幸途中の現場で謡われたと思しきオモロが、『おもろさうし』巻10「ありきゑとのおもろ御さうし」、巻13「船ゑとのおもろ御さうし」、巻19「ちゑねんさいしきはなぐすくおもろ御さうし」（以上1623年編集の巻）すなわち、久高行幸が実行されていた時代に編集された祭祀歌謡集に散見する。試みに経路に沿って該当のオモロを抜き出してみると次のようになる。

表1 『おもろさうし』巻10、13、19に残存する現実の航海のオモロ

オモロ(番)/重複歌	内容	節数
29/147/1531	与那原祭祀	4/2/2
511	与那原、国王臨席の巡拝	7
531	のろ達を載せて東へ船出	8
1295/1532	佐敷寄り上げ森礼拝	2/2
514/1534	浦廻り：久手堅半島周航と斎場御嶽への上陸	20/2
832/1536	斎場御嶽下から帆上	2/2
837	航海を司る久高の神女国笠	5
838	同行する神女あけしの、首里大あむしられ（なよ笠）と首里根神（袖清ら）	10
819/1537	久高渡中での凪祈願	2/2
854	久高島蒲葵森での大君以下神女による国王長寿霊授与	7
1316	久高集め庭にて、「知念見遣り欲しや」の遥拝	(3)
1317	久高集め庭・外間集め庭での暁の新崎遥拝	3
853	久高島からの船出、王国中の聖地と斎場御嶽で神女が航海の安全を祈る	7
852	斎場御嶽への帰帆・御嶽の守護	4
530/1545	洋上を与那原へ帰帆	8/2

以上のように、具体的な往還途上での情景と、久高島での祭祀状況を謡うオモロが確認できる。しかし、収録される巻が分散しており、『おもろさうし』編集の時点で、久高

渡海の慣行の記憶が薄れていたことが推測できる。とはいうものの、オモロ800番台の航海オモロを収録した「船ゑとのおもろ御さうし」(巻13)には、臨場感溢れる航海の情景を叙したオモロが並んでいる。オモロの節数や長さはまちまちで、短いものは2節、長いものは20節にも及ぶ。ただし、与那原出帆を謡うオモロは明確に断定しがたいが、巻10に収録された東方での祭祀オモロ、特に514番に、「与那原―馬天―(浦廻り、即ち知念半島の周航)―斎場御嶽―久高渡島」のルートが謡われており、航路をとって行幸が行われていた時代があったことが確認できる。しかも、斎場御嶽に至る経路のオモロのうち1500番台の重複オモロ6首は、後述の巻22「知念久高行幸之御時おもろ」に収録される短縮2節オモロの形で再登場する点が目を引く。

1-2 渡島の代替祭祀としての御新下り儀礼の登場

　久高島渡島祭祀は、1673年の羽地朝秀による行幸中止(羽地仕置)の措置まで、第一・第二尚王権を通じて二世紀半にわたり行われてきた、王権の祭政的正当性を保証する世界観を反映した重要な国家祭祀であった。しかし、行幸中止以後、主后に固定された聞得大君職[11]に初めて就任する尚貞王妃(号月心)が、記録上初めて斎場御嶽で「御新下り」儀礼を行うのが1677年である。それ以前の聞得大君の就任儀礼が「御新下り」と呼ばれていたかは不明で、筆者は、久高島往還の「新神」儀礼と王城での君手摩儀礼がセットになっていたものと見ている[12]。

　『おもろさうし』全巻を見渡しても、一級の国家祭祀「御新下り」の祭祀歌謡に該当するオモロが見当たらない理由[13]として、斎場御嶽のみを祭場とする「御新下り」儀礼は、『おもろさうし』の主要な巻が編集された後に始まった新しい儀礼である点が想定できる。御新下り儀礼に関係する歌謡クェーナの記録は、1899年に恩河朝祐が編集した『クワイナ・ヤラシイ・オモヒ集』[外間・玉城1980：p.671]や、山内盛彬が採譜したアガリユーのクェーナや道グェーナ、内クェーナ[山内1981]などに尽きるのである。

　祭場を斎場御嶽に固定した御新下り儀礼の概要は、『女官御双紙』「きこゑ大君かなし」の条に1677年の、また「首里之大阿母志良礼」の条に次の1706年の様子が記述されるほか、与那原部分の過程については、1840年の第14代大君の御新下りの詳細が『聞得大君加那志様御新下日記』に記録されている。しかし、斎場御嶽での儀礼内容については、これらの史料が提供する情報は乏しい。

　それを明らかにしたものが、1875年の御新下りに参加した久高・玉城・大里・南風原ノロに取材した山内盛彬による儀礼過程の復元と歌謡の採譜であり[山内1971]、他方、島袋源七[島袋1950]と前掲山内による御新下り儀礼の復元成果を対比し、『クワイナ・ヤラシイ・オモヒ集』に収録されていた御新下りの5首のクェーナ[14]を併せて考察し、儀礼過程を最終的に復元した玉城政美による論考[玉城1975]である。

　その結果、深夜九ツ時から開始される斎場御嶽での御新下り儀礼の過程は次のように推定された。

（1）　斎場御嶽境域外「御待御殿」出発

(2) 御嶽境域内聖所「大庫理」拝礼
(3) 同境域内聖所「寄満」拝礼
(4) 同聖所「三庫理」拝礼
(5) 同聖所「シキヨタユルアマガ美水」（鍾乳石から滴る聖水）拝礼
(6) あから御庭［大庫理］にて御名付け儀礼、久高渡島を謡う「アラシコエナ」［39番］ほか二首のクェーナ［37番、38番］の吟唱
(7) 聞得大君は御待御殿に戻り仮眠
(8) 翌朝、御待御殿前庭にて上記クェーナ3首の吟唱

　ここで重要なことは、久高渡島を現実には行わない御新下り儀礼のクライマックス、すなわち聞得大君就任者に名を付け（職霊「聞得大君みおうしぢ」を久高島の神女外間ノロが憑依させ）、「玉冠」（たまんちゃぶい）を大君に戴せる儀礼の場において、久高渡島（ニライ渡に舟を出す）のクェーナが吟唱されることによって、本来の儀礼が久高島で行われた来歴を示している点である。しかも、大君が仮眠から目覚めた翌朝、御待御殿の庭で再びこのクェーナが吟唱される点を考慮すると、聖地斎場御嶽での大君の宿泊は、かつて、久高島の御殿[15)]に国王と大君が行幸した来歴を想起していることがほぼ確かである。

　御新下りにかつて国王が同行したことは、久高行幸と同じ論理にしたがっている。渡島儀礼によって新たに職霊を身につける王族神女と土地の神女から現場の聖地で長寿霊を授けられ祝福されるのは、先ず国王だからである。東方への国王行幸時に吟唱されたというアガリユウのクェーナ［32番］の内容が、斎場御嶽御待御殿の内部の設えの状況を謡っていることから分かるように、御待御殿の中に整えられた「屏風構え」の仮の座敷に黄金枕が二つ置かれたことも、職霊を身につけた大君に守護される国王の陪席を示しているのであって、神女とカミの聖婚儀礼を意味するものではない[16)]。

　以上のように、1677年以降斎場御嶽で行われた御新下り儀礼の創設は、久高島で行われていたかつての王族神女の就任儀礼「新神」祭祀を、斎場御嶽での儀礼に集約し代替する近世的措置であったことがみえてくるだろう。

　と同時に、ここでは詳述しないが、斎場御嶽の祭場である、大庫裡、寄満、三庫理の名称がいずれも首里城の聖地や祭場となる殿舎の名である点に、首里城で行われるべき儀礼が斎場御嶽に移されているかのような傾向が指摘できる。首里城から移された儀礼とは、1607年以降の執行記録がない君手摩儀礼である[17)]。

　以上のように、斎場御嶽での御新下り儀礼は、久高渡島と首里城巡回の二重の幻影を帯びた聖地儀礼なのである。

1-3　仮想久高渡島儀礼を含む東方行幸のオモロの真相

　1709年の首里城炎上で焼失した「神歌御双紙」の複本が各地に探索され、1710年に再編集してなった『おもろさうし』全22巻のうち、おもろ主取安仁屋家に保管されていた、当時王城で執行されていた公儀儀礼のオモロ集が巻22「みおやだいりおもろ御さう

し」と推測されている［池宮 1982: p.74］。すなわち、当時歌唱法が伝えられていたのは、巻22収録のオモロだけであった可能性が高い[18]。

　収録される「みおやだいり」のうち「知念久高行幸之御時おもろ」は17編からなっている（表2）。全てについて本歌が他の巻に存在し、しかも2節編成のオモロに短縮され統一されている。いわゆる重複オモロであるが、重複の様態を波照間の分類［波照間1996］を参考にして表2の各オモロの末尾に記号を掲げる[19]。オモロは行幸の行程順に並べられていて、詞書が祭祀場所を示している。

表2 『おもろさうし』巻22「知念久高行幸之御時おもろ」の伝える仮想のルート（網掛け部分が仮想ルート）

オモロ/本歌	詞書/本歌要旨	重複分類
1529/0512	「首里城出発」/昔始まりや　国造り	②a
1530/0695	「与那原村稲福親雲上宿」/1545年君手摩百果報/	②a
1531/0029	「同　御打立前に」/「与那覇浜／馬天浜」	②a
1532/1295	「佐敷寄り上げ杜」/同左	①
1533/0034	「斎場御嶽」/寄満：八重山出陣	②a'
1534/0514	「斎場御桟敷」/斎場嶽・三庫理	②a
1535/0747	「乗船」/同左	②a'
1536/0832	「帆上」/東方の大主　ややの真帆押し上げて	①
1537/0819	「久高渡中」/東方の大主　海　凪らちへ	①
1538/1317	「久高外間御殿」/同左	②a'
1539/0346	「知念大川」/知念杜グスク	②a
1540/1315	「玉城たまぐすくやふさつ」/浦バル	②a'
1541/1234	「玉城天頂」/同左	②a'
1542/0830	「暁のおもろ」/東方のあけもどろ［玉城宿泊？］	①
1543/0820	「無題」/東方の大主	②a'
1544/0349	「無題」/斎場下はしり［再び斎場御嶽］	②a'
1545/0530	「御帰城・知念佐敷おもろ」/洋上を与那原へ帰帆	②a

　この一連の「みおやだいりおもろ」については、早くは1924年に伊波普猷が『おもろさうし選釈』において巻22のオモロ全てについて「古来儀式の時に用ゐられたものであるから、煩はず全部略解をつけ」た。しかし、本歌オモロとの比較やその重複の様態、さらには詞書の行幸経路については言及しておらず、久高渡海部分についても、その現実性を疑っていないようである。

　近年の研究では、1985年に外間と波照間が久高島関係のオモロの解釈を行い、「知念

41

久高行幸之御時おもろ」に関しては、重複歌を全て掲げている。両人は行幸の事実については疑問を呈している［外間・波照間1985: p. 88］。久高と知念玉城を同時に行幸する「知念久高行幸」という国家祭祀は、いかなる琉球史料にも名を見出すことができないからであるという。後代の民間の東御廻りの経路と比較して、「斎場御嶽よりの久高遙拝を久高への渡御にかわるもの」と指摘している［同前］。オモロ詞書からみて、その行程を辿って行幸が実際に行われたようにみえるが、以下指摘するようにその現実性には疑いがある。

　先ず問題は、第22巻のオモロのほとんどが、既に他の巻に収録されているオモロばかりを組み合わせたもので、しかも、長いものでも短縮されて二節オモロに統一的に改作して編集された跡が甚だしい。本歌の祭祀状況を再現するのではなく単に暗示をするだけである。斎場御嶽と久高渡島部分について短縮状態を調べてみると、1536番（帆上：0832）、1537番（久高渡中：0819）の完全重複歌を除き、斎場御嶽でのオモロ1533番は本歌34が11節24行を2節6行へ、斎場御桟敷のオモロ1534番は本歌514の20節21行から2節3行に大幅に削り落とされ、祭祀文脈が分からなくなっている。しかも久高島からの復路のオモロがない（表1参照）。したがって、久高島渡島部分は実際に航海を行ったとは見えず、仮想の渡島儀礼を想定したものと思われる。

　次の問題点は、オモロ本歌の祭祀状況が「知念久高行幸」の該当オモロの場面や状況にときに対応していないことである。2番目の「与那原村稲福親雲上宿」のオモロ1530番は稲大祭のオモロ1517番と同一で、それらの本歌695は首里城で行われた君手摩儀礼のオモロで全く状況が異なるオモロ冒頭部の転用である。オモロ1533番「斎場御嶽にて」の本歌34は1500年の八重山出陣の戦勝祈願が寄満で行われた際のオモロであるが、大君の斎場御嶽への降臨を示す冒頭2節だけが借用されている。また、オモロ1534番「斎場御桟敷」の本歌514は、久高渡海を実際に行っていた時代に久手堅半島を周航して斎場御嶽参りの後、東方へ船出するオモロである。「斎場御嶽／ソコニヤ嶽」という冒頭2節のみが借用されている。また、最後の「御帰城の御時」オモロ1545番は、船で斎場御嶽から佐敷を経て与那原に帰帆するときに謡われたオモロと推測できるが、『女官御双紙』記載の1677年と1706年の大君御新下り行幸が陸路をとって行われたことを考慮すると、行幸の現実に即していない。以上のオモロ本歌は、異なる祭祀状況を示しているので、その祭祀文脈を脱落させ、名目的に経路に合わせ順次編集されているかのようである。

　では、果たして「知念久高行幸」の一連のオモロは、本当に詞書の示す現地で謡われたものだろうか。一つの可能性は、1875年執行の最後の御新下りの儀礼のアラシクェーナがそうであったように、久高渡島部分が仮想の航海儀礼であったことである。御新下り以外に「知念久高行幸」が示す経路をとって実際に聞得大君が行幸をした時代があるとすれば、それは国王による東方行幸の廃止以後、つまり1673年以後の麦稲祭祀である。

　かつて国王とともに大君が四月稲のミシキョマの知念・玉城行幸を行っていた際は、

知念城内の御殿で宿泊していたといわれるが、1673年以後、大君のみの「東御廻り」となって、玉城巫殿内での宿泊に変更されたという説もある［湧上1982: p.123］。その経路は巻22の「知念久高行幸」ルートに該当する。とすれば、行幸オモロ17編は1673年と現存『おもろさうし』尚家本の成立年1710年の間に編集された可能性もある[20]。

ところが、既に引いたように、『聞得大君御殿并御城御規式之御次第』によれば、かつて国王と大君は、「五月御祭ニ者、(中略)難有御報恩ニ」久高島と知念玉城を一年交替で御直参したというのである。一年交替で二月の麦のシキョマに久高行幸、四月の稲のシキョマに知念玉城に行幸したばかりか、五月にも「難有御報恩ニ」知念に行幸したと読める。『由来記』巻一「王城之公事」四月「行幸於知念及玉城」の条にも、「隔年一次、五月祭之時、知念行幸、有御祭禮也。御規式四月行幸同。」とある。つまり、両文書を総合すると久高行幸の年か知念玉城行幸の年に、五月にも再び「難有御報恩ニ」知念に行幸していたことになる。二月久高もしくは四月に知念玉城に行き再び五月に知念に行くということは相当の負担であるから、その際には、久高に渡島すべき所を斎場御嶽からの遙拝で済ませる可能性が大となる。

しかし、上記『由来記』の箇所に明記されるように、1673年以降麦稲行幸祭祀が当役の代参になってしまえば、1710年再編集の時点における巻22のミオヤダイリの実態としては、「知念久高行幸」がすべて仮想の祭祀で、行幸を想定して別の場所、例えば首里城でオモロの吟唱だけで済まされた可能性も想定できる。

上記『聞得大君御殿并御城御規式之御次第』の「御城御規式之次第」には、「二月大島［久高島］麦之穂祭之前日、麦之美穂、久葉之根被差上候はヽ、当日、御主加那志前、大君加那志、司雲上按司、各御ささかに而御勤被遊候事。」、また、「四月、知念玉城稲之みしきよま祭。(中略)五月稲之穂祭者、(中略)御規式者二月御祭同断」とある。つまり、久高と知念玉城への行幸が行われなくなって以後、二月麦と四月稲の「みしきよま」祭と五月稲穂祭に、正殿二階の「おささか」(玉座「御差床」)で礼拝が行われていたことが分かる。王城稲之穂祭には、次の節に述べるように、城下の三人の大あむしられと首里根神が北殿で稲穂儀礼を行い、正殿二階のせんみこちやに呼ばれて国王から饗応を給わり下城した後、正殿一階(下庫理)にて、男性官員だけで国王出御の「下こほり之御勤」[21]が行われる。

以上の史料の記述内容から分かることは、王城の五月稲之穂祭には、全国の先鞭を切る主旨のみでなく、前代に知念久高に行幸していた時代の二月久高と四月知念玉城の「みしきよま」祭の「難有御報恩」の祭祀の意味が込められていることである。

とすれば、五月の「難有御報恩」の王城正殿の稲穂祭の祭礼の場で、上記「知念久高行幸」のオモロが吟唱され、かつての行幸に替える代理祭祀が行われた可能性が十分考えられるのである。

そう想定する理由は、巻22所収の他のみおやだいり、すなわち「稲の穂祭之時おもろ」と「稲の大祭之時おもろ」を構成するオモロ群が、上記「知念久高行幸」のオモロ以上に、相異なる祭祀状況のオモロ本歌を取り集め編集した混成祭祀の様相を呈してい

2. 首里城稲祭祀におけるミオヤダイリのオモロの混成状況

　王城での稲二祭の祭式準備と執行経過については、大庫理（正殿二階）での儀礼を除き、幸いにも、鎌倉芳太郎が筆写した王府下庫理勢頭方編集の『稲之二御祭公事』文書（1802年成立）により詳細が判明する。それにより、『おもろさうし』巻22に収録されている「稲の穂祭之時おもろ」と「稲の大祭之時おもろ」が、どのような状況で謡われたものかが明らかになる。

　オモロの編成は、以下のように、1513番を除き他の全てに本歌が確認でき、本歌が長い編成でもすべて2節オモロに編集し直されている。重複の様態は、ほぼ完全重複の1首（1526番）[22]と、本歌第2節以外の後続節を選択するオモロ1508番[23]のほかは、ほとんどが単純短縮の事例に属し[24]、表記の変更はいずれも微細なものに留まる。つまり「知念久高行幸之御時おもろ」と同様、本歌を単純に短縮して祭祀文脈を隠し2節編成のオモロに統一しようとする意図が強く表れている。

表3　『おもろさうし』巻22「稲二祭オモロ」本歌と祭祀状況一覧

オモロ番号／本歌		本歌祭祀状況	参加人物・神女	重複様態
稲の穂祭之時おもろ（＊：二節以上）				
1508／	*242	穂祭	尚真、あまみきよ	②b'
1509／	*722	首里城京の内祭祀	聞得大君、京の内のろ	②a
1510／	*631	国王へのセジ込め	国王、精の君、君よし	②a'
1511／	*672	継世門での稲の王城への供奉		②a
1512／	*330	祭に備え神酒の柄杓の制作	君加那志	②a
1513／		世襲いセジ	煽りやへ、差笠	－
1514／	188	鼓拍子を国王に献ず	差笠	①'
1515／	*237	奥武の嶽での祭祀	玉を履き神衣装の神女	②a'
1516／	239	首里森・眞玉森ぐすく	あまみや	①'
稲の大祭之時おもろ				
1517／	*695	君手摩の百果報（1545年）	聞得大君	②a
1518／	*723	君手摩前年予祝	聞得大君	②a
1519／	*736	君手摩（オボツ・カグラ）	煽りやへ	②a
1520／	*173	国王慶賀	差笠	②a
1521／	*112	京の内	聞得大君	④a
1522／	*205	京の内（君手摩前年予祝）	首里大君	②a

1523/	*732	オボツセジを国王に奉る	聞得大君	②a'
1524/	*040	寄満創建、ニルヤセジを国王に奉る		②a
1525/	*324	帯剣の国王慶賀	君加那志	②a'
1526/	308	御嶽での祈願	君加那志	①'
1527/	*335	首里森グスク	百度踏み揚がり	②a
1528/	*336	今帰仁城金比屋武御嶽	百度踏み揚がり	②a

　『稲之二御祭公事』の記述によれば、王城での稲穂祭のうち、国王が出御する正殿下庫理での「美御前揃之御規式」でこれらのオモロは吟唱されたようである。北殿で城下の神女が「御たむとの御規式」を行っている間に、オモロが吟唱された形跡はない。残念ながら、正殿二階大庫理の御差床で行われたはずの国王と大君による儀礼の次第は記録されていない。オモロ吟唱を担当する男性の「神歌人数座」は、神歌主取一人、神歌親雲上三人、神歌勢頭部四人からなり、四人づつ二手に分れて、正殿孫庇（五者い）の内部の南と北に一列に並んだ。

　四つ時になると漏刻門で鐘が衝かれ、官員全員が下庫理に着座すると、楽が奏せられ、国王の出御となる。国王の玉座（御差床）前には、予め献上の御酒が供えられ、オモロの吟唱が始まっており、入御の際に一端止め、外の御庭の三番目の敷瓦左右（南北）に並んでいる楽隊が吹吶の楽を奏でる。三司官親方当が「三ツ飾之御規式」（『図帳（当方）』絵図参照）を玉座の前で行ない、神酒を国王に献上するときは、外の楽隊が半笙の楽を奏でる。諸官に酒が配られる間、オモロの吟唱が続く。「稲の穂祭之時おもろ」である。酒の後は御茶が国王に献上される時に半笙の楽があり、官員にも配られ一巡すると、三司官三人が席を発ち、正殿入口中央に設けられる「御差床御拝所」に並び、国王に対して立ち御拝を行なう。国王入御の後、禁裏に献上された稲穂が下げられてくると、世子以下王子衆と按司衆、そして下庫理内外に参列の諸官にも配られ、御祝の酒も配られ儀礼は終了、世子以下が退場する。オモロの吟唱は、いわばバックコーラスに過ぎない。

　ところが、稲穂・稲大祭のオモロの本歌の内容をみると、ほとんど全てに王族神女が登場する祭祀の情景を謡っている（表3）。祭場の現実とオモロ本歌の祭祀状況との落差には驚かされる。正殿下庫理には、二階の御差床で国王とともに稲穂を拝礼したはずの大君もいなければ、先刻まで城下から登城して北殿で稲穂祭祀を行っていた三平等の大あむしられも居らず、まして、オモロに謡われている他の王族神女は疾うに廃位されていて登場するべくもない。不在の神女が謡われるというより、神女の不在が示されているともいえる。

　オモロの本歌が示す状況を稲穂祭と稲大祭で比較してみると、興味深い違いが見えてくる。稲穂祭の「稲の穂祭之時おもろ」本歌の連続からは、東方巡拝の痕跡がかすかに読み取れる。東方の知念玉城から始まった農耕神話と建国神のアマミキヨを謡うオモロ1508番で始まり、遥か太古（あまみや）以来の由緒ある首里城（首里森・眞玉森ぐすく）

を謡う1516番でおわる。1509番の本歌722が聞得大君と京の内の神女達を謡うことは、稲穂祭に礼拝されることのない京の内（首里城聖地）巡拝のオモロを正殿下庫理で謡うことによって代替しているかのようである。1511番は東方から豊饒（ユー）が継世門を通って訪れる趣旨を謡う本歌672から、継世門の句が省かれたものである。城下の三箇間切から稲穂が捧げられることを意味すると同時に、かつて東方に稲実成長の報恩に行幸した故事を謡っているともみなせる。他にも、宣の君（1510番）、君加那志（1512番）、煽りやへ（1513番）、佐司笠（1514番）など、かつて王城祭祀に登場した王族神女（三十三君）の祭祀の情景を謡うオモロを並べているが、かつては王城の聖域と御庭で行われていた稲穂祭の儀礼を呼び起こす代償行為にもみえる。

　稲大祭のオモロをみてみよう。12首（1517番～1528番）のオモロもすべて他の巻に出ているものの再録で、2節に短縮されている。君手摩儀礼に関連するものが5首（1517番、1518番、1519番、1522番、1523番）もある。君手摩儀礼とは、薩摩の琉球入り後は廃止されたと見られる、王府神女の就任後に王宮で行われた国王慶賀の儀礼であり[Iyori 2005c]、祭祀の文脈が稲祭祀とは全く異なる。当初、御内原の「かわるめの真庭」で、あるいは首里城の聖域「京の内」で降霊祭祀を行った後、御庭に出て城内の官員参列のなか国王慶賀儀礼を挙行するものであった。ところが、短縮歌では君手摩儀礼の文脈を切り落とし聖地巡回のオモロに再編成されている。

　続くオモロ1524番は、オモロ40番が本歌、すなわち首里城寄満（炊事屋）の竣工を祝うオモロで、従来諸説分立して解釈の一定しない三庫理も登場している。筆者の解釈は首里三平等の大あむしられの参加ということである。詳しくは拙著［伊從2005b: p.511］を参照いただくとして、このオモロの最初の2節、ニライ大主と国王を謡う部分だけを謡い、寄満創建の祭祀文脈は隠されている。続く3首は首里城もしくは聖域で神女が国王の勢力盛んなることを祈る歌である。最後は、今帰仁城聖域金比屋武[25]での神女の祈りで終わる。

　以上、「稲の大祭」のオモロ本歌の選択基準を推測すると、現実には行われない稲大祭の首里城内の聖地巡拝（御内原の「かわるめの真庭」から京の内そして寄満、そして城外の園比屋武御嶽まで）をオモロの引用によって暗示しつつ、最後は前王権の神女百度踏み上がりの礼拝を想起する趣旨が見えてくる。しかし、近世の首里城では、稲二祭に城内の聖域で儀礼が行われた形跡がないのである。今日に残る離島の稲二祭の城上り・御嶽参り祭祀において、必ず城跡や御嶽を礼拝する祭祀過程［伊從1989、同2005a］を重視する原則（久米島・久高島など参照）と比較すると、王城での儀礼現実は非常に奇異である。城下神女の登城儀礼と正殿一階の国王出御の政治儀礼に終わっているのである。いわば、王国の腰当ての首里城で、稲二祭祭祀の核心部分が欠如しているのである。それを補完しているのが、編集されたオモロの吟唱で暗示されるとともに（オモロの短縮によって）隠される、古琉球の失われた稲祭祀の追憶であるかのようである。

まとめ：代理祭祀としてのオモロ吟唱から神女不在の提示としてのオモロ吟唱儀礼へ

　久高島への現実の渡海儀礼が実施されていた時代の現場で謡われた儀礼歌謡が『おもろさうし』には記録されている反面、巻22「知念久高行幸」編にみられるように、架空の航海儀礼歌として本歌が編集し直されている場合が確認できた。さらには、実際には執行されない首里城内の聖地での稲二祭の架空の儀礼を、古琉球のオモロを短縮してつなぎ合わせ編成することによって、現実に行われている政治儀礼と併行してヴァーチュアルに生み出す演出技術が、安仁屋家に伝えられたオモロ吟唱法には含まれていたことになる。

　オモロ古歌に手を加えた巻22の連続演奏は、一面で、かつて行われた古祭祀の現場を暗示しつつ、短縮して編集し直される解釈行為を通じて隠され、最終的に、王族神女の消えた首里城内の政治儀礼の場で、不在の神女の儀礼すなわち古琉球の祭祀世界の不在を示す装置となったといえよう。

注

1)　本稿は、2006年9月14日～16日、ヴェネチア　カ・フォスカリ大学東アジア学科主催で行われた第5回沖縄研究国際シンポジウム「想像の沖縄：その時空間からの挑戦」にて筆者が口頭で発表した英文原稿に邦文に加筆してなったものである。

2)　『女官御双紙』「君南風」の条、『君南風由来并位階且公事』［法政大学1983］参照。

3)　『由来記』玉城間切の稲二祭祭場で謡われるウムイには「オボツヤマ／トウサヤ／アヨレドモ／□□（集落名）ノ／オヒャクメイノ／イシュヅカエニ／ヨヨレタル」（オボツ山は遠くにあるけれども、□□村の長の立派な招請に応じてカミが降臨された）とあり、勝連間切にも相似たウムイが記録されている。オボツ山の解釈については、［クライナー1977：p.96］［小野1982：p.108］参照。また、両解釈に対する筆者の考えと他の代替祭祀の幻視事例については［伊従（1987a）2005b：p.150、p.600 注91］参照。

4)　［玉城1991］所収のオモロにおける祭祀モチーフの分類研究を参照。

5)　［島村1983］［波照間1995］［同1996］参照。

6)　現存『おもろさうし』が1710年に再編された時点で生じた重複・類型オモロの研究や、尚家本と安仁屋家伝来本の異同の書誌的な研究は、オモロが記述する祭祀の内容の研究とともに、オモロ研究の両輪をなしている。その両面における先学の仕事を前提に、重複歌や類型歌のオモロについて、その祭祀的な意味を問うのが本稿の課題のひとつである。

7)　『中山世鑑』（1650年編）巻四尚円王即位の条の前王尚徳王の久高行幸の指摘、正史『球陽』尚円王の条や尚質王20（1667）年の条、『琉球国由来記』（1713年、以下『由来記』）巻一三大里間切友盛ノ御嶽の条、『佐銘川大主由来記』聞得大君漂流の条、『聞得大君御殿并御城御規式之御次第』（1875年編）など参照。

8)　『由来記』大里間切「友盛ノ御嶽御イベ」の条、『遺老説伝』附巻134、『佐銘川大主由来記』参照。

9)　『女官御双紙』記載の二例の御新下りの記録（1677年と1706年）、および『聞得大君御殿并御城御規式之御次第』収録のルートは陸路で、斎場御嶽で泊まり、翌日往路を逆に辿って首里に戻る。知念や玉城には向かわない。

10)　「右ニ付［五月御祭ニ者］、難有御報恩ニ久高島江、御主加那志前、聞得大君加那志、三平等

大主部、親方部以下、御召附け被仰付、御直参、知念玉城江壹年越御直参被遊候処、浮名入之御跡より、御繁多ニ付、御直参不被遊候（後略）」［下線引用者］。

11) 1677年の王府の決定（『球陽』巻七）。後述のように同年、久高島にあった聞得大君の行幸御殿が解体され、尚貞王妃の御新下りが斎場御嶽で行われる。

12) 『中山世鑑』巻1および袋中上人の証言［『琉球神道記』巻5「新神」の条］参照。［伊従（1993）2005b: p. 377］、［Iyori, 2005c］参照。

13) 倉塚曄子は、オモロ514番を御新下りのオモロとみなしている数少ない研究者の一人である［倉塚1979: pp. 150–63］。しかし、その論理には無理がある。本オモロを含む巻10が編集された1623年には、依然として久高島渡島祭祀が実行されていたから、このオモロを斎場御嶽で完結する1677年以降開始される「御新下り」のオモロとみなすことはできないからである。

14) 『南島歌謡大成』巻I（沖縄篇上）所収クェーナ35番〜39番。以下、クェーナ番号で示す。

15) 尚貞王妃の御新下り執行の年の1677年に、久高島に存在した国王と大君が行幸時に使用した御殿が解体された記録がある［『球陽』尚貞王9年］。

16) 御待御殿は聖域外に建てられる仮御殿で神殿ではない。二つの枕の存在を日本天皇の大嘗祭神殿に設けられる真床御ふすまに結びつけて、御新下り儀礼を聖婚儀礼と捉えようとする［島袋1950］［新里1970］［山内1981］などの説が主張されたが、御新下り儀礼の論理の起源が、国王を守護する婚姻禁忌の対象の姉妹がオナリ神に就任するところにあることに対する考慮が欠けている。しかし、聞得大君を主后に固定させた1677年の王府の決定自体は、聞得大君継承のオナリ神原則を放棄して、世俗婚の相手を神職に充てたことを意味している。

17) この点については、拙書［伊従2005b］第10章8を参照。

18) そのうち近代にまで伝わったものは僅かであった。伊波普猷は安仁屋真苅翁から巻22のオモロの歌い方と読み方を習っている［伊波（1925）全集6: p. 216］。山内盛彬も同翁から巻22オモロ1508番、1509番、1517番＝1530番、1550番、1554番のそれぞれ第一節の歌い方を採譜している［山内1981:「王府のおもろ」］。

19) いわゆる重複オモロについて、「表記」「詞句・詞章」「節数」「記載法」を手がかりに重複の様態の分類を波照間［1996］は試み、完全重複（I）、不完全重複（II）、非重複（III）の3種に別けた。波照間の分類は厳密なのだが、本稿が関心する巻22の短縮オモロに関して云えば、完全重複歌（①とする）を別とすると、不完全重複の節数が異なる分類について波照間の分類を参考にすれば足りる。表記・詞句・詞章に異同がなく本歌第3節以下を単純に省略する場合（②a）と、本歌第2節以外の節を選択的に残している場合（②b）にまず別ける。次に、表記に微細な異同（助詞の脱落や相違、仮名と漢字表記の違いなど）があり単純な省略の場合（②a'、波照間の⑥aに相当）と選択的省略の場合（②b'、波照間の③に相当）。詞句・詞章に異同（詞句が一部入れ替わったり脱落）があり第3節以下を単純に省略する場合（④a）と選択的に省略する場合（④b）で分類は足りる。波照間はこれらのうち、②a、②a'を不完全重複歌とみ、他を「改作」の意識があるとみて「類歌」とする。

20) 池宮は安仁屋家本巻22「御冠船之御時おもろ」の行間に尚穆王冊封の時（1756年）にオモロが変更された記録が記されていることから、巻22の改訂が同年にも行われたとみる［池宮編1987: p. 12］。

21) 下庫理に国王が出御して行われる行政儀礼を、『由来記』「王城之公事」「稲之穂祭」は「美御前揃之御規式」と記す。

22) 本歌も2節編成のオモロで、助詞の違いや脱落程度の表記の相違の重複状態を「①'」と表記する。

23) 本歌第3節が稲穂祭であることをより明瞭に示す「穂花　とて　ぬき上げは／塵錆は　付けるな」とあるので、第2節を削除して繰り上げている。形式上は類歌でも意味上では同様と見なせる。

24) 重複様態を「④a」とした1521番は、「②a」の単純短縮の第2節の第2行以下を脱落させたものなので、意味上は「②a」と同等。

25) 伊波はこの金比屋武を首里城歓会門前の園比屋武御嶽ととる真境名安興の説を紹介している［伊波（1924）巻 6: p. 171］。とすれば、稲大祭のオモロの並び方は、城内の御物参の順路とほぼ同じものとなる。

参考文献

畠山篤（1991）「神々の船―久高島の外来神の去来」桜井（編）古典と民俗学叢書一五『久高島の祭りと伝承』桜楓社、東京。
波照間永吉（1995）「重複オモロの実相」『沖縄芸術の科学』8、沖縄。
波照間永吉（1996）「重複オモロの考察：「重複」の実態と「重複」概念の提示」、法政大学沖縄文化研究所『沖縄文化研究』22、東京。
鄭秉哲（編）（1745）『遺老説伝』（『球陽』外巻）、宮本・原口・比嘉（編）『日本庶民生活史料集成』一、三一書房、東京。
外間守善・玉城政美編（1980）『南島歌謡大成』I（沖縄篇上）、角川書店、東京。
外間守善・波照間永吉（1985）「久高島及び周辺聖域の神歌」法政大学沖縄文化研究所久高島調査委員会（編）『沖縄久高島調査報告書』、東京。
法政大学沖縄久米島調査委員会（編）（1983）『沖縄久米島　資料編』弘文堂、東京。
法政大学沖縄文化研究所久高島調査委員会（編）（1985）『沖縄久高島調査報告書』、東京。
伊波普猷（1924）『おもろさうし選釈』；『伊波普猷全集』6、平凡社、東京。
伊波普猷（1925）『校訂おもろさうし』南島談話会、郷土研究社；『全集』6、東京。
池宮正治（1982）「『おもろさうし』の成立」『国文学解釈と鑑賞』47–1；『琉球文学論の方法』1982、三一書房、東京。
池宮正治（編）（1987）『おもろさうし精華抄』ひるぎ社、沖縄。
伊従勉（1987a）「沖縄本島周辺村落の祭場・殿の現象的性格について」『人文學報』（京都大学人文科学研究所紀要）61、京都。
伊従勉（1989）「沖縄久米島の稲祭祀祭場の仮設性について」『人文學報』（京都大学人文科学研究所紀要）63、京都。
伊従勉（1993）「聖なる島への国家的視覚の形成：琉球王国御新下り儀礼に見る久高島の意味」京都大学人間・環境学研究科研究紀要『人間・環境学』2、京都。
伊従勉（2003）「聞得大君の〈御新下り〉儀礼は〈御初地入り〉か：伊波普猷以来の通説再考」『首里城研究』7、首里城公園友の会、沖縄。
伊従勉（2005a）「久米島の三庫理：儀間・嘉手苅の祭祀歌謡にみる首里および首里城の三庫理の記憶」『沖縄民俗研究』24、沖縄民俗学会、沖縄。
伊従勉（2005b）『琉球祭祀空間の研究』中央公論美術出版、東京。
Iyori, T. (2005c). A Culture without Temple: Ritual sanctuarization of landscape and female superiority in the state religion in Ryukyu. In Rykwert, J. & Atkin, T. (Eds.), Structure and meaning in human settlement. University of Pennsylvania Museum.
久米具志川間切（1706 以前）『君南風由来并位階且公事』［法政大学 1983］所収。
クライナー・ヨーゼフ（1976）「南西諸島における神観念・他界観の一考察」『沖縄文化』5–3・4、住谷・クライナー『南西諸島の神観念』1977 再録、東京。
仲原裕（開読）（1998）「五月ウマチーのウムイ」『仲里村史』2、沖縄。
琉球王府（向象賢）（1650）『中山世鑑』、翻刻：伊波・東恩納・横山『琉球史料叢書』5、名取書店、1940、東京。
琉球王府御近習方（1706）『女官御双紙』；小島瓔禮（編）1982『神道大系』神社編 52　沖縄、1982 所収、東京。
琉球王府内裏言葉及女官糺奉行（編）（1710 再編）『おもろさうし』全 22 巻；外間・西郷校注岩波思想大系本（1972）、外間校注岩波文庫本（2000）；外間・波照間（編）『定本おもろさうし』

（2002）、東京。
琉球王府（1713）『琉球国由来記』；翻刻：伊波・東恩納・横山『琉球史料叢書』1～2、名取書店、1940、東京。
琉球王府下庫理勢頭方（1802）「稲之二御祭公事」（嘉慶7年成立）沖縄県立大学附属図書・芸術資料館所蔵「鎌倉芳太郎ノート」35B（旧尚侯爵家所蔵本書写ノート）。
琉球王府大里間切（1840）『聞得大君加那志様御新下日記』；小島（編）『神道大系』神社編52 沖縄、1982；法政大学沖縄文化研究所、沖縄研究資料4、1984、東京。
作者不詳『佐銘川大主由来記』琉球大学附属図書館伊波文庫所蔵。
島袋源七（1950）1971「沖縄の民俗と信仰」、谷川（編）叢書我が沖縄第四巻『村落共同体』三一書房、東京。
島村幸一（1983）「『重複オモロ』―諸本が指示する『重複オモロ』を中心に―」『沖縄文化』61、東京。
新里恵二（1970）「沖縄における太陽神崇拝と聖婚儀礼」『沖縄史を考える』勁草書房、東京。
玉城政美（1975）「聞得大君御新下りの構造」『沖縄文化』12-1、東京。
玉城政美（1989）「神女が降りるモチーフ」『沖縄文化』72、東京。
玉城政美（1991）『南島歌謡論』砂子屋書房、東京。
湧上元雄・比嘉康雄（1982）『沖縄の聖なる島々』日本の聖域、第7巻、東京校正出版社、東京。
山内盛彬（1971）「聞得大君と御新下り」谷川（編）叢書我が沖縄第4巻『村落共同体』三一書房、東京。
山内盛彬（1981）『神と人の結婚―聞得大君と御新下り』根元書房、東京。

Romanticizing the Ryukyuan Past: Origins of the Myth of Ryukyuan Pacifism

Gregory Smits*

理想化された琉球の歴史：琉球における平和主義の起源

グレゴリー・スミッツ

　昔から、琉球は人々の空想や願望を反映させる空白の画面として機能してきた。ここでこの現象の一側面、すなわち琉球は平和主義の王国であり、軍や警察力を持たなかったという考えについて述べる。このエッセイは4つの主要部分で構成される。最初は沖縄の平和主義という現代神話の考察である。次に、琉球の平和主義の神話は事実に基づく根拠がないということを明らかにするために、琉球軍の構造体や武器、戦闘などを見てみる。その後、「沖縄は平和主義の歴史がある」という神話の19世紀から、20世紀初期までの展開を論じる。最後に架空の構造としての沖縄・琉球について結論する。

Introduction

　On August 28, 2009 the Okinawa Association of America marked its 100th anniversary by hosting the musical *King Sho Hashi — Dynamic Ryukyu* at the Redondo Beach Performing Arts Center in Los Angeles. The poster promoting the event characterizes it as "an ultra modern *kumiodori* musical in Japanese and English," and the main visual image of the poster features a young man wielding a sword. The sword is not poised for violence. Instead it is held backwards, blade against the forearm, as a dance prop[1] The following passage from an article describing the musical quotes from its producer: "Discussing his purpose in creating the work, producer and stage director Daiichi Hirata said, 'For Okinawans, King Sho Hashi was the first historical figure to have a truly positive impact on the country. I want to take that passionate Okinawan tradition and convey it to future generations using King Sho Hashi as the motif.'"[2] The promotional poster for the musical says of Shō Hashi that "His vision united a kingdom."[3]

---

* Associate Professor, Pennsylvania State University　ペンシルベニア州立大学

Perhaps the most obvious critical detail that comes to mind in examining the discourse surrounding *King Sho Hashi — Dynamic Ryukyu* is the peculiarly modern conception of Okinawa's distant past that assumes some kind of meaningful "Okinawan" identity already existed when Shō Hashi began his conquests. Both Hirata and the promotional poster suggest that there already was a "country" or a "kingdom" of Okinawa, and that Shō Hashi (1372–1439; r. 1422–1439) performed a glorious service for the people living in this place by uniting them. In this view, Okinawa has become a timeless entity, a screen onto which contemporary people can project identities, values and aspirations. Significantly, the promotional literature connected with *King Sho Hashi — Dynamic Ryukyu* is silent about the potentially problematic issue of Okinawa's relationship with Japan. Moreover, the celebratory nature of this musical drama and the literature surrounding it elides something that might seem essential to even the most basic telling of Shō Hashi's story: military violence. Shō Hashi ruled Chūzan at a time when Okinawa was home to three small states. He waged bloody military campaigns in the north and south of Okinawa to conquer Hokuzan (also called Sanboku, destroyed in 1416) and Nanazan (also called Sannnan, destroyed in 1429). Shō Hashi was surely ambitious, but if his main goal was anything other than personal gain, there is no good evidence of it. Prior to their violent unification, the three Okinawan states maintained tributary relations with the Ming Chinese court via the Ōsōfu, a quasi-independent office located in Chūzan and staffed by Chinese expatriates.[4]

Let us consider a different celebratory version of Shō Hashi's unification, that found in the *Chūzan seikan* (Mirror of Chūzan, hereafter "*Seikan*") The *Seikan* was Ryukyu's first official history, completed in 1650 by Shō Shōken (Haneji Chōshū). Interestingly, the *Seikan* account of Shō Hashi's conquest is much longer than that of Satsuma's conquest of Ryukyu in 1609. Roughly like *King Sho Hashi — Dynamic Ryukyu,* the 1650 account of Shō Hashi contained an agenda that spoke to its contemporary audience. In the classical Chinese manner of writing history, Shō Shōken described Shō Hashi as a virtuous man who brought order to a chaotic Okinawa. Indeed, Shō Hashi "went hungry himself when the people were starving and suffered cold himself when the people were cold." One might wonder how severely the people of Okinawa suffered from the cold, but such language was boilerplate praise in the manner of classical Chinese literature. Furthermore, Shō Hashi was sagacious, his words and deeds were good, and he was free of desires — like King Wen, celebrated founder of the Zhou dynasty in China. By contest, the king of Sannan frequently hosted "large, drunken pleasure banquets" and was without decorum or loyalty[5] Historical sensibility throughout East Asia in the seventeenth century required that the founder of a dynasty be virtuous and the last ruler of a state be depraved. Similarly, though for different ideological reasons, modern Okinawan nationalism tends to romanticize the Ryukyuan past.

The major difference between the seventeenth century account of Shō Hashi and the contemporary musical drama was the emphasis on military conquest. The bulk of the description of Shō Hashi in the *Seikan* details the battles and troop movements that resulted in his ultimate victory. In response to an alleged plan to conquer Shuri by the king of Sanboku, Shō Hashi appointed the *aji* (local warlords) of Urasoe, Goeku, and Yomitan as generals, assembled an army, and set out from Shuri Castle, arriving in Nago several days later. At one point the Chūzan forces outmaneuvered the enemy and their arrows "fell upon them like rain."[6] Another fight involving 200 defenders of a northern castle and 500 Chūzan attackers "stained the grass with blood, and corpses sprawled along the roadway." In addition to swords and arrows, a small band of twenty attackers crept quietly into the castle and set fires.[7] Blood-stained grass and copses lining the roadway were, of course, stock metaphors for describing warfare.

The main point here is that the *Seikan* account is generally accurate in pointing out that Shō Hashi's accomplishment was the result of hard-fought battles in which many Okinawans perished. From the standpoint of 1650, there was no particular reason to cover up or minimize Shō Hashi's warfare, unlike the case of Ryukyu's disastrous war with Satsuma in 1609. Indeed, that war with Satsuma is described only in the histological overview that serves as the *Seikan*'s introduction, and only in brief sterile terms. We read that Shimazu Iehisa dispatched Yokoyama Kenzaemon as a general, who invaded Ryukyu and captured the king. There is no account of specific battles, Iehisa is described as "benevolent and decorous," and a few lines later "wise ruler" Shō Hō reinstated Ryukyu's "old ceremonial customs and music," thus presumably restoring harmony to Ryukyu in classic Confucian style.[8]

Particularity after 1609, Ryukyu's elites had to tread very carefully to maintain some degree of political autonomy. Their general approach was to use connections with China, bakufu fears of military conflict with the Qing court, and features of the Tokugawa-era hierarchy as a counterbalance to Satsuma's power.[9] As part of this process, Ryukyuan elites became increasingly skilled at managing the kingdom's image. They sought to convey to outsiders the image of a small, peaceful kingdom, where Confucian-style virtue mitigated or even eliminated the need for coercive force to maintain domestic order or to defend against external threats such as pirates. Herein lies the basic origin of the myth of Ryukyuan pacifism, which retains widespread currency today. This paper has four interrelated goals. First I survey the contemporary myth of Okinawan pacifism. Second, I survey the structure, weapons, and select battles of the Ryukyu Kingdom's military forces, in part to make it clear that the myth of Ryukyuan pacifism is without a factual basis. Next I discuss the nineteenth and early twentieth-century development of this myth. Finally, I draw some brief conclusions about Okinawa or Ryukyu as an imaginary construct. My basic argument is that Ryukyu has long functioned as a blank screen upon which people have projected fantasies and desires.

1. The Contemporary Myth of Ryukyuan Pacifism

Searching the Web using combinations of terms pairing "Okinawa," or "Ryukyu" with words such as "peace," "weapons," and "rape" reveals a large number of sites, whose topics include the problem of U.S. military bases, the infamous 1995 rape of a twelve-year-old girl, Okinawan martial arts, other Okinawan arts and crafts, and Okinawan history. The content of these sites ranges widely in quality, and some include essays by scholars or others claiming familiarity with some aspect of Okinawan history or culture. Despite diverse content, what many of these sites have in common is the perpetuation of a romantic myth of Okinawan or Ryukyuan pacifism, typically in the service of a contemporary political agenda.

Active or passive acceptance of the myth of Ryukyuan pacifism is common even among historians and other scholars. The usual approach is to juxtapose an alleged pacifistic past with a militarized present. Consider, for example, Laura Hein discussing an article on Okinawan pop music:

> James Roberson discusses Okinawan pop musicians who . . . envision Okinawa as "betwixt and between" powerful external forces but also as embodying social and moral virtues that set them apart from other Japanese and from Americans. Two themes stand out in particular. The first is peacefulness, or "gentle kindness," as the Rinken Band phrases it. That band claims in its songs a long history of diplomacy beginning before Okinawa came under Japanese rule and evokes modern Japanese (and American) bellicosity and Okinawan peacefulness by including a projected photograph of the Okinawa Peace Memorial in its live performances.[10]

When deployed skillfully, this juxtaposition of a peaceful past versus militarized present helps assert that, in addition to the obvious problems associated with the military bases, their presence also violates the very spirit or soul of the peaceful Okinawan people. Such a rhetorical strategy thereby enhances poignancy of the image of Okinawans as victims. This approach often relies on questionable assumptions that Okinawa's people are and have been a singular entity in terms of culture and viewpoint and that conditions obtaining in the rather distant past (the Ryukyu Kingdom ended in 1879) necessarily apply — or presumably *should* apply — in the present.

Perhaps the most prominent figure who regularly alleges past pacifism in addressing the base problem is former governor and Ryukyu University professor Ōta Masahide. For example, in a speech delivered in 1997, while still governor, he asserted that:

> The [Ryukyu] kingdom's predominant features were devotion to peace and an absence of weapons. The people's wide recognition as an unarmed land of courtesy was stressed by the late Professor William Lebra of the University of Hawaii, whose *Okinawan Religion: Belief, Ritual and Social Structure* (1966) argues that the cultures of Japan and Okinawa differ fundamentally. In contrast to Japan's "warrior culture," Okinawa's is notable for an "absence of militarism."[11]

This claim sets up a lengthy discussion of the militarization of Okinawa from 1945 to the present. Notice that Ōta cites the authority of anthropologist William Lebra, most likely in this case because his audience was a U.S. congressional study group.

Although Lebra did not take up the topic as an issue for serious investigation, he perpetuated the myth of Ryukyuan pacifism in the context of presenting background information about Okinawa. Almost certainly the passage to which Ōta refers is one in which Lebra compares Okinawa with the mainland of Japan. While pointing out the relatively more prominent status of women in Okinawa society, he stated that one reason might be:

> the absence of militarism during the past five hundred years . . . Nearly all Western visitors since the time of Captain Hall have commented on the mildness and lack of overt aggression in Okinawan behavior. The absence of any martial spirit save where infrequently inculcated by the Japanese was particularly apparent in the battle for Okinawa during World War II, when virtually every Japanese fought until killed or committed suicide while Okinawans were not averse to surrender when they could.[12]

As we will see, Lebra was incorrect about the absence of militarism for 500 years and the lack of battle-related suicides among Okinawans. We will also see that "Captain Hall" and other British sailors who visited Naha in 1816 were indeed influential perpetrators of an idealized image of Ryukyu. We will return to Hall later, but here it is interesting to note that although Ōta appropriated Lebra's authority in the passage above, it is highly unlikely that Ōta or others who seek to expose Okinawan suffering would actually quote from Lebra as I have here. The reason is that we now have strong evidence pointing to a scenario precisely the opposite of that described by Lebra. In other words, Japanese soldiers during the Battle of Okinawa often surrendered, whereas many Okinawan civilians killed themselves and their families, often in especially gruesome ways. Indeed, these group suicides have become a major grievance in the contemporary narrative of Okinawan victimization.[13]

The juxtaposition of an allegedly idyllic land without weapons or violence and the militarized islands of today, leads almost inevitably to the metaphor of rape. In an essay entitled "The Rape of Okinawa," George Feifer takes the usual rhetorical approach, setting the stage as follows:

> Throughout the centuries when Japan was almost hermetically sealed against foreigners, Okinawans welcomed their ships with a graciousness that startled passengers and crews. Although fear may have prompted it, the callers did not think so. Another eighteenth-century [sic] Englishman spoke for almost all such travelers when he reported Okinawans' most prominent characteristics as "their gentleness of spirit and manner, their yielding and disposition, their hospitality and kindness, their aversion to violence and crime." "For gentle dignity of manners, superior advancement in the arts and general intelligence," another sailor maintained, "the inhabitants . . . are by far the most interesting, enlightened nation in the Pacific Ocean." The Russian writer Ivan Goncharov was skeptical of such praise when he arrived in 1853. But "What a place, what people!" he found. "All exuded such a feeling of peace, simplicity, honest labor and plenty that it seemed to me . . . a longed-for haven."[14]

The paragraphs that follow this passage describe the U.S. military bases and the suffering they inflict on Okinawa's inhabitants. The title of Feifer's essay was surely prompted by an actual incident, which he mentions in the preliminary paragraphs: the 1995 rape of twelve-year-old schoolgirl by three U.S. soldiers. Although sexual assault had long been a scourge connected with the bases, this particular incident became a *cause célèbre* among women's advocacy groups and the anti-base movement. The victimization of this young, innocent girl quickly came to symbolize the larger-scale rape of the former "peaceful kingdom."[15]

While there are many good arguments for eliminating or reducing the U.S. military presence on Okinawa, the rhetorical strategy of invoking contrast with an allegedly peaceful kingdom of centuries past is based on dubious assumptions about the normative force of history and the social and cultural coherency of "Okinawa" across time. More fundamentally, it is simply incorrect. The Ryukyuan state, like all states, relied ultimately on coercive force — or the threat of it — to maintain order. Military force created the Ryukyu Kingdom, first to unite Okinawa under Shō Hashi and then to subjugate the other Ryukyu Islands and bring them under Shuri's control. In consolidating its empire and maintaining it, the Okinawan polity in Shuri sometimes clashed militarily with southward-expanding polities based in the province of Satsuma. To the south, Shuri relied heavily on tribute trade with China, and pirates often attacked its ships and sometimes even the port of Naha. In short, the Ryukyu kingdom did not lack police and military forces or occasions to use them.

2. Military Affairs in the Ryukyu Kingdom

Soon after military force placed Okinawa under one ruler in 1429, the conquest of the other Ryukyu Islands began. Let us consider the example of Amami-Ōshima and nearby Kikaijima. In 1450 (1451 in some accounts), six shipwrecked Koreans drifted to Gajashima, a small island in the Satsunan chain. They reported that the island was half under the control of Satsuma and half under the control of Okinawa. Later, four of these Koreans were taken to Sasari at the northern end of Amami-Ōshima. The local Okinawan military commander there sent the Koreans on to Shuri, where they met with the king and other officials. From their account, we know that Amami-Ōshima was under Okinawan military control by that time but that the fight to control Kikaijima was still in progress. Several Korean accounts point to the 1440s as the time Okinawan forces conquered Amami-Ōshima. On nearby Kikaijima, residents resisted the Okinawan invaders vigorously, finally causing King Shō Toku personally to lead an invasion of the island in 1466.[16]

The observations of the Koreans in 1450 are significant in several respects. Notice, for example, that at this time Okinawans controlled half of Gajashima, an island very close to Satsuma. The many islands between Satsuma and Okinawa served as potential objects of conflict between a northward-expanding Ryukyu Kingdom and the southward-expanding ambitions of some of the warlords who controlled Satsuma. Gajashima seems to have been the all-time northernmost limit of Shuri's military control. The Chikama family, retainers of the Hōjō, controlled Satsuma at the turn of the fourteenth century, and they forged a network of trade routes throughout the northern Ryukyu Islands. In 1493, a force from Satsuma invaded Amami-Ōshima and clashed with an army under Shuri's command. In a bloody battle, the Ryukyuans drove off the Satsuma invaders.[17] In 1537, King Shō Shin (r. 1477–1527), often credited by modern myth-makers with creating the "peaceful kingdom" by confiscating and locking up all weapons, led an invasion force of Okinawan soldiers to quell a rebellious Amami-Ōshima. The *Kyūyō*, an official history, states that Shō Sei dispatched soldiers to Ōshima in 1538. Some accounts record King Shō Gen as leading an invasion of Amami-Ōshima in 1571, though there is some debate among historians regarding the veracity of the 1571 campaign.[18] Invasions of Miyako, Yaeyama, and other islands also took place during the fifteenth and sixteenth centuries. In short, the Ryukyu Kingdom functioned as a small-scale empire, created, expanded, sustained, and defended by the use of military force.

From the Koreans who drifted to Gajashima in 1450 we know that Ryukyuan firearms (hand cannon) at this time were of advanced design, "similar to those of our own country." The Koreans reported that they studied these weapons with the aid of a royal official charged with the oversight of firearms. Such firearms almost certainly came from China. Ming court records include a 1452 decree by the Board of Justice forbidding the practice by residents of the Fujian coast of conveying military hardware to Ryukyuans in private trade deals. The inhabitants of coastal areas of Fujian often stockpiled weapons to repel *wakō* pirate attacks.[19]

Other shipwrecked Koreans described military affairs in and around Shuri castle in detail in a 1462 account. The soldiers guarding the perimeter of the castle served yearly tours of duty, with a member of the royal family appointed to train and oversee each year's new conscripts. The basic unit of the army was a 100-man group, several of which guarded the castle. When the king ventured out, a 300-man contingent of mounted soldiers accompanied him. Within the castle, about 100 people serving in five-day rotations administered the military forces and made logistical arrangements. Outside of Shuri, a local warlord administered a stone castle in each of the nearby districts. The Korean account did not specify the number of these castles, but other sources list sixteen of them in addition to Shuri.[20]

This early system of military organization was almost certainly the direct predecessor of the *hiki* system established by Shō Shin, a pivotal monarch in Ryukyuan history. Throughout his long reign, he strove, with considerable success, to strengthen the power of the king vis-à-vis the hereditary warlords (*aji*), to enhance the ideological and symbolic authority of the king, and the build a centralized, efficient military system. It is therefore ironic that Shō Shin figures prominently in one variant of the myth of Ryukyuan pacifism: the story of karate. Because the king confiscated weapons and forbade their use, the basic story line goes, Okinawans became adept at fighting with their empty hands or using farm implements as weapons.[21] Modern myth-making notwithstanding, Shō Shin pursued two basic strategies with respect to military affairs. On the one hand, he sought to place all Ryukyuan military power under direct royal command. On the other, he sought to strengthen Ryukyu's military by implementing a more efficient organization and improved infrastructure.

Shō Shin required all local warlords to reside in Shuri, bestowing great social prestige on them while eliminating their military power. To fill the local power gap thus created, the king implemented the so-called *magiri-shima* system. "*Magiri*" were local administrative districts, and the term "*shima*" refers to villages within the districts (probably relying on the metaphor of villages as "islands" within districts). Shō Shin and his successors appointed non-warlord officials to oversee the districts, and the former warlords involved themselves with the aristocratic society of the capital and central government politics. Significantly, references to local military forces in monuments erected between 1522 and 1554 used the term "*magiri gun*" (district forces) instead of *aji gun* (warlord forces). We do not know the details of the composition of these forces, but they were all under Shuri's direct command by the end of Shō Shin's reign.[22]

The *hiki* system was the core of Shō Shin's new military organization. Perhaps the easiest way to grasp the logic of this arrangement is think of "*hiki*" rather literally as meaning "to pull together." Each *hiki* pulled together various officials and military forces into networks capable of dealing with emergencies. The *hiki* combined in one organization both military and police functions, including guard duty, administration of government, and administration of trade. Ryukyuan ships were the governing metaphor of the *hiki*. The *hiki* were led by officials with the title *sedo* (O. *shiidu*), a variant of *sentō*, ship's captain. The names of the *hiki* all ended with *–tomi,* which was also the suffix for the names of large ships (like *–maru* for Japanese vessels). This terminology is indicative of the central importance of oceanic trade, a royal monopoly, for Ryukyu's prosperity. Takara Kurayoshi has characterized the *hiki* as "overland ships" (*chijō no kaisen*) and ocean-going vessels as "floating *hiki*" (*umi ni ukanda hiki*). Not surprisingly, the *hiki* also provided shipboard military forces for Ryukyuan trade vessels, all of which were armed from 1421 onward. The *hiki* were grouped into three watches (*ban*), each of which contained four *hiki*. It is likely that the heads of these three watches evolved into the Sanshikan (O. Yoasutabe), the highest organ of government in Ryukyu from the sixteenth century until the end of the kingdom.[23] In modern military terminology, one might characterize the *hiki* as rapid deployment forces.

In conjunction with these networks of rapid deployment forces, Shō Shin sought to strengthen the underlying infrastructure of the military, a policy continued by his immediate successors. A famous 1509 monument inscription at Urasoe tells of the king's storing weapons there to reduce the need to obtain them from outlying areas. It is this inscription that is typically cited in connection with claims that Ryukyu became a society without weapons as a result of Shō Shin's policies. The king also walled in the northern face of Shuri castle and in 1522 built a road for military use between Shuri and Naha. In 1546, Shō Sei extended the network of defensive walls around Shuri Castle and constructed Yarazamori Castle to defend the entrance into Naha Harbor. Shō Shin also established an official to oversee artillery deployment and technology.[24] As we will see, the combination of the Yarazamori Castle and effective cannon served the kingdom very well when an invasion force from Satsuma attempted to enter Naha Harbor in 1609. It also helped repel major attacks by pirates in 1556 and 1606.

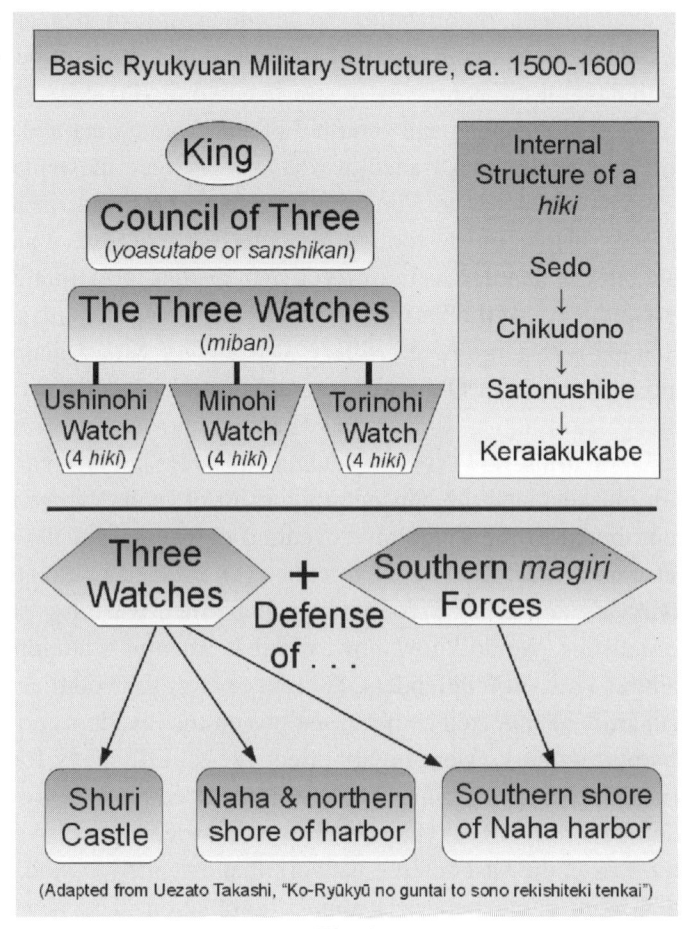

Basic Ryukyuan Military Structure, ca. 1500-1600

King
Council of Three (*yoasutabe* or *sanshikan*)
The Three Watches (*miban*)
- Ushinohi Watch (4 *hiki*)
- Minohi Watch (4 *hiki*)
- Torinohi Watch (4 *hiki*)

Internal Structure of a *hiki*:
Sedo → Chikudono → Satonushibe → Keraiakukabe

Three Watches + Southern *magiri* Forces → Defense of...
- Shuri Castle
- Naha & northern shore of harbor
- Southern shore of Naha harbor

(Adapted from Uezato Takashi, "Ko-Ryūkyū no guntai to sono rekishiteki tenkai")

Fig. 1

By the middle of the sixteenth century, Ryukyu's military had reached its full development, and figure 1 illustrates its basic organization. One general point reflected in this diagram is that Shō Shin's military reforms were in part designed to focus the kingdom's resources on guarding the central organs of state, namely the port of Naha and Shuri Castle. This organizational structure was supported by a network of castles and roads throughout the Shuri-Naha area. Yarazamori Castle and Mie Castle were on opposite sides of the narrow entrance to Naha Harbor. An iron chain boom could be drawn between the two castles to close off the entrance to ships. Large-bore artillery pieces were concentrated in this area as well. Iō Castle, nearby but further into the harbor, functioned as the main arsenal, distributing weapons to the *hiki* soldiers as they assembled at their defensive positions. Tomi Castle, deep inside the harbor, was the command and control center.

The Pearl Road, built explicitly for military purposes, connected these castles to each other and to Shuri Castle.[25]

In terms of the size of Ryukyuan armies, documents connected with Okinawan invasions of other Ryukyu Islands, mobilizations to defend against pirates, and the mobilization to defend against the Satsuma invasion of 1609 indicate a range of between 1000 and 3000 soldiers, with naval flotillas ranging in size from 46 to 100 ships.[26] Ryukyu manufactured some of its own weapons and acquired others from China and Japan. There is abundant evidence that Ryukyuans traded in weapons between these places, most commonly bringing Japanese swords to Ming China, where they were in great demand.[27] Ryukuans often made adaptations to foreign weapons. For example, many sword blades came from Japan, but the handles were of Ryukyuan design to facilitate wielding them with one hand.[28] On the eve of the Satsuma invasion, the kingdom's major port was well fortified and defended with large-bore artillery pieces (shot with a diameter of 7–9 cm was most common). The *hiki* in Okinawa were able to muster an army of about 3,000 soldiers on relatively short notice. Ryukyuan swords and bows were of effective design. Small-bore personal firearms, however, while abundant, were not on a par with Satsuma's muskets. Superior muskets, and the concentration of Ryukyuan defense resources in the port of Naha contributed to the kingdom's eventual defeat, as did the battle-hardened quality of the Satsuma invaders.[29]

Although Ryukyu's defeat by Satsuma is well known, there are surprisingly few details on battle statistics. We do know, however, that Satsuma's attempt to enter Naha Harbor was a failure. The 3,000 defenders, the two castles, the boom across the harbor, and the Ryukyuan artillery inflicted heavy casualties on the invaders and caused them to retreat. The Naha port defenses were highly effective. Unfortunately for the defenders, the various overland approaches to Shuri castle were guarded much less effectively. After a Satsuma force broke through Ryukyuan defenses at Urasoe, it quickly surrounded Shuri Castle, cutting it off from the vast defense network that extended around Naha Harbor.[30]

After 1609, Ryukyu came under Satsuma's domination. The new political order undoubtedly resulted in changes to its military affairs, but many details of this period await further research. Overall, however, it is important to stress that post 1609 Ryukyu was not without armed military and police forces. Pirate attacks on Ryukyuan shipping remained a common problem, and Satsuma occasionally complained that Ryukyuan sailors did not defend their ships vigorously enough (Satsuma typically put up most of the capital for Ryukyu's tribute trade after 1609).[31] Ryukyuan ships sailing to China continued to be armed for their voyages and to need those arms. Seventeenth-century bureaucratic reforms reduced the status of the *hiki* but did not eliminate them. One document points out that in response to the appearance of a foreign ship at Yaeyama in 1640, "soldiers from Satsuma and several hundred Ryukyuan soldiers" were dispatched.[32]

After 1609, Ryukyu's tributary relations with China became crucially important for the kingdom's political autonomy. The kingdom's greatest military challenge, therefore was to ensure that tribute relations and trade took place without incident. Numerous accounts of Ryukyuan tribute ships battling pirates are found in the *Kyūyō,* an official history. An entry for 1672 describes Ryukyuan tribute ships surrounded by pirates who attacked with flaming arrows. After a "bloody battle," the Ryukyuan ships broke through the ring of pirate boats, at a cost of six sailors killed and twenty-four wounded.[33] In another incident during the reign of Shō On (r. 1795–1803), two Ryukyuan ships on their way to China fought a pitched overnight battle with three pirate ships. The Ryukyuan crew members brandished weapons (*heiki*) and used "a new type of cannon" (*ifū no teppō*) in their defense, which was ultimately successful—at least according to the official version of events.[34] Apparently these same ships were attacked again near Fujian, and the *Kyūyō* explains that the Ryukyuans manned their battle stations and defended themselves with cannon and pikes. The pirates sent out smaller boats that surrounded the tribute ships, and the battle took many twists and turns before the damaged Ryukyuan ships were able to enter Fujian.[35]

The importance of trade and diplomacy for the kingdom's prosperity both before and after 1609 required it to maintain naval forces capable of repelling the pirate attacks that were endemic in the South China seas. Moreover, the post-1609 Ryukyuan state sometimes wielded coercive force vis-a-vis internal dissenters. For example in 1632, King Shō Hō punished a number of allegedly derelict officials who oversaw the China trade by banishment to remote islands. One was even sentenced to death, but Satsuma intervened to reduce that sentence to banishment.[36] More well-known cases include the execution of Heshikiya Chōbin, Tomoyose Anjō, and fifteen of their supporters in 1734, following a failed bid to topple Sai On's (1682–1761) administration, and the severe punishment of some prominent residents of Kumemura who protested the 1802 change in how Ryukyuan students sent to Beijing were selected (the *kanshō sōdō*). In short, even after 1609, Ryukyu was a normal country, and this normalcy included, for better or worse, state deployment of coercive force for political and economic ends.

3. Origins and Development of the Myth of Ryukyuan Pacifism

One general point to make regarding the image of Ryukyu a pacifist kingdom is that by the nineteenth century Ryukyuan officials had become extremely adept at manipulating the kingdom's image vis-a-vis outsiders. The most important group of outsiders was Chinese investiture envoys (*sakuhōshi*). Let us consider the case of vice-envoy Li Dingyuan in 1800. In *Shi Ryūkyū ki,* Li's detailed record of his stay in Ryukyu, he described with much enthusiasm the plot of the *kumiodori* play *Kōkō no maki* (Tale of filial piety) and concluded with an exclamation that heaven greatly rewards those who give their lives for filial piety.[37] During the eighteenth century, Ryukyuan officials began the practice of entertaining Chinese envoys with *kumiodori* designed to impress upon them the image of a refined and virtuous kingdom. *Kōkō no maki,* based on a legend from the time of King Gihon (r. 1249–1259), involves a daughter who offers her life for the good of society and her impoverished mother, only to be saved by miraculous cosmic intervention. She ends up marrying the king's son. The play was first shown to Chinese envoys in 1756. In Li's case, just before his departure, royal envoys unexpectedly showed up with fans, incense, and other gifts. It was the birthday of his mother in China, but Li had not told anyone in Ryukyu about it. Ryukyuan officials had done their research well, and Li was most impressed by this display of filial consciousness on their part.[38] My point in mentioning Li's experience in Ryukyu is simply to emphasize the skill with which Ryukyuan officials worked to portray positive images to foreign visitors. In classic Confucian values, a state governed by virtue would have little or no need for coercive force. Ryukyuans presented this same general image to European visitors as well as Chinese.

Starting in the early nineteenth century, European ships made their way to Naha with increasing frequency. These visits produced a variety of reports about the inhabitants of Okinawa or other Ryukyu Islands, some of which were published and reached an audience of armchair travelers. The relative obscurity of Ryukyu added to its exotic appeal in such contexts. According to a summary of these accounts by George H. Kerr, "The visitor was invariably struck by the absence of arms or incidents of violence, by the unfailing courtesy and friendliness of all classes, by the intelligence of the gentry, and by the absence of thievery among the common people."[39] Kerr's general history of Ryukyu, the only such work available in English, quotes these European writings at great length, without any serious critique of their contents. Because he did not read Japanese, Kerr depended on assistants to translate or summarize Japanese materials into English. His book, though well-written and intelligent, did not even reflect the state of Japanese scholarship on Ryukyu circa the 1950s. The *hiki* system, for example, a foundational institution in premodern Ryukyu, receives no mention even though Iha Fuyū had already published a widely-known analysis on this topic some two decades earlier. In short, Kerr seems to have had no knowledge of Ryukyuan military affairs and took the nineteenth-century European reports of a pacifist society at face value. I make these points not to criticize Kerr, who did a superb job given his the limitations of his circumstances. His book, however, has been and continues to be, a prominent vehicle for perpetuating the myth of Ryukyuan pacifism.

A major development of myth of Ryukyuan pacifism came from the visit to Naha in 1816 of two British ships, the Lyra and Alceste. The ships were on a mission to survey parts of the Korean coast and the Ryukyu Islands, and they stayed at Naha from September 15 through October 27. Several members of the crew recorded observations of Okinawa, but Basil Hall, captain of the Lyra, and John M'Leod, physician on board the Alceste wrote lengthy accounts that were later published and widely read. These accounts gushed with praise over the kindness, gentleness, and intelligence of the Okinawans, whose behavior compared especially well with the alleged boorishness and arrogance of "the Chinese." According to Hall and M'Leod, Okinawa was a land of peace and serenity. Its residents bore no weapons and its people committed no crimes. According to Hall: "We never saw any punishment inflicted at Loo-choo; a tap with a fan, or an angry look, was the severest chastisement ever resorted to, as far as we could discover."[40] Hall's account of social order enforced by fan taps was destined to be repeated many times and remains a potent image to this day.

It is perfectly likely that Hall's account is accurate as far as it goes. Why would Hall and the other crew members, whose movements were restricted to a small area, ever have had occasion to observe police and judicial activities during their short stay? Obviously Hall was unaware of the kingdom's law court, the *hirajo* or with the Ryukyu's two detailed law codes. Likewise, he was unaware of the offenders against these laws, who had been arrested, tortured, fined, exiled, had their property confiscated, or faced the death penalty.[41] It is hardly surprising that the accounts of Hall and M'Leod describing an idyllic Oriental land of peace and tranquility, free of the scourges of war, weapons and animosity, would have appealed to Europeans in the wake of the Napoleonic Wars. Interestingly, Hall discussed Okinawa with Napoleon himself when the Lyra put in at St. Helena, and reported in his account that:

> Several circumstances . . . respecting the Loo-Choo people surprised even him a good deal; and I had the satisfaction of seeing him more than once completely perplexed, and unable to account for the phenomena I related. Nothing struck him so much as their having no arms. "Point d'armes!" he exclaimed; . . . "Mais, sans armes, comment se bat-on?"
> I could only reply, that as far as we had been able to discover, they had never had any war, but remained in a state of internal and external peace. "No wars!" cried he, with a scornful and incredulous expression, as if the existence of any people under the sun without wars was a monstrous anomaly.[42]

One striking thing about this passage is the implication superior moral virtue for those who hold to a belief in Ryukyuan pacifism, in contrast to a rogue Napoleon who scoffed at it. One suspects that scholars like Ōta, who surely know that the myth is unfounded, are of similar mind. In any case, given the degree of ignorance of Ryukyu and other parts of East Asia that prevailed in 1816, it is conceivable that thoughtful or worldly people might have believed Hall's tale, even if Napoleon did not. Certainly many of them would have wanted to believe in a country without weapons.

At the end of the nineteenth century Basil Hall Chamberlain, a relative of Captain Hall and noted authority on Japan, visited Okinawa Prefecture briefly and published a lengthy analysis in *The Geographic Journal*. His account vigorously endorsed the myth of Ryukyuan pacifism. Part of Chamberlain's account of Ryukyuan history reads:

> In some important respects the country really deserved the title bestowed upon it by a Chinese emperor in 1579, and is still proudly inscribed on the gate of its capital city, the title of "The Land of Propriety." There were no lethal weapons in Luchu, no feudal factions, few if any crimes of violence. . . . Confucius' ideal was carried out — a government purely civil, at once absolute and patriarchal, resting not on any armed force, but on the theory that subjects owe unqualified obedience to their rulers . . .[43]

Here, of course, Chamberlain takes the descriptions of Hall and M'Leod and explains them in terms of classical Confucian values. In Chamberlain's version, Ryukyu was not only a rare or unique example of a society without war, weapons or aggression, but also a rare or unique instance of a Confucian paradise.

Later in his account, Chamberlain restates the matter in terms of the prevailing tenets of racial science. After discussing the physical qualities of Ryukyuans in some detail and comparing them with the qualities of Japanese, Chamberlain states:

> The most prominent race-characteristic of the Luchuans is not a physical, but a moral one. It is their gentleness of spirit, their yielding and submissive disposition, their hospitality and kindness, their aversion to violence and crime. Every visitor has come away with the same favourable impression — Captain Broughton, whom they treated so hospitably on the occasion of his shipwreck in 1797; Captain Basil Hall, Dr McLeod, Dr, Guillemard — even the missionaries, poor as was their success, and all the Japanese. For myself, I met with nothing but kindness from high and low alike.[44]

Today's advocates of the myth of Ryukyuan pacifism similarly speak of "the" Okinawans as if they are and were a singular entity. Instead of relying on notions of racial characteristics, however, the preferences is to rely on a romantic version of history.

The famous scholar of Ryukyu Iha Fuyu (1876–1947) is the final link between more recent conveyors of the pacifist myth like Kerr, Lebra, and Ōta and the original nineteenth century European myth-makers. Iha is a more ambivalent figure in this respect because some of his writing does acknowledge Ryukyu's military past. For example, in the 1930s he analyzed accounts of military affairs in the *Omoro sōshi,* discussing weapons, defense works, the military character of the *hiki,* and related topics.[45] Elsewhere, however, Iha argued that Shō Shin enforced a policy of pacifism (*hisen shugi*) by confiscating weapons and prohibiting their use. He did acknowledge, though, that these moves were also aimed at suppressing internal rebellions and defending against pirates. As Uezato points out, in part owing to an imprecise conception of key concepts such as "defense" or "pacifism" Iha's exact stance is hard to discern.[46]

Conclusion

Among scholars of Ryukyuan history in the early twentieth century, there were explicit critics of the notion of a pacifist Ryukyu kingdom. Yokoyama Shigeru, for example, vigorously criticized Basil Hall's assertion of a land without weapons. Among postwar scholars, Nakahara Zenchū criticized Iha's portrayal of a pacifist Shō Shin, arguing that Shō Shin's policies were moves intended to strengthen the kingdom's military capabilities. Nakahara also argued that it was not the case the Shimazu confiscated the kingdom's weapons after 1609. In recent decades, scholars such as Takara Kurayoshi, Maehira Fusaaki, Teruya Masayoshi, Tomiyama Kazuyuki, and Uezato Takashi have confirmed and further developed the arguments of Yokoyama and Nakahara, shedding much light on the details of Ryukyuan military organization, equipment, and tactics.[47] Abundant evidence of the Ryukyu Kingdom's military and police structures and capabilities is available for anyone who cares to take a close look the academic literature.

Simply a glance at the headlines of the entries in the *Kyūyō* should be sufficient to dispel the notion that Ryukyu was a land without weapons, crime or conflict.

If Orientalism is the process of Europeans projecting desires or fantasies onto distant "eastern" lands, then the nineteenth-century version of the myth of Ryukyuan pacifism might accurately be regarded as a variety of Orientalism, albeit one abetted by Ryukyuan officials. Indeed, all parties were involved in conjuring up a Ryukyu that suited their purposes. The modern and contemporary manifestations of the myth now include a substantial number of residents of Okinawa among its proponents. The details of the Ryukyuan past are sufficiently remote that Ryukyu's history can be molded to serve contemporary political agendas fairly easily. Obviously, interpreting the past is always a contentious issue, and many aspects of Okinawa and Ryukyuan history remain the subject of scholarly debate and disagreement. That said, however, the effacing of all forms of coercive activity on the part of Ryukyuans throughout history goes beyond the usual boundaries of academic debate. It is a remarkable propaganda accomplishment, first seriously attempted by eighteenth-century Ryuyuan officials.

It is understandable, of course, that thoughtful people would be distressed by the propensity of humans to behave badly. The myth of Ryukyuan pacifism undoubtedly resonates with a deep desire to believe that human nature is potentially good enough that societies free of coercive force are possible, while also adding poignancy to the narrative of modern Okinawa victimization. This psychological mix is powerful enough to anesthetize the critical thinking function that should be part of any scholarly or journalistic endeavor. I am not convinced that a fairy tale version of Ryukyuan history has much to offer by way of practical benefits. Insofar as the U.S. military presence has been a corrosive force in Okinawan society, relevant arguments against it should be made in the context of the present and recent past without recourse to an impossible version of history.

Notes

1) http://okinawa-information.com/blog/king-sho-hashi-dynamic-ryuku (accessed 5 Nov. 2009).
2) Keiko Uchida, "How the Musical 'King Sho Hashi' United the Power of the Okinawan People," Matthew Galgani, trans (14 Sep 2009) at: http://www.discovernikkei.org/en/journal/2009/9/14/king-sho-hashi/ (accessed 5 Nov. 2009).
3) http://okinawa-information.com/blog/king-sho-hashi-dynamic-ryuku (accessed 5 Nov. 2009).
4) Maeda Giken, *Okinawa, yogawari no shisō: hito to gakumon no keifu* (Naha, Japan: Dai'ichi kyōiku tosho, 1972), pp. 64–67.
5) Yokoyama Shigeru, Iha Fuken (Fuyū), and Higashionna Kanjun, eds., *Ryūkyū shiryō sōsho*, vol. 5 (Hōbun shokan, 1940, 1988), p. 37.
6) Ibid., p. 39.
7) Ibid., p. 40.
8) Ibid., p. 12.
9) For more details, see Gregory Smits, *Visions of Ryukyu: Identity and Ideology in Early-Modern Thought and Politics* (Honolulu: University of Hawai'i Press, 1999), pp. 15–49.
10) Laura E Hein, "Introduction: The Territory of Identity and Remembrance in Okinawa," *Critical Asian Studies*, 33:2 (2001), p. 209. Here I quote Hein, not Roberson, because Roberson does not actually go as

far as Hein in juxtaposing the bellicose present with an allegedly peaceful past.
11) Ōta Masahide, "Okinawa Calls for a Just Peace: Speech to the U.S. Congressional Study Group on Japan," in http://www.iwanami.co.jp/jpworld/text/okinawa01.html (accessed 20 Mar. 2006).
12) William P. Lebra, *Okinawan Religion: Belief, Ritual, and Social Structure* (Honolulu: University of Hawaii Press, 1966, 1985), p. 13. Lebra's Japanese translator, the late Mitsugu Sakihara, himself a Battle of Okinawa veteran, found this passage so contrary to everything he had observed, that he convinced Lebra to have it omitted in the Japanese version of the book (personal communication).
13) See, for example, the chapter "The War Comes Home to Okinawa" in Haruko Taya Cook and Theodore F. Cook, *Japan at War: An Oral History* (New York: The New Press, 1992), pp. 354–372. See also Ōta Masahide, "Re-Examining the History of the Battle of Okinawa," in Chalmers Johnson, ed., *Okinawa: Cold War Island* (Cardiff, CA: Japan Policy Research Institute, 1999), esp., p. 29.
14) George Feifer, "The Rape of Okinawa," *World Policy Journal*, 17:3 (Fall, 2000), pp. 35–36.
15) For a scholarly analysis of the significance of the 1995 rape, see Linda Isako Angst, "The Sacrifice of a Schoolgirl: The 1995 Rape Case, Discourses of Power, and Women's Lives in Okinawa," *Critical Asian Studies*, vol. 33, no. 2 (2001).
16) Ishigami Eiichi, "Ryūkyū no Amami shotō tōchi no shodankai," *Rekishi hyōron*, No. 603 (2000), pp. 5–9; and Uezato Takashi, "Ryūkyū no kaki ni tsuite," *Okinawa bunka*, vol. 36, no. 91 (2000), p. 76. The Korean source on which these authors rely is the *Joseon Wangjo Sillok*. See also Entry #115. Kyūyō kenkyūkai, eds., *Kyūyō* (Yomikudashi edition) (Kadokawa shoten, 1974), p. 11.
17) Ishigami, "Amami," pp. 3–4, 9; and Uezato Takashi, "Ko-Ryūkyū no guntai to sono rekishiteki tenkai," *Ryūkyū Ajia shakai bunka kenkyūkai kiyō*, no. 5 (October, 2002), pp. 113–114.
18) Uezato, "Guntai," p. 114 and entry #202 and #227. Kyūyō kenkyūkai, *Kyūyō*, p. 14. Regardless of the details, it seems clear that Amami-Ōshima resented Shuri's control and often resisted with violence.
19) Uezato, "Ryūkyū no kaki," pp. 76–78.
20) Uezato, "Guntai," pp. 108–109.
21) Perhaps the most prominent example of this narrative is Nagamine Shoshin, "Okinawan Karate and World Peace," found at many web sites such as http://www.renseikan.com/WorldPeace.shtml (as of 11-7-2009). Although rare, some martial arts writers acknowledge a more realistic interpretation of Shō Shin's actions. For example: "Although it is documented that King Shoshin ordered his provincial lords, or aji, to live near his castle in Shuri, many historians no longer believe that he totally disarmed his ruling class. Although a famous stone monument, the Momo Urasoe Ran Kan No Mei, which is inscribed with the highlights of King Shoshin's reign, tells of the King seizing the aji's swords and how he amassed a supply of weapons in a warehouse near Shuri castle, some Okinawan historians believe that King Shoshin was actually building an armory to protect his ports and prepare for any potential invasion by wako, or pirates, not that he was stripping the Okinawan samurai or the general population of their weaponry" (accessed 21 Mar. 2006) at http://tkdtutor.com/16Weapons/Offensive/Offensive.htm.
22) These events are well documented in any general history of Okinawa. Uezato explains their significance in the context of military affairs with great clarity. See "Guntai," pp. 110–112.
23) For a detailed analysis of the *hiki, see* Takara Kurayoshi, *Ryūkyū ōkoku no kōzō* (Yoshikawa kōbunkan, 1987), pp. 103–119. See also Uezato, "Guntai," p. 112, pp. 118–119.
24) Uezato, "Guntai," p. 113; and Uezato, "Ryūkyū no kaki," p. 78.
25) Uezato, "Guntai," pp. 117–119; and Uezato, "Ryūkyū no kaki," pp. 82–87.
26) Uezato, "Guntai," pp. 120–121; and Uezato, "Ryūkyū no kaki," p. 84.
27) Uezato, "Guntai," p. 124; and Uezato, "Ryūkyū no kaki," pp. 82–83.
28) Uezato, "Guntai," p. 123.
29) Uezato, "Guntai," pp. 115–116, pp. 121–124; and Uezato, "Ryūkyū no kaki," pp. 82–88.
30) Uezato, "Guntai," pp. 115–116; and Uezato, "Ryūkyū no kaki," pp. 82–88.
31) For example, in 1670 pirates connected with Ming loyalist forces captured a Ryukyuan ship, and Satsuma criticized the Ryukyuans as "cowards in the extreme." See, Tomiyama Kazuyuki, *Ryūkyū ōkoku no gaikō to ōken* (Yoshikawa kōbunkan, 2004), p. 80.
32) Uezato, "Guntai," pp. 116–117.

33) Entry #464. Kyūyō kenkyūkai, *Kyūyō*, p. 211.
34) Entry #1465. Kyūyō kenkyūkai, *Kyūyō*, pp. 439–440.
35) Entry #1487. Kyūyō kenkyūkai, *Kyūyō*, pp. 445–447.
36) Tomiyama, *Ryūkyū ōkoku no gaikō to ōken*, pp. 176–7.
37) Li Dingyuan, *Shi Ryūkyū ki*, Harada Nobuo, trans., ed. (Gensōsha, 1985), 335–337.
38) Li, *Shi Ryūkyū ki*, pp. 407–408. See also Kakazu Takeshi, "Rikuyu engi: Tei Junsoku ga fukkokushi fukyū" *Ryūkyū shinpō*, 4–24–1993 (#17 in the series *Ryūkyū kanshi no tabi*).
39) George H. Kerr, *Okinawa: The History of an Island People* (Rutland, VT: Charles E. Tuttle Company, 1958), pp. 250–251.
40) Kerr, *Okinawa*, p. 255. For extensive excerpts from the crew members of these two ships, see pp. 249–260.
41) There are many accounts of Ryukyuan judicial proceedings and law codes. One excellent source is *Okinawa no hankachō*, which details criminal cases before the Hirajo in the 1860s and 70s. One case, for example, involved the investigation into the actions of police officials who tortured a suspect excessively, thus causing his death. See Higa Shunchō and Sakihama Shūmei, eds., trans., *Okinawa no hankachō* (Tōyō bunko 41) (Heibonsha, 1965), 85–94. See also "Satsuma-han shihaika no saibanken," Chapter 3 of Tomiyama, *Ryūkyū ōkoku no gaikō to ōken*, pp. 170–197.
42) Kerr, *Okinawa*, p. 259.
43) Basil Hall Chamberlain, "The Luchu Islands and Their Inhabitants: I. Introductory Remarks," *The Geographical Journal*, vol. 5, no. 4 (April, 1895), pp. 310–311.
44) Chamberlain, "The Luchu Islands," pp. 318–319.
45) Iha Fuyū, "Ko-Ryūkyū no bubi o kōsatsushite "karate" no hattatsu ni oyobu." Hattori Shirō, Nakasone Masayoshi, Hokama Shuzen, eds., *Iha Fuyū zenshū*, vol 5 (Heibonsha, 1974), pp. 196–215 (originally published 1932); and "Ko-Ryūkyū no "hiki seido" ni tsuite—Ryūkyū bunka no ranjukuki ni kansuru ichi kōsatsu," *Zenshū*, vol. 9, pp. 279–322 (originally published 1935). See also Uezato, "Guntai," p. 105.
46) Uezato, "Guntai," 105; and Iha Fuyū, "Ko-Ryūkyū no seiji," *Zenshū*, Vol. 1., 419–495, esp., pp. 431–440.
47) For a concise summary of these arguments and a listing of the key essays, see Uezato, "Guntai," pp. 105–106.

References

Angst, L. I. (2001). The sacrifice of a schoolgirl: The 1995 rape case, discourses of power, and women's lives in Okinawa. *Critical Asian Studies*, 33 (2), 243–266.
Cook, H. T., & Cook T. F. (1992). *Japan at war: An oral history*. New York: The New Press.
Chamberlain, B. H. (1895, April). The Luchu Islands and their inhabitants: I. Introductory remarks. *The Geographical Journal*, 5(4), 289–319.
Feifer, G. (2000, Fall). The rape of Okinawa. *World Policy Journal*, 17(3), 33–40.
Giken, M. (1972). *Okinawa, yogawari no shiso, hito to gakumon no keifu*. Naha, Japan: Dai'ichi kyōiku tosho.
Hein, L. E. (2001). Introduction: The territory of identity and remembrance in Okinawa. *Critical Asian Studies*, 33(2), 209–210.
Higa, S., & Sakihama S., (Eds., Trans.) (1965). *Okinawa no hankachō*. (Tōyō bunko 41), Heibonsha.
Iha, F. (1974). "Ko-Ryūkyū no bubi o kōsatsushite "karate" no hattatsu ni oyobu" in Hattori, S., Nakasone M., & Hokama S.,(Eds.). *Iha Fuyū zenshū*, vol 5, (pp. 196–215), Tokyo: Heibonsha. (originally published 1932)
Iha, F. ("Ko-Ryūkyū no "hiki seido" ni tsuite — Ryūkyū bunka no ranjukuki ni kansuru ichi kōsatsu," In Hattori S., Nakasone M., & Hokama S. (Eds.), *Iha Fuyū zenshū*, vol. 9, pp. 279–322 (originally published 1935).
Ishigami, F. (2000). Ryūkyū no Amami shotō tōchi no shodankai. *Rekishi hyōron*, 603, 2–15.
Kakazu, T. (1993, April 24). Rikuyu engi: Tei Junsoku ga fukkokushi fukyū. *Ryūkyū shinpō*, (#17 in the series

Ryūkyū kanshi no tabi).

Kerr, G. H. (1958). *Okinawa: The history of an island people*. Rutland, VT: Charles E. Tuttle Company.

Kyūyō kenkyūkai. (1974). (Eds.) *Kyūyō* (Yomikudashi edition), Kadokawa shoten.

Lebra, W. P. (1985). *Okinawan religion: belief, ritual, and social structure*. Honolulu: University of Hawaii Press. (Originally published 1966)

Li, D. (1985). *Shi Ryūkyū ki*, Harada Nobuo, trans., ed., Tokyo: Gensōsha.

Nagamine, S. Okinawan karate and world peace. (n.d.), Retrieved November 7, 2009, from http://www.renseikan.com/WorldPeace.shtml

Ōta, M. Okinawa calls for a just peace: Speech to the U.S. congressional study group on Japan. (April, 1997), Retrieved November 7, 2009, from http://www.iwanami.co.jp/jpworld/text/okinawa01.html

Ōta, M. (1999). Re-examining the history of the battle of Okinawa. In Johnson, C., (Ed.), *Okinawa: Cold war island*. Cardiff, CA: Japan Policy Research Institute.

Smits, G. (1999). *Visions of Ryukyu: Identity and ideology in early-modern thought and politics*. Honolulu: University of Hawai'i Press.

Takara, K. (1987). *Ryūkyū ōkoku no kōzō*. Tokyo: Yoshikawa kōbunkan.

Tomiyama, K. (2004). *Ryūkyū ōkoku no gaikō to ōken*. Tokyo: Yoshikawa kōbunkan, 2004).

Uchida, K. (2009, September 14). How the musical 'King Sho Hashi' united the power of the Okinawan people. Galgani, M., Trans. Retrieved November 5, 2009, from http://www.discovernikkei.org/en/journal/2009/9/14/king-sho-hashi/

Uezato, T. (2002, October). Ko-Ryūkyū no guntai to sono rekishiteki tenkai. *Ryūkyū Ajia shakai bunka kenkyūkai kiyō*, 5, 105–128.

Uezato, T. (2000). Ryūkyū no kaki ni tsuite. *Okinawa bunka*, 36(91), 73–92.

Yokoyama, S., Iha, F. (Fuyū), & Higashionna, K. (1988). (Eds.) *Ryūkyū shiryō sōsho*, 5, Hōbun shokan. (Originally published 1940).

Okinawan Labor and Political Activists in Hawai'i: Race, Ethnicity, Class and Social Movements in the Mid-20th Century

Joyce N. Chinen*

ハワイの沖縄系労働運動・政治活動家たち：
20世紀中庸の人種、エスニシティ、階級、そして社会運動

ジョイス・N・チネン

21世紀を生きるハワイの住民は概して他のアメリカ国民よりも優れた市民権と労働権を享受している。これらの権利がどのように獲得されたかということについて、社会的には二つの説明の仕方が定着している。一つは多民族的労働組合主義を基盤とした組織化に成功した労働運動によるものとしての説明である。二つ目は、以前の民主党支持者、労働組合、そして特に第二次世界大戦に従軍し多大な犠牲を払った日系退役軍人たちが共闘しながら社会で政策決定過程における平等を要求し、半世紀にもわたる共和党支配をひっくり返した「民主党革命」によるものとしての説明である。いずれにおいても、沖縄人と沖縄アイデンティティは一般的日本人の括りの中に埋没し、評価されることはなかった。また、一方では、一般的沖縄人は、経済的、社会的成功を勝ち取るべく起業家精神にあふれ、民族的連携を図り、ハワイ農業で苦役に従事する一世として説明される。公文資料と口述史料を基に、本稿では沖縄人が起業家としてではなく社会の活動家として果たした役割を強調したい。特に人口統計学的要素や社会史的要素がどのように活動家としての役割を後押ししたのかを明らかにする。結論として、言祝がれ流布するハワイにおける沖縄人の「立身出世話」とハワイ社会における沖縄人共同体の将来の方向性について再検討を促す。

Student: "Uchinanchu — they're kanemochi (wealthy)."
Professor: "Really?"
Student: "OK, maybe not all — but lots."
— a conversation with a gosei University of Hawai'i Ethnic Studies student in Fall 2008

---

* Professor, University of Hawai'i-West-O'ahu ハワイ大学ウエストオアフ校教授

Introduction

Uchinanchu (Okinawans) in Hawai'i are often perceived to be affluent and successful. Indeed, the perception of their "model minority" status is not only widely held by non-Okinawans, but also uncritically accepted by local Okinawans. At a time when social resources are shrinking, when immigrants and disadvantaged ethnic minorities in multi-ethnic Hawai'i are competing for access to educational oppotunities and jobs, and when indigenous Hawaiians are struggling to regain their lands and sovereign rights, the belief that Okinawan success is based on their cultural "exceptionalism" is inappropriate, if not outright offensive. How did Okinawans in Hawai'i transform from being a discriminated and ridiculed group (e.g., by the use of a common epithetical saying: "*Okinawa-ken-ken, buta kaukau*" — "people from Okinawa, pig food"), to being perceived as wealthy — as "*kanemochi*?"

Hawai'i residents, including Okinawans, generally do enjoy an extensive array of civil rights and, because of progressive labor laws, better working conditions compared with residents of other states in the USA. How did this occur? Motivation, hard work, and collective institutions such as traditional *moai* or *tanomoshi* (Okinawan revolving credit associations) are often given explanations of Okinawans' success. Social scientists however, realize these kinds of practices only can have limited effects. That is, they may facilitate upward *individual mobility* but only mobility which occurs on the *micro-* or small scale level. To raise the status of a whole group, i.e., *social mobility*, requires larger-scale collective actions or *social agency*. Furthermore, to understand how these large-scale changes in social status occur, we need to look at *macro-level* changes, including demographic shifts and socio-historical contexts. Connecting the *micro-* and *macro-levels*, at the *meso-level*, we need to examine collective actions taken within formal organizations which address the dominant social *structure* (Giddens, 1984). In short, critically examining the myth of Okinawan exceptionalism requires focusing on labor and political movements and the organizations which transformed the landscape, history and social structure of Hawai'i in the mid-twentieth century. It also requires examining where and how Okinawans were located in those social movements, and their contributions therein.

In this paper, I tie the social mobility experienced by Okinawans in Hawai'i to larger social forces such as demographic patterns and the labor and political movements which were sweeping across the United States and fomenting in Hawai'i in the mid-twentieth century. I contend that it was the labor movement, and Okinawans' participation in it, which accounted for the rise in the standard of living of Okinawans and the population at large. Complementing this was the rise of the Democratic Party in 1954, another (and related) arena where Okinawans' participation was significant. Together, these two social movements laid the foundation for significant reforms which lifted the living standards of the general population in Hawai'i and consequently also that of Okinawans as a group. Furthermore, I maintain that Okinawans were both serendipitous and purposeful actors in these movements. By examining demographic composition, the political and economic history of this period, I believe important lessons can be learned about personal and social responsibility, about agency and structure, about public policy and civil society.

This paper relies on a linked analysis of various archival materials. These include items from oral history interviews conducted by the University of Hawai'i at Mānoa Center for Oral History (COH) and the University of Hawai'i-West-O'ahu Center for Labor Education and Research's (CLEAR) *Rice and Roses* (labor history series). It also uses newspaper accounts and other archival documents found in both the International Longshore and Warehouse Union Local 142 (ILWU Archives) and the ILWU International Archives in San Francisco, the San Francisco State University Labor Archives (SFSU Archives), and the Okinawa Prefectural Archives (OPA).[1] In examining these materials, I pay attention to what the historical sources have to say about Okinawan individuals in the particular context of Hawai'i. I attempt to correlate these different available data on Okinawan individuals, their thoughts as expressed in the interviews, with the historical events going on in both Hawai'i and American society at the time, and sometimes in Okinawa. This investigation reveals some of the ways in which Okinawan activists negotiated their ethnic and progressive identities while engaging in socially significant work.

1. The Myth of the Model Minority

The term "model minority" is often used to refer to ethnic minorities who have achieved a higher socio-economic status in a multi-ethnic society. The designation is often double-edged, both applauding the accomplishments of the minority group, while retaining the group's minority or subordinate status vis-à-vis the "majority" group. It maintains that in spite of the group's status as minority, it has been able to attain its higher status without the benefit of social "assistance" or "hand-outs." Consequently, it reinforces the idea that there are "good minorities" and "problematic minorities" who don't play by society's rules. This conception divides minority groups and has traditionally benefited the dominant group (Wilson, 1973). In short, embracing of the "model minority" status and logic reinforces the *status quo* of inequality and injustice.

In this section of the paper, I briefly sketch out the socio-historical context in Hawai'i into which the Okinawan issei arrived. I describe how they were paradoxically not only targets of racism, but also beneficiaries of it. I then discuss the political, economic, and historical contexts into which the Okinawan nisei in Hawai'i came of age and how they were socially positioned to participate in the events of the mid-20th century. In other words, I attempt to show how Okinawans both aided and then benefited from the reforms instituted by progressive social movements in the mid-twentieth century. All these were possible because they were serendipitously in the right place at the right time. They were, as the title of Jon Shirota's novel describes, *Lucky Come Hawaii* (1965).

2. Background on Modern Hawaii and the United States in the 19th and early 20th Centuries

Throughout the nineteenth and twentieth centuries, the Hawaiian archipelago underwent rapid and radical social changes. Starting in the late eighteenth century, the Hawaiian Islands were visited by explorers, traders and missionaries representing various nations. Through wars and consolidations, the islands were rapidly transformed from a set of autonomous mini-kingdoms into a single kingdom headed by Kamehameha I. However, the indigenous Hawaiian population imploded, decimated by the introduction of infectious diseases and disruptions of their established social and cultural patterns. Over the next few decades, the indigenous people and the Hawaiian Kingdom grappled with the accelerating encroachment of commercial interests.

A Reciprocity Treaty of 1876 between the United States and the Kingdom of Hawai'i crystallized the expansion and domination of a sugar industrial economy, and greater American influence in Hawai'i's affairs. King Kalākaua was forced to sign a new constitution (often called the "Bayonet Constitution") in 1886; it granted greater powers to commercial interests while limiting the powers of the Hawaiian people. In her attempt to reverse those conditions, Queen Liliu'okalani was overthrown in 1893, in a coup led by business interests linked to the United States of America. Failing immediate incorporation by the U.S. because of the election of President Grover Cleveland, whose administration which was less sympathetic to expansionism, the islands languished as a Republic for a time. Hawai'i was finally annexed by the U.S. in 1898 under President William McKinley via a Newlands Resolution (rather than a treaty, which is the customary procedure) because there were not enough votes for ratification. Hawai'i became a Territory in 1900 and remained in that political status until 1959 when it became the fiftieth state of the United States of America. Statehood status is still viewed as illegitimate by certain segments of the Hawaiian community.

This history serves as an important backdrop when examining the status of Okinawans in Hawai'i. So were the events and broad historical patterns and changes unfolding on the continental U.S. In addition to its expansionist moves in Asia, the Pacific and the Caribbean, America was dealing with the transformation of its workforce. The numbers of European and Asian immigrant workers kept increasing just as the descendants of earlier Euro-Americans were organizing into trade unions to improve their wages and working conditions. Threatened by "coolie labor" (cheap, super-exploitable labor) undercutting their efforts, Euro-American nativistic unionists such as Dennis Kearney organized the Workingman's Party. This political party, most influential in California, lobbied for legislation barring Chinese immigrant labor from California and other western states, and eventually nationally. Their efforts culminated in the passage of the first immigration law targeting a specific national group: the Chinese Exclusion Act of 1882, renewed in 1892, and finally made permanent in 1902. As low-wage Japanese immigrant labor filled the vacuum created by the lack of Chinese laborers, anti-Japanese sentiment also emerged.

On the U.S. continent, the resentment of cheap coolie labor continued to grow, for Asian labor often worked for wages which undercut white workers. Calls by the white working-class to exclude the "yellow peril" from the U.S. intensified. Simultaneously, the U.S. expansion into Asia, the Pacific, and the Caribbean was bringing together a series of events which had positive consequences for Uchinanchu immigrants. After the exclusion of Chinese workers, Japanese sojourning laborers increasingly became the target for racial exclusion; the Gentlemen's Agreement of 1907 was the result. Since Japan's central government was somewhat stronger than China's in this period, the provisions were less unequal. The Gentlemen's Agreement provided that Japan would limit the numbers of male laborers it sent to the U.S., and in exchange, the U.S. would permit Japanese already in the U.S. to reunite with their families. Eventually, this would lead to the Immigration Act of 1924, also known as the Asian Exclusion Act, which set restrictive quotas for immigrants from different nations — ultimately reducing the numbers of Asian immigrants to virtually zero.

These two laws had important implications for Okinawans. First, Okinawan issei were incorporated into Hawaii's political economy at a particular historical moment and into a particular socio-political context. On April 30, 1900, a scant three months after the twenty-six men from Okinawa arrived on the island of Oʻahu, the Organic Act was passed, preparing the way for Hawaiʻi to officially become a Territory of the United States on June 14, 1900. With this, the previously signed labor contracts were nullified; the Okinawan men were free to leave. More important, those Okinawans who chose to stay in Hawaiʻi, entered into a labor environment where their pay and working conditions, while not great, were substantially better than those experienced by the Naichi (mainland) Japanese and Chinese laborers who had come much earlier. Okinawans were free from the most egregious provisions of the Masters and Servants Act of 1850, including those which had permitted bounties (monetary rewards) for the capture of workers who had run away from plantations, and extended labor time for contracts violations, etc. (Beechert, 1985; Hiura and Terada, 1981). Therefore, Okinawans experienced labor conditions which, according to some social movement theories, were more favorable for organizing. They experienced — *relative deprivation* (rather than *absolute deprivation*).

Second, by the time of the Gentlemen's Agreement of 1907, the dream of many Japanese laborers of returning to the homeland as wealthy men had evaporated; settling in the U.S. and Hawaii was becoming more realistic. Japanese were shifting from a *sojourner* mentality to a *settler* one, as they realized that their paltry earnings were inadequate for returning to Japan (Takaki, 1983). As they gave up their dreams of returning to their homeland, and instead adjusted to settling and raising families in Hawaii, they sent for their wives and children. Those who were not already married, petitioned their families to locate wives for them in an arranged marriage practice which came to be known as "Picture Brides" (Chai and Kawakami, 1986). Some of the more adventurous "Picture Brides" even negotiated their own marriages. The demographic patterns which resulted from the Gentlemen's Agreement had profound social implications for the fortunes of the Japanese in Hawai'i i in general, and Okinawans in particular.

Demographers focus on birth, death and migration because the interactions of these factors affect population size, characteristics, and resource availability. Between 1907 and the passage of the Immigration Act of 1924, the numbers of women coming to Hawai'i from Okinawa skyrocketed. Japanese (and Okinawan) migration which has been masculinely gendered up to that point, flipped and became more balanced and, in some years, even female-dominated (Nordyke, 1989, p. 66). Nearly 10,000 Picture Brides entered in this interval, many of whom were Okinawans. In 1918, for example, women made up 38% of the Okinawans in Hawai'i (Ishikawa, 1981, p. 90).

The more evenly balanced sex ratio among the Japanese and Okinawans had two consequences. One consequence was the creation of families and veritable a "baby boom." Japanese males were more likely than other males of other ethnic groups to be married, consequently, the population of Japanese (and Okinawans) increased substantially (Nordyke, 1989). In one area, Puna, where a large population of Okinawans resided, "older residents recalled life in a big family in a small plantation house that consisted of parents and many siblings (sometimes including grandparents or in-laws)" (Kinoshita, 2002, p. 10). It was common for families to have eight to twelve children, with older children helping to raise younger siblings and/or terminating their formal schooling to earn income to aid their parents support their families.

The second result of the more balanced sex ratio was the possibility of second incomes. As Tomonori Ishikawa (1981) has shown, the level of remittances, funds sent back to Okinawa, substantially increased after women arrived. This is hardly surprising. "Bachelor societies" tend to promote hyper-masculinized activities such as drinking, gambling and prostitution which are counter productive to capital accumulation. The introduction of wives, at minimum, reduced participation in those activities, and provided the possibility of a second income for the household. Accounts of "Picture Brides" tell of daily work routines which began hours before sunrise and continued late into the night (Chai and Kawakami, 1986). Many of these women worked in the fields, usually at 60% of wages their husbands earned. In the days before automation, they often worked alongside their husbands gathering and bundling the harvested cane stalks for their husbands to do *happaiko* (carry the 50–60 pound bundles on their shoulders, climb up a narrow plank, and unload the cane into the mule-drawn carts or trains for transport to the mill); or in *kachiken* (cutting cane into foot-long segments to be water-flumed to the mill), or *hole-hole* (stripping dry cane leaves from the stalk), or *hoehana* (weeding with a hoe). After completing their paid work, they returned to their "second shift" (Hochschild and Machung, 1997), the unpaid household work of cooking, cleaning and raising children. Often, they would supplement their meager wages and/or those of their husbands with informal economic sector activities such as cooking, or doing laundry for the bachelor workers, including Filipino workers, to earn extra cash. Other entrepreneurial work such as making *tofu* (bean curd), or *sake* (rice wine), tending the *furo*, relying on unpaid family labor, and other activities generated even more cash (Chinen, 1990). Consequently, the remittances from Okinawans in Hawai'i surpassed those of other diasporic Okinawan communities (Ishikawa, 1981).

Several significant social structural factors affected Okinawans' family and community formation. The first of these was their social location in the society at large, and in the social hierarchy of the plantation economy in particular. As one of the later groups incorporated into the paternalistically managed plantation workforce, indeed entering at a time when many Naichi were leaving the plantation, Okinawans were given the worst and lowest paying jobs. They were assigned the least desirable housing, often on the periphery, away from the center of the plantation's activities. Second, they faced double discrimination in Hawai'i. As Asian workers, they faced racism and the institutional discrimination imposed by the *haole* (white) plantation system. Additionally, having arrived at least some fifteen years after the *Kanyaku Imin* (government sponsored immigration), Okinawans were also a minority within the minority Japanese population — a "double minority." Incorporated as a prefecture in 1879, only six years before the government-sponsored immigration from Japan would begin, Okinawans lacked an established infrastructure for formal education. With limited access to schools, Okinawans' verbal and written Japanese language proficiency was lower than those of the *Naicha* (Japanese people living on mainland Japan). Moreover, isolated from people on the mainland of Japan, it was not until they were in Hawai'i, that the Uchinanchu and Yamatunchu first encountered each other *en masse* — as prefectural groups with noticeably different languages, customs, taste, dress, habits and mores. Prejudice and discrimination were frequently the result (Ikeda and Toyama, 1981; Shirota, 1990; Ige, 1981); there are many accounts of discrimination and psychic injury. Epithets like "hey, Okinawa!" or "*Okinawa-ken ken, buta kaukau*! (people from Okinawa, pig food) were often leveled against Okinawans, because of their pig-raising practices which included gathering garbage and preparing it for pig feed. Even other ethnic groups noticed that Okinawans were "not-quite-Japanese," referring to them as "Japanee-Pake" (Japanese-Chinese).

Okinawans' responses to this socially structured "double discrimination" took several forms. Some Okinawans, especially the nisei, coped as individuals by adopting various impression management techniques, presenting a more American or Japanese "self." This included speaking better Japanese, dressing in Japanese or Western styles, forgoing Okinawan food or cultural habits. Others, especially the issei, coped collectively, by forming locality clubs or *kumiai*, by in-marrying, and by participating in revolving credit associations called *moai* or *tanomoshi*. Finally, Okinawans also tended to gravitate to geographical areas where other Okinawans tended to reside, creating small communities of familiar folk (Ishikawa, 1981). Both strategies — individuals "passing" as well as congregating in Okinawan communities — probably were used, depending on the particulars of the situation.

3. Okinawans and the Labor Movement

The labor movement in Hawai'i is multifaceted, but the union best known for its influence in twentieth century Hawai'i is the International Longshore and Warehouse Union Local 142 (ILWU). Coming out of the "industrial organizing" framework of the Congress of Industrial Organizations (CIO), the ILWU organized workers along the waterfront, in the sugar, pineapple, tuna packing, auto industries, just to name a few. Their ability to organize workers in multi-ethnic Hawai'i was a major feat since the "divide-and-conquer" strategies used by management, especially on the plantations, had been effective for nearly a century. Techniques such as ethnic-related differential pay levels, access to promotions, health services, housing and other benefits had kept workers fighting amongst themselves, deterring effective labor organizing. Consequently, the CIO-led ILWU took a multi-ethnic approach. Rallying around the slogan "An Injury to One is an Injury to All," it ensured representation of the major ethnic groups, printed key documents in various languages, and was successful in organizing workers. In contrast to the craft-oriented American Federation of Labor (AFL) approach, the CIO-led ILWU organized whole workplaces, whole industries. This narrative of multi-racial unionization, however, blurs the role ethnicity might have played in the lives of key individuals who pushed this collective enterprise on. Particularly in the 1940s and '50s, those individuals included several Okinawans. In this section, we will explore the roles played by some of these Okinawan activists.

Even before the arrival of Okinawans, sugar plantation workers already had established a history of resistance to the oppressive working conditions they faced (Beechert, 1985). These worker actions often were referred to as "riots," or "walk-outs," and were fairly spontaneous responses to specific incidents or conditions. They were usually localized to a particular plantation or short-term strikes lasting about a week or so, but they functioned as learning opportunities for future actions. The large-scale labor organizing that took place in the mid-20th century came about because of the confluence of several factors. Locally, these included changes in the plantation labor force, the rationalization of sugar production, the increasing migration of Asian workers off the plantations and into the urban areas; the backdrop of unionization on the continental U.S. also played a part, for the external support that the national labor organizations provided external support (Beechert, 1985, p. 179).

When Hawai'i was incorporated into the U.S. in 1900, skilled trade workers from the continental U.S. were attracted to the island territory. Along with their trade they brought craft unionism, and several skilled trade unions were established in the islands. Organizers associated with the American Federation of Labor began to move into Hawai'i. The unionized higher wages attracted some of skilled workers off the plantations and into the urban areas which changed the composition of the plantations' workforce. Japanese workers who were formerly not able to get skill trades jobs a decade earlier, began moving into these higher-paying positions on the plantations, and eventually joined the workers of other ethnic backgrounds who previously had moved off the plantations and into urban areas.

In 1909, the Higher Wage Association organized a strike of mainly Japanese sugar workers from Waipahu, Aiea, and other plantations on Oʻahu. That strike was ultimately broken by the introduction of "scab" workers (i.e., replacement workers hired to break a strike). What is important is that the strike lasted from May 9 to August 5 — nearly three months — because it had the support of sugar workers on the neighbor islands. Moreover, four months after the strike ended, the planters raise the wages and made many of the improvements demanded by the strikers. The Higher Wage Association was led by Fred Makino, Yasutaro Soga and Tomoyuki Negoro, Japanese community leaders and intellectuals who were largely based in urban Honolulu; they served an important organizing function. Makino was publisher of the *Hawaii Hochi*, while Soga was publisher of the *Nippu Jiji* (which, after the Second World War, became the *Hawaii Times*). What roles Okinawans played in this strike needs to be further researched, but two items are noteworthy here. The first item is that Ishikawa (1981) had identified Waipahu, ʻEwa and Aiea as areas where large numbers of Okinawans resided. Second, Waipahu workers were especially noted for their militancy, and Seiyei Wakukawa (1981, p. 235) notes that Okinawans were active in this strike, and even were leaders in the subsequent 1920 strike.

In the interval between the 1909 Japanese strike and the 1920 Japanese and Filipino strike, the islands continued to be visited by organizers associated with various trade unions, e.g., even the International Workers of the World ("Wobblies") organizer Joe Hill. Moreover, through newspapers, workers were being exposed to labor actions in other industrial sectors, notably among harbor and dock workers. As Japanese (and Okinawan) families grew, the demands of sugar workers also changed to include women's concerns. In the 1920 Japanese and Filipino Strike which lasted nearly six months, the coalition between the two ethnic-based unions initially included demands for maternity leave and other concerns of women. Since the Filipino labor force was mostly single males, this demand came mainly from the Japanese union and, not surprising, many the strikers were Japanese women. After this strike, many Japanese, including Okinawans, began leaving the plantations for urban areas.

Sensing future trends, the plantation elites used various strategies to retain the next generation of plantation workers. The Americanization Movement was designed to encourage Japanese and Okinawan youth to speak English, to adhere to American values, and to remain on the plantations (Tamura, 1994). It divided the Japanese community, with some community leaders like Reverend Takie Okumura actively supporting it, and others like *Hawaii Hochi* publisher Fred Makino rejecting it. Probably the most notorious case embodying the contradictions inherent in the Americanization Movement was the disposition of the Miles Fukunaga case. In 1928, a bright young mentally ill nisei male, frustrated by unattainable college aspirations, kidnapped and then killed the young son of a trust company officer. After an island-wide manhunt, Fukunaga was captured, arrested, confessed, tried, convicted and executed — despite questions about whether an insanity defense should be explored. Scholar Iha Fuyu visited Hawai'i around this time and it is thought that his subsequent work was informed by this furor caused by the case (Oshiro, 2007).

According to Seiyei Wakukawa (1981), there was considerable discussion going on about labor and social justice in the various Japanese language newspapers in the 1920s. One of the publications Wakukawa (1981) points to as a decidedly left-leaning newspaper, was the *Yoen Jiho* (Hawaii Star) which was published on Kauai; in its early days, it served mainly an Okinawan readership. Methodist minister, Reverend Seikan Higa took over the paper from 1923–1924 and it took on a pro-labor editorial stance, according to Wakukawa (1981), especially interesting since this is about the time of the 1924 Filipino strike in Hanapepe, Kaua'i. Chinyei Kinjo, subsequently took it over for a while, but publication was suspended during the war when Japanese language newspapers and other community institutions were shut down. Kinjo was arrested, detained and subsequently sent to internment camp during World War II. Helen Geracimos Chapin, in her study of newspapers in Hawai'i has this to say about the paper:

> "*Yoen Jiho* [Hawaii star] (1921–1941), also called the *Koloa Times*, was sponsored by the Kauai Labor Union and was the most radical of the ethnic language papers in that it was Marxist in orientation. Editor Ichro Izuka was joined by future labor leaders Jack Kimoto and Ginjaro Arashiro. With a hefty circulation of 1,000, *Yoen Jiho* gained inclusion in the list of "dangerous periodicals compiled by a territorial commission on "subversive activities" (Sakamaki 1928)." (Chapin, 1996, p. 136)

By the 1930s and '40s, Okinawan nisei, who straddled three cultures (Okinawan, Japanese, and American) were coming of age — but they were entering a society fraught with contradictions. The Great Depression had pummeled both the nation's and Hawai'i's economies, causing bankruptcies and widespread unemployment. Labor agitation increased. The Roosevelt Administration's New Deal economic recovery program included the National Labor Relations Act in 1935 (NLRA, also known as the Wagner Act); it gave manufacturing workers the legal right to organize into unions and to collectively bargain with their employers. Both the American Federation of Labor (AFL), whose unions organized along *craft* lines, and the unions affiliated with the Congress of Industrial Organizations (CIO), which organized workers along *industrial* lines, sent organizers to Hawai'i. But the CIO organizers were far more effective organizing Hawai'i's industrial labor force. Their ideological position of multiracial organizing resonated better with the sugar and pineapple workers whose experiences had been characterized by one ethnic group being pit against another under management's divide and conquer strategy.

The CIO's starting point in Hawai'i was organizing workers in the shipping, stevedoring and longshore industrial areas; eventually, however, their organizing spread to restaurant and laundry workers, and especially the workers employed in the sugar mills and canneries. One Okinawan who was involved in the labor movement from the start was

Matsuki "Mutt" Arashiro who was involved in organizing the Port Allen Waterfront Workers' Association. Associated with him in organizing plantation workers on Kauai was another Okinawan, Unsei Uchima. They worked with Jack Hall (who later became regional head of the ILWU) and Jack Kimoto in labor organizing efforts. Arashiro, was a gifted strategist. As early as 1939, he attempted to persuade dockworkers that securing a law permitting agricultural workers to organize would ultimately help secure longshore workers' interests, as well (Beechert, 1985, p. 277).

The problem with the NRLA was that it only applied to industrial workers. Agricultural workers were excluded, even though they were the majority of the workers in both the sugar and pineapple industries. Thus, most of the organizers for the ILWU who organized the two industries with the largest workforces came from jobs in the mill or other industrial positions. Thomas Yagi, an organizer and later Maui Division Director of the ILWU Local 142, became involved with the union when he transferred from Waihee Farm to Wailuku Sugar Warehouse. He had recently graduated from St. Anthony's School for Boys in 1939. By simply moving from field work into the warehouse, from the status of an agricultural worker to an industrial worker, Yagi became eligible to join the union and participate in its activities under the NLRA. He was encouraged to join the union by "a fellow worker by the name of James Gushiken. And Jimmy was — I was working under him, too, and he's always nice to me about working" (Yagi interview, 1989, p. 475). At this point, Okinawan identity probably only played a part in enhancing his "social capital," providing Yagi with some beneficial social networks (since Gushiken is an Okinawan surname), but it did not appear to play a central part in his activism. Probably that was because the union de-emphasized ethnicity, and promoted the message of inclusiveness.

> "In the twenties, the difference is this, that in 1946, we had all of the workers together, all ethnic groups, all racial groups — the Filipinos, the Japanese, Portuguese, Hawaiians. All of them together. In the 19 — in the early twenties, they had only the problem of Japanese, they struck, themselves. The Filipinos, they struck, themselves. And these are the kind of problems, 1936, the Filipinos had. They didn't have the support of the Japanese people, the workers, nor the Portugese workers to support their strike because they were not in it together with them, although they would benefit by it. But that's the kind of problem they faced. So this strike, 1946 strike, was a first that we struck the plantations in that fashion." (Yagi interview, 1989, p. 483)

Just as the labor movement was gaining traction, Pearl Harbor Naval Base was attacked by Japan, transforming people of Japanese ancestry into "the enemy." In Hawai'i, martial law was declared immediately. There were curfews, black-outs, rationing. Many of the Japanese and Okinawan community leaders — Buddhist ministers, Japanese language school principals and teachers, journalists and publishers — were immediately arrested, detained and/or imprisoned. "Things Japanese" (flags, memorabilia, etc.) were destroyed or repressed. Japanese language newspapers and Japanese language schools were all shut down by military order. Wages were frozen, and restrictions were imposed on job changes, travel, and labor organizing. Meanwhile, defense workers and active duty military personnel flooded into Hawai'i — inflating prices, causing crowding, shortages — and unequal wages.

As attention shifted to the war effort, labor organizing took on different forms. These included organizing patriotic support of recreational activities for the armed forces at USOs, blood drives, preparation of medical supplies for the troops, etc. "Organizing" is based on gaining access and developing relationships with people. One of ILWU's most effective organizers, Yasuki "Yasu" Arakaki of Olaa was involved in the Surfrider Athletic Club, a team initially composed of "rejects" of the Japanese baseball league. While the all-Japanese baseball league was closed down by order of the military governor, the Surfriders were permitted to continue for morale purposes because they were multi-ethnic. In the process of playing baseball on a team with a non-Japanese name, Arakaki was permitted to travel around the island, meet others at baseball games, and to establish contacts with potential union members (Arakaki interview, 1991, pp. 117–119).

Martial law lasted nearly two and a half years. When it was removed, labor organizing took off. The fiery Yasu Arakaki became a major organizer and leader in the labor movement on Hawai'i island, and in the ILWU. As one of the top students in his high school class, he had aspirations to attend Waseda University in Japan, but like Tom Yagi, Arakaki was only able to attain a high school education. With some ten siblings, most of them younger than he, Arakaki was forced into the workforce immediately after graduating from high school. Luckily, he was able to begin in the carpenter's shop of the plantation where he maintained the flumes, but eventually passed the examination to work in the warehouse in charge of purchasing; this meant he became an industrial worker, eligible to join a union under NLRB rules.

4. California Labor School and International Labor Education Program

Transforming interested workers and potential activists into organized, focused, and competent unionists required exposing these budding leaders to an analysis of the capitalist economic system, the philosophical ideas of organized labor, and the practical or technical aspects of unionism. To accomplish this, the ILWU leadership, together with other supportive Leftist instructors, put together an institution which, in the span of three to five months, provided an intensive training and learning experience for CIO-oriented unionists from around the country. This was the California Labor School (CLS). Participants went to lectures on economic and political theories, learned public speaking skills, visited sites where strikes and picketing were taking place, observed soup kitchens, the process of negotiating contracts, and the costing out of contract proposals. They also came into contact with African Americans and white working-class unionists. Historians continue to debate how closely the CLS was linked to the Communist Party of America (CPA) since many if not most of the instructors were members of the CPA. However, the CLS also operated as a free-standing educational institution and, for a brief time, veterans could use

[Figure 1. Participants in the ILWU and California Labor School leadership training program for Hawaii unionists with ILWU President Harry Bridges, San Francisco, February-April 1946. Source: ILWU Local 142 Archives.]

their Veterans Administration educational benefits to attend it (Holmes, 1994, p. 185).

Since the CIO's philosophy and organizing position was that of racial and ethnic inclusivity, the students who were selected to attend the California Labor School came from a variety of ethnic backgrounds and included Japanese, Filipinos, Hawaiians and other ethnic groups in the industrial workforces. Several rank and file unionists from Hawai'i were sent to San Francisco for this labor education in 1946 and 1947. Among the "Japanese" unionists attending in 1946 class were Yasuki Arakaki and Thomas Yagi of Maui, seated second and third from left respectively in the photo below.

Both Yagi and Arakaki regarded their education at the California Labor School as transformative. Both spoke of the experience as the "college education" that they could not afford. Yagi noted that:

> "Well, back in 1946, when we had the first [ILWU] conference in Hilo, I together with [ten or eleven] others were selected to attend this special training school in California, known as the California Labor School. And also the training with the officers, and training me how to conduct the various union meetings, parliamentary procedures, news bulletins, and seeing first hand of the international executive board meeting at that time, and meeting with the international officers, discussing union problems. . . . firsthand information on seeing how grievances are processed, how the international officers negotiate contracts. All this has been the topics that which we — strike strategy, political action, economics. . . . " (Interview with Thomas Yagi, 1989, p. 473).

A similar view of the curriculum offered at the California Labor School was provided by

Yasu Arakaki. The curriculum provided him with skills, but also with a chance to contribute something that was long lasting and useful to the union--a strike manual.

> "Because I had California Labor School experience, while I was there, we had to attend night classes listening to progressive speakers. We were asked to visit the strike situation, look at the soup kitchen. So when I came home, I wrote, I drafted the strike strategy manual for the sugar workers in Hawaii. The manual is still there. There is some amendments, some corrections there, some improvement, but the strike manual that I prepared is still in the ILWU file." (Interview with Yasuki Arakaki, 1991, p. 1126).

It also provided Arakaki with some intellectual grounding for him to think deeply and broadly about different kinds of social structures and the kinds of issues which might be generated by them.

> "In 1946 I was sent to California Labor School. We were taught American labor history, different 'isms', different types of unions. When I say 'isms," it means socialism, communism, capitalism, imperialism. So we got a background of different type of 'isms" that existed in the society at the time." (Interview with Yasuki Arakaki, 1991, p. 1126)

How did these rural working-class men, both with only high school degrees, manage to travel from Hawai'i to San Francisco to attend the California Labor School? The solution was quite ingenious, and reveals the degree to which the CIO-affiliated unions cooperated with one another. According to correspondence in ILWU archives, the men were transformed from sugar workers or dock workers into ship's kitchen workers. In a cooperative arrangement with another CIO-affiliated union, the Cooks and Marine Stewards Union, the ILWU was able to gain "temporary membership" for the students attending the California Labor School and permit these men to work off their transoceanic passage. Arakaki confirms this.

> "The first thing they did was to send me to California Labor School. One of the eleven selected in the Territory. Two from the Big Island. I was one of them. We left on the S. S. Matsonia. I worked as a scullion. We peel potato on a ship. After five days, I was in San Francisco in February 28." (Interview with Yasuki Arakaki, 1991, p. 1129).

In San Francisco, Arakaki developed a friendship with Harry Bridges, the President of the ILWU, and along with a hand-full of other ILWU delegates, even attended the Chicago Peace Conference in 1951, where Bridges was a speaker. The conference brought together Leftist intellectuals, scientists, and artists such as W.E.B. DuBois, Linus Pauling, Dashiell Hammett, Paul Robeson, and others and set out a platform protesting American involvement in the Korean War and the escalation of the nuclear arms race — "Ban the Bomb." One can only imagine the heady experience it must have been for a warehouse inventory worker from a small plantation town on the Big Island.

The next few years were busy ones for these unionists, the ILWU, as well as other unions. The ILWU aggressively implemented organizing drives and collective bargaining, and their growing strength could be seen in a series of strikes beginning in September of 1946. The "Great Hawaiian Sugar Strike of 1946," which lasted 79 days, dealt a blow to the paternalistic forms of control which had previously dominated the plantations. Although it was not successful, the Pineapple Strike of 1947 demonstrated that over 18,000 workers would indeed walk out. Finally, the "Great Hawaiian Dock Strike of 1949," nearly brought Hawai'i's economy to its knees. But just as labor was flexing their muscle, events on the international stage — the Cold War — intervened. The perceived threat of encroaching communism in the U.S., known as the "Red Scare," shook up American society once again. Its effects were also felt in Hawai'i, and will be discussed further in the next section.

While it gained power and influence, the ILWU also worked to establish itself as a respectable institution and major player in Hawai'i's economy and society. The ILWU developed service programs within the union, setting up a social welfare department and eventually hired Ah Quon Leong McElrath, wife of union official Robert McElrath, to work with the union members' families on budgeting, family planning, retirement planning, etc. It also set up an education department, hiring David Thompson, to help the rank-and-file unionists understand contemporary issues, institutionalize the education of union officials, etc. One of the programs the union established was an International Labor Education Program in which three-member teams of rank-and-file unionists, competitively selected, were sent abroad to observe the labor and industrial conditions, and other relevant issues in countries around the world. In providing an opportunity to engage rank and file workers in international affairs, it helped them to develop an internationalist perspective on labor conditions and relations with their union brothers and sisters. In this period union about two dozen or so unionists were exposed to Australia, New Zealand, Greece, Yugoslavia, etc. Some, like the study trip to Cuba by the ILWU's Secretary-Treasurer Newton Miyagi, were controversial both within and outside of the union; however, most of the educational study teams went to less controversial places, broadened members' perspectives, and grounded the policy positions taken by the union.

In 1960, Yagi applied for the International Education Program offered by the union. The ILWU was still committed to the doctrine of organizing and cooperating with workers around the world, and Okinawa was chaffing under the continuing U.S. Occupation. After completing the union-funded three-country study tour portion of the trip, he took a self-funded side trip to Okinawa.

> "But the whole concept came on the basis — that's the reason why we were, in 1960, I went as a chairman of a three-man committee to Japan, India, Calcutta, Hong Kong, and later I went to Okinawa. These were the overseas delegation. Some of them went to Cuba, some of them went to the European countries. To Greece as well as... This was to make us fully understand worldwide problems or worldwide workers' problems and see how that ... We were advised, warned, that don't compare the standard that we are living with the other countries, poor countries. And these are the kinds of things they made us understand. But prior to that we have lots of disagreements." (Interview with T Yagi, December 19, 1989 p. 501).

Upon his return, Yagi briefed ILWU's Education director, Dave Thompson, about the

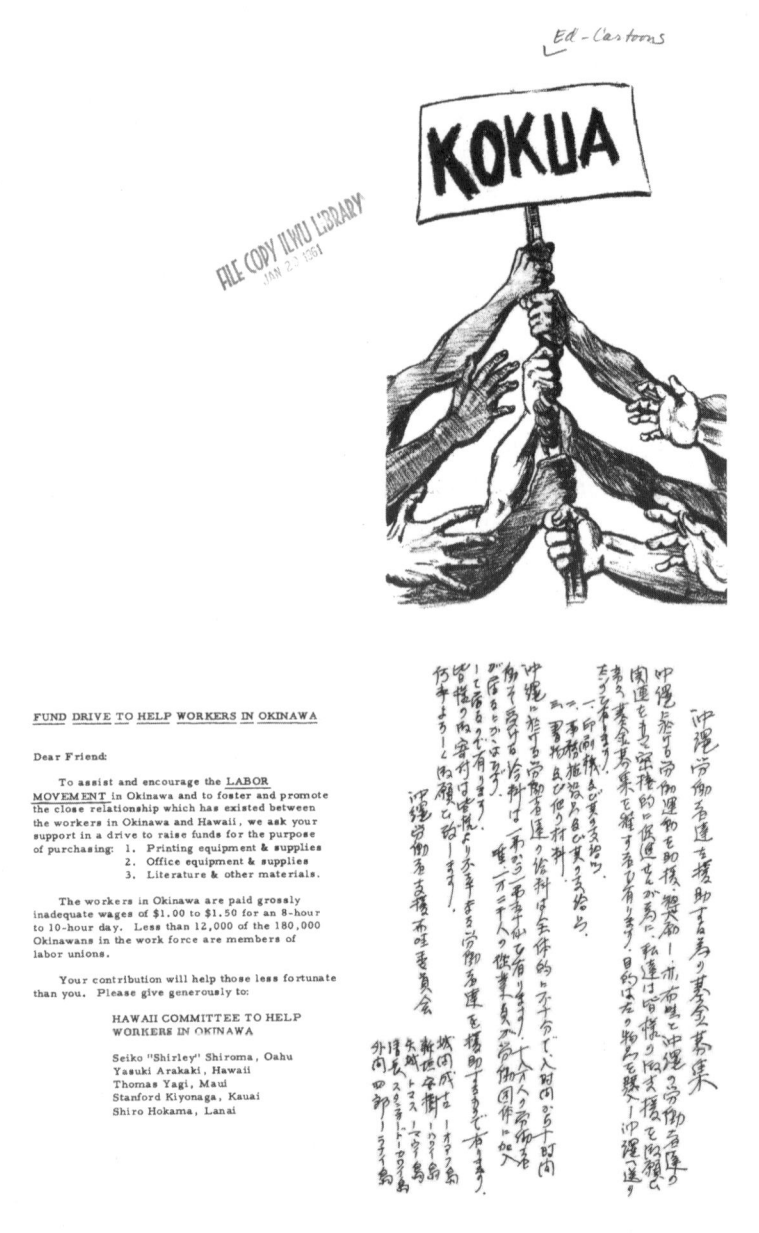

[Figure 2. KOKUA Flyer of FUND DRIVE TO HELP WORKERS IN OKINAWA.
Source: ILWU Local 142 Archives]

conditions he witnessed in Okinawa. They then organized an effort to support workers in Okinawa. The flyer shown below was one of the results of Yagi's actions. The illustration of raised arms and a sign "KOKUA" (help out) was drawn by Thompson. In addition to Yagi, contact persons on the flyer include other Okinawan names: Seiko Shiroma, Yasuki Arakaki, Shiro Hokama. Clearly, the degree of cooperation between the ILWU and the

Okinawan labor movement is an area where further research is required.[2)]
Perhaps this accounts for why Yagi was among the few Okinawan nisei who supported the reversion movement. At a time when most Okinawan nisei, even some of his colleagues in the labor movement, questioned the wisdom of Okinawa returning to Japan, Yagi's was one of the few voices that countered the dominant narrative of Okinawa's great progress under the U.S. Occupation.

Many, if not most nisei Okinawans' positions on reversion mostly mirrored the American military's — that the "Ryukyuans" should remain under American control. Since the post-war Relief and Reconstruction efforts of Okinawa in Hawai'i had depended so much on U.S. military cooperation to transport the items, Okinawans in Hawai'i were generally used to working with the U.S. military. As second generation Okinawans, and first-generation Americans, the nisei were mostly educated in the American educational system in the midst of the Americanization movement (Tamura 1994), and inculcated with patriotism and supported American militarism In this sense, Thomas Yagi was probably one of the few nisei who was able to consciously link his Okinawan identity with his organizer identity and critique the buildup of American bases.

5. "Democratic Revolution" and Okinawan Politicians

Unions focusing exclusively on the collective bargaining process can only be partly effective for their membership. Workplaces are as much governed by conditions, frameworks and regulations determined outside the workplace as within the contract. Recognizing that influencing that larger social arenas would ultimately help their rank and file members, Hawai'i unions got involved in electoral politics as well. They established Political Action Committees (PACs). They lobbied for raising the minimum wage, enacting worker's compensation, occupational safety and health laws, temporary disability insurance (TDI), civil rights, health insurance, etc. — as *social rights* for all workers, even those workers not covered by negotiated contracts. Since these social rights function as parameter setters (i.e., as *minima* or "floors"), unions were able to stabilize their own gains and improve their positions in their collective bargaining process.

For more than a half century after becoming a Territory, the Republican Party was the dominant party in the Hawaii Territorial Legislature. The Republican Party was closely aligned with the business elites of the major corporations which dominated the economy of the territory. These corporations — Alexander and Baldwin; Castle and Cooke, C. Brewer, American Factors, and Theo. H. Davies — were known as the "Big Five" and, through interlocking directorates and intermarriage among the upper class families, controlled much of the economic and social life of the Hawaiian Islands (Shoemaker, 1940; Beechert, 1985).

As early as 1944, the ILWU had worked to elect politicians in both parties who might be friendly to their interests — 16 House members and 8 Senators in the Territorial legislature. A year later, in 1945, the Territorial Legislature enacted the Hawaii Employment

Relations Act (now HRS 377), often called the "Little Wagner Act," which extended the "right to organize a union and collectively bargain" provisions of the National Labor Relations Act of 1935 to all of Hawai'i's workers. In so doing, Hawai'i became the first place in the United States to permit even agricultural workers the right to unionize and collectively bargain with their employers. The following year, from September to November in 1946, the ILWU led 21,000 sugar workers throughout the islands in a successful 79-day strike against the Hawaii Employer's Council — winning many important provisions such as the discontinuation of the perquisite system, the mechanism which had been used to capriciously reward or punish, and therefore, control workers.[3] A pineapple strike followed in 1947, and then in 1949 dock workers struck for a contentious six month period to win parity with dockworkers on the West Coast. The power of the ILWU and the CIO-model of organizing to shut down everything from sugar plantations to the docks was amply demonstrated.

However, organized labor's increasing power in Hawai'i and on the continent also brought other challenges. Another "Red Scare" was spreading across the nation and unions and their leadership were targets. In Hawai'i, Governor Ingram M. Stainback declared war on communism in Hawai'i 1946. On November 25, 1947, teachers Dr. John and Aiko Reinecke were suspended indefinitely without pay from their public school positions. Among the 11-point charges, mostly for being Communists, was the charge "for not possessing the ideals of democracy" (Holmes, 1994, p. 46). The territorial legislature passed a concurrent resolution requesting that the U.S. House Un-American Activities Committee (HUAC) investigate the degree of internal subversion in the territory. Seven individuals, several of them directly or indirectly connected to the ILWU, were charged with being Communists and with plotting to overthrow the government of the United States. The "Hawaii Seven," as they were called, were Jack Hall, John Reinecke, Koji Ariyoshi, Jack Kimoto, Jim Freeman, Charles Fujimoto and his wife Eileen Fujimoto.[4]

The HUAC required union officers to testify at these hearings, and the organizers were subpoenaed. When they and others refused to testify, citing their Constitutional rights under the Fifth Amendment of the Bill of Rights against self-incrimination, they became known as the "Reluctant Thirty-Nine." Many nisei were among this group, and the Okinawans included Yagi, Arashiro, Arakaki, and others. The dilemma facing many of these subpoenaed men and women was that many of them indeed had signed Communist Party member cards, but only to access the skills and assistance required in organizing, and to bring more democratic practices into their workplaces. Indeed, they were more "unionists" than "Communists." For Yagi and others, refusing to respond to the question by citing the Fifth Amendment against self-incrimination, was the most accurate and appropriate response. It also meant that he faced social ostracism in the community because he was "indicted, though, but was acquitted, and was not convicted." (Yagi interview, p. 490).

In the midst of the anti-Communist hysteria, another arena was undergoing change — politics. Here a coalition of three interest groups were organizing to revitalize the lackluster Democratic Party. One part of the coalition was an assortment of traditional Democrats. Another part of the coalition included organized labor. The third were returning young, educated nisei veterans of units such as the 100th Infantry Battalion, 442nd Regimental Combat Team, and the Military Intelligence Service. This demographic bump of young, educated nisei desiring to participate in the political life of the territory was significant. Having demonstrated their bravery and loyalty to the U.S. at extraordinary high costs, having survived the Second World War--even as some of their families were internment camps--this last group of Democrats were not about to return to the same paternalistic society they had left during the war. Together, with the leadership of a former police officer (and later Governor) named John A. Burns, the coalition was able to pull together a grass-roots campaign that gave the Democratic Party the dominance in the Legislature which it has held over the past fifty-plus years.

Probably the best known Okinawan in Democratic Party politics was the late Robert "Bob" Oshiro. For over thirty years, his name was the synonymous with Democratic Party politics as one of the key grass-roots strategists. Born and raised in the pineapple plantation town of Wahiawā, of parents who had immigrated from Okinawa, he graduated from Mid-Pacific High School (because Leilehua High School, where he had been attending, had been taken over by the military during the war). While attending the University of Hawai'i, he was drafted and trained as a Military Intelligence Service interpreter; the war ended just as he was en route to Japan, making him one of the first soldiers in the occupation of Japan. After discharge, he returned home and completed his education at the University of Hawai'i; however, his graduation was ill-timed. The 1949 Great Hawaiian Dock Strike was on. Unable to find a job, he decided to use his remaining veteran's educational benefits and went to Duke University Law School. Inspired by one of his professors, who had taught about the potential of lawyers to be social engineers, he returned in 1953 to set up a law office in his home town of Wahiawā. Oshiro got involved in precinct politics just on the eve of the 1954 elections and the "Democratic Revolution" which swept the Democrats into the status of majority party in the Territorial Legislature. After a half century of Republican Party rule, Oshiro reflected:

> "I think the most exciting thing about it all is that all of us came out with a conviction that it can be done. I think that's the most significant thing that came out of that election, and you know, that's very important. Today, when you look at the world over, you find all kinds of methods of trying to change society. I think in '54, that gave us hope, tremendous hope, that this is the avenue that we should work towards, if we want to bring about changes — whether it's political, economic or social . . . That reinforced the thinking of many of us. (Oshiro Interview, p. 1374)

Oshiro went on to serve in the Legislature as a Clerk, and then as an elected Representative from his district of Wahiawā. Although he is often credited for having put together successful campaigns for at least three governors and a number of congressional officials, he was most proud of helping to pass legislation that consolidated the multiple school boards in the Territory (later, the State) to a statewide Board of Education where schools could count on uniform levels of funding, and provide a measure of equity for students among the different school districts.

Another Okinawan legislator, Representative Yoshito Takamine eventually became the long-standing chair of the House Labor Committee. He was born and raised in Honokaʻa. Unlike his two older sisters, he was able to finish high school; however, like many other nisei on the sugar plantations, he could not afford to go on to college. Consequently, he went to work for the sugar company, working in the field machinery department unloading the sugar cane for processing. Like Yagi and Arakaki, it was because he worked on the industrial side, that he got involved in the labor movement — He signed up in July of 1944. In the 1946 Strike, he was assigned to look over the needs of strikers along the Hamakua coast. Takamine remembers it as a well-run strike with a host of committees (e.g., communications, picketing, soup kitchen, hunting, fishing, "bumming," social morale, etc.). He recalled the only problem was one of providing striking workers with white rice (the CIO partners on the West Coast had mistakenly sent brown rice). In 1958, Takamine reluctantly got into politics, at the last minute when the ILWU and the Democratic Party couldn't find anyone else to run for the seat of Representative from the Third District. He won by a scant thirty-two votes, but thereafter repeatedly reelected for the next twenty-four years. Takamine noted:

> "I spent most of my time chairing the labor committee. Because there was much work to be done in the area of minimum wage, workmen's comp, unemployment comp, safety, and all those basic labor laws. . . . Dave Thompsons was deeply involved in education. Education, you know, for children, uh the future of children, the future of the state. So it was the Department of Education, University of Hawaii." (Takamine interview, p. 18)

Indeed, during his tenure as Representative and Chair of the House Labor Committee, the Legislature enacted several important pieces of legislation which have made the State of Hawaiʻi as one of the most progressive in the nation: increases in the Minimum Wage; the Hawaii Worker's Compensation in 1963; Temporary Disability Insurance Act in 1969; and the Employer Pre-paid Health Insurance Act in 1974.

Other Okinawans politicians elected to the Legislature included Matsuki "Mutt" Arashiro, whose career on the island of Kauai spanned both labor and politics; Akira Sakima who was part of the group that delivered milking goats to Okinawa in the Relief and Reconstruction period, chaired the Education Committee for many years; Peter Iha; Robert Taira; Marshall Ige; Ken Kiyabu and the first woman Uchinanchu Legislator, Patsy (Miyahira) Young, just to name a few. All ran as Democrats; the only Republican Legislator was Robert Teruya.

The Legislature was not the only political arena in which Okinawans were involved. Another Okinawan labor activist who was also involved in the political arena was Seiko "Shirley" Shiroma. As an organizer for Kahuku Plantation, Shiroma was active both within the ILWU, and in the community. Realizing that most workers' children attended public schools, he ran for and won a seat on the Board of Education. At the time he was the general manager of the Union Insurance Service (which had been started by the ILWU and United Public Workers unions, and which was later purchased by the AIG). Union Insurance Service provided unionized workers with affordable automobile and other forms of insurance, a service that had previously been unavailable to them because of the expensive rates that the large commercial corporations charged. Shiroma was an advocate for better educational standards, confronting schools principals on the way in which civics education was being presented. He advocated for a tougher curriculum with clearer expectations of content mastery rather than simply teaching general attitudes. In a speech to the annual State Secondary Principals' Conference, he said "Our experience is that where the schools teach attitudes on labor questions they are anti-union attitudes." (HA 11/29/1969).

6. Consciousness of and Relevance of Okinawan identity

In several conversations I had with the late Ah Quon Leong McElrath, retired ILWU social worker, life-long community activist, and former member of the Board of Regents of the University of Hawai'i, we often discussed the differences that characterized the Okinawan union organizers and membership (compared to the Japanese). According to her, "The Okinawans were different, more militant. You should check out the *Yoen Jiho*." It seems that the *Yoen Jiho*, the Japanese-language paper might have played an important part in the formation of the ideas of the Okinawan issei radicals (Wakukawa, 1981); how much these ideas might have affected the nisei remains an area that requires further study.

What we do know is that most labor and political leaders acknowledged their Okinawan ancestry without hesitation. While Okinawan identity may not have been the primary impetus of their activism, it was "in the mix." For example, Yasuki Arakaki was conscious about the discrimination that he and other Okinawans faced vis-à-vis the Japanese. He described how his relationship with his Naichi girlfriend had to be terminated because he was Okinawan. It angered him to be rejected because of her parents' prejudice, but he also recalled his mother's comments about avoiding relationships with people whom she called "Molokai-hito." Arakaki subsequently married a Hawaiian woman, whom his mother accepted unconditionally. Arakaki's ability to recognize parallels in the discrimination against Okinawans and against people whose relatives had contracted Hansen's Disease and had been sent to Kalaupapa on Molokai island probably enhanced his ability to connect with people of various backgrounds, critical to his success in organizing.

Probably the person who most identified with his Okinawan identity and could see its transnational implications, was Tom Yagi. In late January and early February of 1960 six legislators of Okinawan ancestry visited Okinawa for ten days as guests of the United States Commission on Civil Administration of the Ryukyu Islands (USCAR), transported by U.S. Military Transport. They included: Rep. Yoshito Takamine (D); Robert C. Oshiro

(D); Rep. Akira Sakima (D); Rep. Peter S. Iha (D); Robert E. Teruya (R); Sen. Matsuki Arashiro (D). The delegation later issued statements marveling at the progress Okinawa had made since the war's end. They spoke about the new roads, new buildings, etc. and, for the most part, favored the continuation of American Occupation of Okinawa, this despite the increasing volume of voices within Okinawa petitioning have Okinawa returned to Japan (HSB 1, 26, 1960). It appeared that USCAR's objective of the delegation's visit was generally accomplished. However, Maui Division's Tom Yagi presented a counter argument based on his own site visit to Okinawa; he was one of the lone voices among Hawai'i nisei Okinawans to counter USCAR's and the six legislators' perspectives.

In many respects, then, this examination of Okinawans and their roles in the labor and political moments in Hawai'i has found patterns similar to those discovered earlier by Jung (2006). Like Jung, I submit that Okinawans conceptualized and practiced interracial politics and they did not merely give up "race" and/or "culture" for "class." It was in particular movements that for them *class* became *racialized*, as in their attacks against the "Big Five" which became *haole-ized (made"white')*. At the same time, Caucasians like John A. Burns or Jack Hall, was de-racialized, made "Local" or "one of them." After all, Harry Kamoku, the Hawaiian activist-organizer on the Hilo docks, workers were "brothers under the skin." (Puette, 1986, p. 4) Similarly, while the Okinwans were conscious of and critical of the Naichi Japanese disregard of Okinawans as a group, they did not forego opportunities to work with them, or with Filipinos, or other ethnic groups. In other words, Okinawans in the progressive movements of the mid-twentieth century negotiated their Okinawan identities by the particular requirements of specific situations; in the end, it was a strategy which helped them to bring about modern Hawai'i.

Discussion and Conclusion

Okinawans *sojourned* to Hawai'i at a particular historical moment, and *settled* here just as critical historical events were occurring. Additionally, the resulting sizeable nisei generation came of age at the critical moments of Hawai'i's labor and political history. They participated in the social structural changes the islands underwent in the mid-twentieth century, in the both the labor movement and the political ousting of the hegemonic Republican Party. Together, these movements disrupted and transformed the society, both in terms of industrial relations and civil society, into a modern-day Hawai'i.

In this paper I have argued that the results of Okinawan and other multi-ethnic labor and political activist were the mandated access to employer pre-paid health insurance, worker's compensation, unemployment benefits, etc. — some of the rights taken for granted by workers in the fiftieth state today. Civil rights which exceed the national floor — for women, in education, etc. These are some of the reforms that Okinawans nisei facilitated, in conjunction with their other fellow workers and legislators. The Congress of Industrial Organizations (CIO) organizing style in the ILWU might have been the overall strategy, but on the ground in Hawai'i, it took individual organizers like Tom Yagi, Yasu Arakaki, Matsuki Arashiro, Shiro Hokama, Toyo Oshiro and many others. In the government, it was through people like Yoshito Takamine, Goro Hokama, Robert Oshiro, Akira Sakima, and so many others, that progressive legislation could take place — many of the programs and policies that we take for granted today.

In conclusion, it may be true that Okinawans in Hawai'i, as a social category, currently live relatively comfortable middle class lives; they are often home-owners, employed, hard-working, playing by the rules, etc. However, especially in a multi-ethnic societal context like Hawai'i, where ethnicity is often correlated with social class, it is inappropriate to tautologically explain socioeconomic status in terms of ethnicity. Variations in educational and income attainment, housing, etc. are not simply a result of adherence to cultural norms, values and practices. This "good values" reasoning can lead to an uncritical acceptance of the "model minority" myth, and block seeing how larger social forces have affected, and continue to affect their lives. The affluence that is taken for granted today is as much, if not more, a product of the labor and political movements of the mid-1900s, as from individual or small collective efforts. These social movements, in which nisei Okinawans were located and contributed to, came about because of their demographic and class location. They worked on behalf of the all workers and citizens, not just themselves, and in the process, benefited themselves. Conditions in the 21st century are quite different. Okinawan sansei and yonsei have smaller families, or no children. The entry of new immigrants from Asia and the Pacific, the reassertion of Hawaiian nationalism, and the rise of reactionary politics dismantled the progressive gains there needs to be much more reflection on the part of Okinawans to be more reflective about their present status and the extent which the past upward trajectory can be sustained. Perhaps the conversations should instead Okinawans should ask: what can we learn from previous generations of Uchinanchu to bring about a more just and peaceful society so that <u>everyone</u>, not just Uchinanchu, can benefit?

INTERVIEW TRANSCRIPTS AND MATERIALS

University of Hawai'i at Mānoa, Center for Oral History Interviews
Interview with Thomas Yagi, November 9, 1989.
Interview with Robert Oshiro, April 7, 1988
Interview with Yasuki Arakaki, March 19, 1991.
University of Hawai'i -West O'ahu, Center for Labor Education and Research, *Rice and Roses* Hawaii Labor
    History Interviews
Interview with Yoshito Takamine, June 17, 1996 Rice and Roses
Interview with Seiko Shiroma, April 4, 1996, Rice and Roses
Interview with Ah Quon McElrath, May 26, 2004
Okinawa Prefectural Archives.
National Archives and Records Administration, Record Group 260 Records of the United States Occupation
    Headquarters, World War II Records of the U.S. Civil Administration of the Ryukyu Islands (USCAR),
    The Public Affairs Department, The Information Division, Box No. 339 of HCRI-PA, Cataloged by the
    National Diet Library Japan and the Okinawa Prefectural Archives.

Figure 1. Description: "Participants in the ILWU and California Labor School leadership training program for Hawaii Unionists with ILWU President Harry Bridges, San Francisco, February-April 1946."
Arakaki (second from left), Yagi (third from left)
Credit: ILWU Local 142 archives.
Figure 2. "'KOKUA' flyer for Okinawa." Sketch of 10 arms holding a picket sign "KOKUA"
Credit: ILWU Local 142 archives

Notes

1) I gratefully acknowledge the assistance that Rae Shiraki, archivist at the ILWU Local 142, and Gene Vrana, librarian at the ILWU International Library, provided me with their collections. Also, Yuko Kakinohana at the Okinawa Prefectural Archives provided me with much assistance accessing the Kotani-Kimoto Interviews. I also thank Bob Ellefson and the *IJOS* reviewers for their editorial assistance.

2) There were three separate conferences ostensibly organized by Harry Bridges, President of the ILWU, although the official organization was the "All Pacific & Asian Dockworkers Corresponding Committee." The first was held in Tokyo beginning on May 11, 1959 and running three days. Harry Bridges and regional directors of the ILWU, including Hawaii's Jack Hall attended. From Okinawa, Mr. Makoto Motomura participated. In his report which ran some nine pages, Mr. Motomura spoke of the occupation of Okinawa, noting " . . . there is an Okinawa among U.S. military bases." He refers to nuclear bases taking land from Okinawans: "Hundreds of farmers, workers and students who fought in opposition were arrested and put in prisons."
A second conference was held again in Tokyo from June 15–17, 1961. The report on the Hawaii Labor Situation was delivered by Mr. Noboru Miyamoto, basically on the history of the development of the ILWU in Hawai'i, concluding with a concern over mechanization and automation. The Report on the Okinawan Labor Situation was delivered by Mr. Hideo Taira (pp. 58–64). He noted that "at least five of the thirteen members of the Okinawan delegation were refused their passports." A third conference was held in Djakarta, Indonesia from Oct 4–9, 1963. No Okinawans were listed among the delegates from Japan. (ILWU Archives, Honolulu, HI, "International Workers connections" file).

3) Perquisites included "free" housing, health care, charge accounts at the plantation store, etc. Because they were "given" to workers, they could be assigned at the will of the plantation managers. When workers were not compliant, they could be reassigned to lower quality homes or, as frequently occurred during strikes, evicted from their housing. Without the perquisite system, workers no longer could be evicted from their homes as long as they were up-to-date in their rental payments.

4) Of the seven, only Hall was directly related to the ILWU. Mrs. Fujimoto worked in a secretarial position for the union for a time.

References

Arakaki, M. (2001). Hawaii Uchinanchu and Okinawa: Uchinanchu Spirit and the formation of a transnational identity. In R. Nakasone (Ed.), *Okinawan diaspora*. (pp. 130–141) Honolulu, HI: University of Hawai'i Press.

Beechert, E. D. (1985). *Working in Hawaii: A labor history*. Honolulu, HI: University of Hawaii Press.

Conybeare, C. (Producer). (1996). 1946: The great Hawaiian sugar strike. (Television documentary video): Honolulu, HI: Center for Labor Education and Research, Rice and Roses.

Conybeare, C. (Producer). (1999). 1946: The great Hawaii dock strike. (Television documentary video): Honolulu, HI: Center for Labor Education and Research, Rice and Roses.

Chai, A. Y., & Kawakami, B. F. (1986). *Picture brides: Lives of early immigrant women from Japan, Okinawa and Korea*. Rice and Roses [Television series].

Chapin, H. G. (1996). *Shaping history: The role of newspapers in Hawai'i*. Honolulu, HI: University of Hawaii Press.

Chinen, J. N. (1990). Okinawan women: Continuity and change. In J. N. Chinen & R. Adaniya (Eds.). *UCHI-*

NAA: Okinawan history and culture. 1900 Okinawan Celebration Education Committee. Honolulu, HI:Fisher Printing Co. Inc., supported by the Hawaii Committee for the Humanities.

Chinen, J. N. (2000). Uchinanchu today. In *To our issei . . . Our heartfelt gratitude* (pp. 12–18). Honolulu, HI: Centennial Celebration Committee.

Ethnic Studies Oral History Project and the United Okinawan Association of Hawaii. (1981). *Uchinanchu: A history of the Okinawans in Hawaii*. Compiled and edited by the Ethnic Studies Oral History Project and the United Okinawan Association of Hawaii. Honolulu, HI: Ethnic Studies Program, University of Hawaii.

Fujikane, C., & Okamura, J. Y. (Eds.). (2008). *Asian settler colonialism: From local governance to the habits of everyday life in Hawai'i*. Honolulu, HI: University of Hawai'i Press.

Giddens, A. (1984). *The constitution of society: Outline of the theory of structuration*. Berkeley, CA: University of California Press.

Hiura, A. T., & Terada, V. K. (1981). Okinawan involvement in Hawaii's labor movement. In *UCHINANCHU: A History of Okinawans in Hawaii* (pp. 223–232). Honolulu, HI: Ethnic Studies Oral History Project and the United Okinawan Association of Hawaii.

Hochschild, A. R., & Machung, A. (1997). The second shift: Working parents and the revolution at home. New York: Avon.

Hokama, L. Y. (1981). Okinawan partcipation in the legislature. In *UCHINANCHU: A History of Okinawans in Hawaii* (pp. 243–232). Honolulu, HI: Ethnic Studies Oral History Project and the United Okinawan Association of Hawaii.

Holmes, T. M. (1960, January 26). 10-day trip to Okinawa. Honolulu star-bulletin.

Holmes, T. M. (1962, November 29). ILWU Official Says Labor Gets Rough Time At School. Honolulu Advertiser.

Holmes, T. M. (1994). The specter of communism in Hawaii. Honolulu, HI: University of Hawaii Press.

Ishikawa, T. (1981). A Study of the historical geography of early Okinawan immigrants to the Hawaiian islands." In *Uchinanchu: A history of the Okinawans in Hawaii* (pp. 127–142). Compiled and edited by the Ethnic Studies Oral History Project and the United Okinawan Association of Hawaii. Honolulu, HI: Ethnic Studies Program, University of Hawaii.

Izuka, I. (1947). The truth about communism in Hawaii. (31-page pamphlet)

Jung, Moon-Kie. (2006). *Reworking race: The making of Hawaii's interracial labor movement*. New York: Columbia University Press.

Kawakami, B. (1993). Immigrant clothing in Hawaii. Honolulu, HI: University of Hawaii Press.

Kimura, Y. (1981). Social-historical background of the Okinawans in Hawaii. In *Uchinanchu: A history of the Okinawans in Hawaii* (pp. 51–71). Compiled and edited by the Ethnic Studies Oral History Project and the United Okinawan Association of Hawaii. Honolulu, HI: Ethnic Studies Program, University of Hawaii.

Kinoshita, G. (2002). Telling our roots in the sugar plantation: Collective identities of Japanese American elderly in Puna, Hawai'i. In J. Y. Okamura (Ed.), The Japanese American contemporary experience in Hawai'i, social process in Hawai'i, 41 (pp. 1–20). Honolulu, HI: University of Hawai'i Press.

Nakano Glenn, E. (2002). *Unequal freedom: How race and gender shaped American citizenship and labor*. Cambridge, MA: Harvard University Press.

Nakasone, R. (2001). *Okinawan diaspora*. Honolulu, HI: University of Hawai'i Press.

Nordyke, E. C. (1989). *The peopling of Hawaii*, 2nd edition. Honolulu, HI: University of Hawaii Press.

Okamura, J. Y. (2008). *Identity and politics in Hawai'i*. Philadelphia: Temple University Press.

Oshiro, G. (2007) Hawaii in the life and thought of Ifa Fuyu, father of Okinawan studies. In J. N. Chinen (Ed.), *Uchinaanchu diaspora: Memories, continuities and constructions, social process in Hawaii* 42 (pp. 35–60). Honolulu, HI: University of Hawaii Press.

Sakihara, M. (2000). The twenty-six men. In *To Our Issei...Our Heartfelt Gratitude* (pp. 12–18). Honolulu, HI: Centennial Celebration Committee.

Shirota, J. (1965). *Lucky come Hawaii*. New York: Bantam.

Shirota, J. (1990). The dawning of the Okinawan." In *UCHINANCHU: A pictorial tribute to Okinawans in*

Hawaii by United Okinawan Association. (pp. 16–49) Hawaii: EastWest Magazine Co., Ltd.

Shoemaker, J. (1940). *Labor in Hawaii*. Washington, D.C.:Government Printing Office.

Tamura, E. H. (1994). *Americanization, acculturation and ethnic identity: The nisei generation in Hawaii*. Urbana: Univeristy of Illinois Press.

Toyama, H., & Ikeda, K. (1981). The Okinawan-Naichi Relationship. In *Uchinanchu: A history of the Okinawans in Hawaii*. Compiled and edited by the Ethnic Studies Oral History Project and the United Okinawan Association of Hawaii (pp. 127–142). Honolulu, HI: Ethnic Studies Program, University of Hawaii [Reprinted from *Social Process in Hawaii* 1950].

Ueunten, W. I. (2007). *The Okinawan revival in Hawaii: Contextualizing culture and identity over diasporic time and space*. Unpublished manuscript, University of California, Berkeley.

Wilson, W. J. (1993). *Power, racism and privilege*. New York: Macmillan.

Zalburg, S. (1979). *A spark is struck! Jack Hall & The ILWU in Hawaii*. Honolulu, HI: The University Press of Hawaii.

ハワイへの憧憬・アメリカへの違和
――宮城聰とハワイ――

仲 程 昌 德*

A Longing for Hawai'i, Discomfort towards America: Satoshi Miyagi, Hawai'i, and Okinawan Literature

NAKAHODO Masanori

There was an Okinawan writer named Satoshi Miyagi, who was active from the 1930s until the beginning of the 1940s. Leaving Okinawa for Tokyo in 1921 and getting involved with the journal *Kaizo* as an editor, Miyagi went to Hawai'i to promote a collection of Japanese literature that his company, Kaizo-sha, published. While in Hawai'i, his longtime yearning to be a professional writer became stronger, and Miyagi published his first short stories, "The Earth — Our Home" and "The Birth of a Living." Miyagi was instantly recognized as one of the most promising young writers, and he again went to Hawai'i in 1935. He published a collection of short stories titled *Honolulu Stories* in July 1936, which was based on his visits to Hawai'i. He revised *Honolulu Stories*, and it turned into *Hawai'i* in April 1946. The present discussion focuses on Miyagi and his 1946 work *Hawai'i* in the context of Okinawan literature, suggesting Miyagi's cross-cultural experience in Hawai'i was the driving force for him to create his story.

はじめに

　宮城聰は、昭和の初期、2度ハワイに渡っている。
　第1回目は、1927年（昭和2年）5月、横浜から「サイベリヤ丸」で出帆している。宮城によれば、「五月一日の夜、改造社の日本文学全集のための講演へ出かける芥川龍之介を上野駅で見送った」「その翌々日の三日」のことで、「サイベリヤ丸」がホノルルに着いたのは出発してから「十一日目」のことであったという[1]。
　宮城の目的は、ハワイ在住「日本人へ日本文学全集を宣伝するため」であった。改造社の営業部では「ノボリ、横幕、ポスター類」を沢山船に積み込んでいた。宮城が渡布したその頃「ハワイや米本国へ旅行する人は、今日とは異り、極めて少数であったので、

---

* 元琉球大学教授 Professor (retired in 2009), University of the Ryukyus

移民としては随分多くの日本人が行っているのに、ハワイがどんなところであるか、よくわかって」いなかった。宮城は「知人の一人もいない未知の土地なので、不安もあった」[2]が、船のなかで、郷里広島を訪問しての帰りである「山城ホテルの若主人」[3]と知り合い、ホノルルの同ホテルに宿泊する。そして、ホテルの近くでハワイ産業会社を経営していた平良牛助を知り、彼の紹介でドクター小波津の知遇を得、新城銀次郎と出会う。

　新城は、宮城を連れて、ホノルル中の書店を廻り、宣伝の手配をしてくれた。さらにホノルル在住者に協力を依頼し「書店の歩道に面する表に、改造営業部が積み込んであった横幕を張って、自動車の車体を赤地の布に日本文学全集と改造社の社名を白抜きにした横幕で張り廻らした十数台の自動車を連ねて」街頭を走るとともに、「改造社のタスキを肩から掛けて、ホノルルの街を練り廻って宣伝」してくれた。

　6月4日、ホノルルで発行されていた邦字新聞の1つ『布哇報知』は「雑誌『改造』の記者、宮城久輝氏は今朝入港のサイベリア丸にて来布したが、改造社発行の現代日本文学全集の件の要件にて滞在する由で、山城ホテル宿泊中」の記事を出していて、それも大きな宣伝になったはずである。

　宮城の最初の渡航は、宮城自身の回想や、『布哇報知』の記事からわかるように改造社社員として改造社発行の日本文学全集を売り込むためであったが、ハワイに来た宮城に大きな転機が訪れる。そのことについて、彼は次のように書いていた。

　　日本文学全集の宣伝に刺戟されてか、東京に帰って、自分も勤めるかたわら作品にとりかゝり度いという欲望が、心底深く燃えていた。米本国へ行こうと思えば、ロスアンゼルスかサンフランシスコでは、移民局の調べも必要なかったのであったが、米国への旅行は、文壇にさえ出れば、いつでも行けるから、早く帰って、文学をしたい、という心が強く、米本国旅行の意欲は全くなかった[4]。

　宮城は、ハワイで、俄然「文学をしたい」という思いにとらわれ「行こうと思えば改造社は、全集景気で、金に制限など」なく米本国まで行くことが出来たにもかかわらず、一等船賃を請求しただけで、帰ってしまう[5]。

　宮城の2度目の渡航は、1935年5月[6]。秩父丸の三等船客としてハワイに向かったのは、「改造社の費用節約」ということもさることながら、「前田河広一郎にならって」[7]のことで、いわゆる「作品の取材」[8]のためであった。

　1935年6月25日付『日布時事』は「宮城久輝氏が新進作家になつて再来布す　創作資料蒐集のため」の見出しで「数年前改造社の日本文学全集宣伝のため来布せる宮城聰氏（久輝）は既報の如く二十日秩父丸で再来布した、氏は当地から帰朝後改造社を退き文筆に志ざし全ゆる艱難を嘗めつゝ精進の結果昨年三月東日大毎に中篇小説発表の機会を与へられ引きつゞき三田文学に「生活の誕生」、八月号の改造に「樫の芽生」を発表し新進作家としての地位を確保し、その前途を嘱目されてゐるが、氏は現状に満足□□□□□□□ため来布、二三ケ月滞在のはずである、氏は目下『プレシデント・マッキンレー

号送還記』といふ題で創作執筆中であるが、その余暇に数種の雑誌にも寄稿して居り、七月号の『短歌研究』には「想ひ出のハワイ短歌」といふ題下で潮音詩社の集まり等を紹介してゐる」（□は不明箇所）との記事を出していた。

　25日の記事は「既報の如く」と記してあるように、21日の記事を受けて書かれたものである。21日の新聞は「新進作家宮城氏昨便で来布」として「大毎の懸賞小説に当選し文壇の新進作家に列せられてゐる雑誌改造社記者宮城久輝氏（沖縄県出身）は所報の如く昨日の秩父丸で来布したが今回の来布の目的の大半はハワイを材料にした創作の材料蒐集にあるそうでワザと三等船客の中に雑つてゐた、同氏は元改造記者で例の円本全盛時代にこの用件で特派来布したこともあり当地に知人も多い、現在又改造社に再入社し山本社長の顧問社員である」と報じていた。

　宮城の渡布の目的は、1度目と2度目とでは大きく変わっていた。1度目のハワイは改造社の日本文学全集の宣伝のためであったが、2度目のハワイは、作品の素材を収集するためであった。

　改造社社員宮城久輝は、新進作家宮城聰へと変貌していた。『日布時事』の2度にわたる宮城の来布を報じた記事は、そのことをよく伝えている。

　宮城は、『日布時事』からわかるように「東日大毎」に「中篇小説」を発表する機会を得て新進作家への第一歩を踏み出したといっていいが、その記念碑的な作品「故郷は地球」は、ハワイでの見聞をとり入れていた[9]。

　ハワイは、作家宮城聰の誕生を促した地であった。そして「故郷は地球」をはじめとして数多くの作品を輩出させていく地になっていく。

1. 理想郷の現実――「故郷は地球」

　「故郷は地球」は、「日本の代表的二大新聞の一つである東京日日新聞、大阪毎日新聞が、六人の流行作家に一人ずつ新人を推薦させ、挿絵も名声の高い画壇の大家によって新人を推薦させて貰い、夕刊連載創作純文学を企画した」[10] ことから、里見弴の推薦で連載された作品の一つで、「島国根性の強い沖縄差別への鬱憤をこめたものであった」[11]と宮城は回顧している。

　1934年（昭和9）2月13日から3月17日にかけて『東京日日新聞』の夕刊に連載された作品[12]は、東京の雑誌社で働く主人公の目前で、日々繰り広げられる沖縄差別のさまざまな様態を抉り出していたが、その終わりをハワイで閉じていた[13]。

　ハワイの場面は、とってつけたかのようで、唐突の感をいなめない。それだけに、評価の分かれるところだが、そこには、大切な出来事が2つ取り出されていた。その1つは「サントスの従兄」から届いた手紙と関係するものであり[14]、あとの1つは「国際村」に関するものである。2つは、前者がローカリズム、後者がグローバリズムを表象するものとなっているが、その後者に、何故ハワイの場面をあえて付け加えたか鮮明にしてくれる箇所があった。

次は、その部分である。

　やがてヌアヌパリの崖を築いた道を下つて、海の開けた裏オアフへ出た。
「ココカヒつて如何いふ意味ですか…」
「カナカの言葉で兄弟といふことらしいですね、あの土地を持つてゐるリチャーズさんが国際村、日本でいへば別荘地を建設しようとしてゐるんですよ。君が四五年後にまた来る時には立派な村が出来てゐるだらう。僕がいい家を作つて置くからそこで一年位本を読むんだね…」
　ココカヒ村建設地は自動車を下りて一時間ばかり歩いた。すでに大勢の人が行つてゐる。スロープの草原と藪を歩いてゐる様は、三百年の昔欧州人がはじめてアメリカへ来たのを想像させた。

宮城は、ここに取上げられている場所について「裏オアフの記」でも触れている。そこでは次のようになっている。

　　先の旅、私はRさんに連れられて、この島を目近かに見る岬へ行つたことがあつた。そこはこの湾へ傾く藪であつたが、そこにココカヒといふ村を建てるといふことであつた。ココカヒはカナカの言葉で、血或ひは兄弟と云つた意味だと聞いたが、我等は、グワベといふジャムを作る野生の果物の繁茂する中の道や、小丘や溝なども通つてそこへ行き着いた。分譲しようといふアメリカ人は牧師とかで、この不毛の土地を売るのに一生懸命であつた。理想郷を建設するといふ宣伝が利いたのであらう。随分多勢の人が、人種の差別なく土地の見立てに集つていた。中腹にオハイの大木のある広場があつたが、そこではココカヒ村建設の儀式が始められ、星条旗を中央にして各国の旗が真直に立ち、自国の国旗を前にして、人種と装ひの異る娘等が横列に並んでゐた。同胞娘はたしか三人と憶えるが、お太鼓の振り袖姿で支那人娘や比島娘に並んでゐた。賛美歌を歌ひ、地主が何か話して、それが儀式であつた。私はその過ぎた日を懐ひ乍ら、その辺りを心にとめて見るのであつたが、ココカヒの村らしい姿は何処にもなく、昔を語り顔に草に被はれた緩かな傾斜の原ばかりだつた。

「故郷は地球」の場面は、第1回目の渡布の際、「Rさん」に案内されて見た情景を取り入れて書かれたものであったことが「裏オアフの記」の記述からわかる。そしてそれはほぼ事実に即していたこともわかるが「島国根性の強い沖縄差別への鬱憤」をこめて書かれた作品に、とってつけたかのようにその体験がつけ加えられたのは「国際村」構想に強く魅かれるものがあったことによるであろう。

「国際村」建設現場は、宮城にとってまさに「理想郷」だと受け取られたのである。そこには差別などあるはずはないと考えたことで、「差別」を取り上げた作品の結びに相応しいものとしてつけ加えられたのである。

　ハワイが憧れの地として見られていた。

宮城が、同地を再訪したのは「理想郷」がどのようになっているか知りたいという思いがあったからであろう。さらには「君が四五年後にまた来る時には立派な村が出来てゐるだらう。僕がいい家を作つて置くからそこで一年位本を読むんだね…」といわれた言葉にある期待感を持っていたのではないかとも思われるが、計画は、本体そのものが破綻していた。

　「故郷は地球」と「裏オアフの記」とでは、違いが見られた。それは、前者が「理想郷」実現へ向けての計画が進行中であった時期が扱われていたこと、後者が「理想郷」計画が挫折した後のことが書かれているといった違いではない。もっと微妙な違いである。

　「理想郷」実現にむけての建設が進む現場について、「故郷は地球」では「あの土地を持つてゐるリチャーズさんが国際村、日本でいへば別荘地を建設しようとしてゐるんですよ」と書いていたのに対し、「裏オアフの記」では「分譲しようといふアメリカ人は牧師とかで、この不毛の土地を売るのに一生懸命であつた」と書いていた。

　「国際村」建設の実際は、「裏オアフの記」に見られるとおりであったに違いない。それが「故郷は地球」では消されていた。「国際村」構想が、「不毛の土地」を売らんがための事業であったことを隠蔽したのである。

　「故郷は地球」は、「理想郷」を描こうとしたのである。そこには、宮城の夢が託されていたといってもいいだろう。しかし、ハワイの現実は、「理想郷」とは遠く隔たっていた。「ジャガス」が書かれる由縁である。

2．移民の現実――「ジャガス」

　宮城が、ハワイから戻ってきて、再び渡布するまでの間に書いた、ハワイに取材した作品は「故郷は地球」だけではなかった。そのことに関して宮城は「昭和九年から同十年の四月頃までの目ぼしい物語は、週刊朝日の特別号に掲載された『人種の復讐』[15]と、（中略）それに木誌に掲載して貰った『ジャガス』[16]であると書いていた。

　宮城は「ジャガス」について「『ジャガス』は、改造社の「文芸」（文学雑誌）へ持ち込み依頼したが、編集者が採ってくれないので三田文学へ持って行った。そうしたらこれも五、六日ばかりで活字になった」と述べていた。宮城は作品に自信があったので、改造社の山本社長に送ったところ、「いい作品」だと褒められたばかりでなく、「もう一度ハワイへ行って見ないか」[17]といわれ、即座に2度目のハワイ旅行が決まったというおまけつきのものであった。

　「ジャガス」は、『三田文学』1934年（昭和9）12月号に発表された宮城の「唯一の戯曲」[18]で、「序景」を含め全六景からなっている。

　「序景」は、「カナカ人」同士の土地の売買をめぐる抗争、「一景」は、移民たちが入耕可否の検査を受ける場、「二景」は、古参の日本人が、入耕したばかりの移民の掘立小屋を訪れてくる場、「三景」は、少年と監督の忠実な助手である男との口論の場、「四景」

は、耕地の火事の場、「五景」は、焼死した男の墓を詣でる場といった構成になるもので、ハワイの抱えていた問題とともに、日本人移民の惨苦を刻みこんだものとなっていた。

例えばそれは、大切な土地が二束三文で売られていくこと（序景）、妻が駆け落ちしていくこと（一景）、移民はジャガスと同様だと見られたこと（二景）、食事が極度に貧弱であること（三景）、「パケーに体を売つた方がよかつた」といった話がなされること（四景）、ジャガスを撃ち殺すピストルの音が聞こえてくる（五景）といったことが取上げられていて、金のなる木があると思ってやって来た国が、実は地獄のようなところであったというものである。

劇は、焼死した親友の墓を詣でた男が、地獄のような耕地で働くものたちを「救ふ」ために「一生懸命やらう」という言葉で幕を下ろす。

「ジャガス」は、最初ハワイに渡ったとき、世話になった先輩から「初期の移民が、日本での契約とは異り、牛馬同様の過酷の労働を強いられた委しい具体的な話を」[19] 聞いて書かれたものである。

「ジャガス」に出てくる話は、決して珍しいものではなかった。ホノルルで発刊されていた２大邦字新聞『布哇報知』および『日布時事』をめくればいくらでも出てくる。例えば「物価は二重三重に騰貴しても給金は依然として昔のまゝなので、耕地労働者は生計難に苦しみ、色々の哀話を産みつゝある」として、1919年10月21日付け『布哇報知』に掲載された「資本家の冷酷」、耕主の「冷酷無情」を批判した記事[20]、「昔の布哇は、女と云つたら百人に対する一人にも当ら無いと云ふ有様なりし事とて若し日本から女が来たと云へば、他人の女房であらふが娘であらふが将た又、渋皮の剥けた女であらふがあるまいがそんな事には少しもお構ひなしで独身者は直ちに人の女を包囲攻撃し甚だしきに至りては亭主の留守を狙つて盗み出すと云ふ騒ぎ」と書き出された1916年8月10日付け『布哇報知』の記事[21]、また「沖縄県人屋賀妖善と云ふは今より三ケ月前妻カマトを呼寄せたるに此の女元来蓮葉な性分に生れ付いたるため来布当座より博愛主義を施し宜からぬ噂を流したる事再三に止まらず然る所カマトは毒を喰へば皿までとの大それた度胸を据へ数ある姦夫の其の中一番虫の好いた新垣某と手に手を取りワイアルアより何れへともなく逃走したり」といった『日布時事』1913年3月26日に報じられた記事[22]等、同種の話は枚挙に暇が無い。

「ジャガス」で扱われている出来事は、特別なことなどではなく、初期移民の哀史として、よく知られていたといっていい。

「ジャガス」は『三田文学』に発表された後、1942年（昭和17）4月発刊された『ハワイ』に収録する際、手を入れていた。それは間違いの訂正にはじまり、注記の削除、不備な文意の補筆そして主要な登場人物の名前の変更といった点に及んでいる[23]が、それだけに留まらなかった。

次は『三田文学』に発表された「ジャガス」の最後の場面である。

新田。今迄あんなに云ふまゝに諾いて牛馬以上に働いてゐた自分が俺は可笑しく考
　　へられるよ。長岡が死んだので始めて覚めた。耕主も吾々も同じ人間だ。何故あ
　　んなに出鱈目な酷い仕打ちを受ける訳があるか。私はきつと⌒長岡の魂を安め
　　る為めに、ここの耕地の労働者皆を救ふ考へだ。
　　きよ子。ええ！　妾も出来るだけやりますわ。
　　新田。一生懸命やらう…。

それが、『ハワイ』に収録された「ジャガス」では、次のようになっている。

　　藤田　今迄あんなに云ふまゝに諾いて、牛馬以上に働いてゐた自分が、俺は近頃可
　　笑しくなつたよ。長岡が死んだので初めて目が覚めた。耕主も吾々も同じ人間だ。
　　何故あんなに出鱈目な酷い仕打ちを受ける訳があるか。ここの耕主は顔だけは人
　　間だが、それこそ地獄の鬼でもこんな酷い心は持つてゐないのだ、鬼は人間にゐ
　　ると聞いたが、耕主のことだつた、いや耕主ばかりではない、アメリカ人は皆鬼
　　だ、鬼でなくて、どうしてピストルで脅して火の中に飛び込まして殺すことが出
　　来るか、さうだ、鬼を退治するのは日本の男だ、俺は生命を賭けてやる考へして
　　ゐる。それで初めて長岡の魂も安まる。われわれ同胞が心を合して当れば、欲の
　　深い鬼はきつと退治できるのだ。
　　きよ子　ええ！　きつと出来ますわ。
　　藤田　生命を賭けて出来んことはない。きつとやらう…。

　藤田（初出は新田）のセリフを、宮城は『ハワイ』に収録する際、大きく書き変えていた。

　『ハワイ』が刊行されたのは1942年4月である。日米の戦争が始まったのがその前年41年（昭和16）の12月であった。そのことを知れば「ここの耕主は顔だけは人間だ、それこそ地獄の鬼」にもまさるといった言葉から「アメリカ人は皆鬼だ」と続いていく「藤田」のセリフの増補が、何ゆえであったかを理解するのに難渋するといったことはないであろう。

3. アメリカへの憤り──連作作品と「アラモアナ事件」

　真珠湾への奇襲攻撃に沸いた年が明けて間もなく刊行された『ハワイ』は、その題名から、多分に真珠湾での大勝利に関する戦記だと想像されたに違いないが、『ハワイ』の中で戦争と関わるものといえば「大東亜戦争勃発の日──『都新聞』」の付記がある「爆撃された布哇」と題された短い随筆1編だけである。他は真珠湾爆撃以前のハワイを背景にしたもので、「ジャガス」を別にすれば、題材を求めて渡布した2度目の体験を踏まえて書かれた作品が採られていた[24]。

　「創作」の部に収録されている「三等渡布記」「ホノルル移民局」「ホノルル」は連作と

いってもいいものである。新進作家と目されるようになった宮城が、作品の素材を求めるためにあえて三等船客として乗り込んだ体験を下敷きにしている。

「三等渡布記」は、乗船1週間前「アメリカ領事館」で「査証」の発行を依頼するところから出帆、船中での出来事そして上陸するにあたっての検疫検査までが書かれていて、それぞれの場面で思わぬ障害に出会い狼狽、反発、憤激する主人公の姿が描かれていた。

主人公の進登は、切符を買う前に、旅行事情に詳しい旅館に行って相談しようと思い訪ねる。するとそこに、かつてハワイで一緒に遊び廻った知人がいた。偶然の出会いを喜ぶと共に彼に一切を打ち明ける。彼は「帰りは三等で結構だから往きだけは二等にしなさい、でないと、大体米国の官憲が人間扱ひしないぞ、理屈もへちまもない、一二等は紳士で、三等は米国の大嫌いな労働する動物と見做してゐるのだからね」と忠告する。進登は、彼の忠告に従わず、三等でいくが、上陸にあたっての検査が、彼の忠告通りであったことがわかる。

次は、検査を前にした主人公進登の胸をよぎった思いが綴られている箇所である。

　やがて彼は、それを、日本に対する米国からの侮辱として感じた。すると、その侮辱の原因を思ふのであつた。それは、我等日本同胞が、自由に移住していい筈のわれ等東亜民族の土地、即ち、マレイ、スマトラ、ボルネオ、ジャバ、豪州などへ、イギリスやオランダが、しめ出しを喰はせて、自然、アメリカに移民しなければならなかつた。そして米国は、不毛の地を、血と汗で美田にしてやつた我々の同胞を人種的差別で虐待するのである。──祖国の力が身内に湧いた、何時かはこのハワイが、移民官がなくて来られるやうな想ひになり、そして豪州を始め南太平洋の島々が日本と同じ一色に塗られた地図を頭に描くのであつた。

「三等渡布記」は、そのように日本人の三等船客を人間扱いしない「米国の役人達」の態度に憤慨し、「豪州を始め南太平洋の島々」とともに、ハワイが、日本の領土になる日の来ることを考えるところで終わっていた。そのことは、他でもなく、日米戦の勃発が実感される状況にあったことを語っているが、それは乗り合わせた「夫人」たちとの船中での会話にも現れている。

2世たちが日本の「軍歌や唱歌」ばかりを歌っているという一「夫人」の話から、「人種の差別」に話が移り、その後に次のような会話が続いていく。

　『へえ？、そんなに酷い差別をするのですか。ぢや万一日米戦争があると、親子がほんとに敵味方になりますな』
　『いや。二世は、アメリカの国民だからアメリカの軍隊になつて戦ふが、然し**鉄砲は後へ向ける**と云ひますわ』[25] 二世の谷口夫人が答へた。
　『戦争になると日本ははあ、それや強いですけん、アメリカは飛行機を威張つてゐるが、はあ、日本の飛行機もなかなかやるさうだ、わしは今度聞いてきたが…』

「2世」たちは、アメリカの敵日本にではなく、味方のアメリカに銃をむけるそうだ、

といった話や日本の飛行機もアメリカの飛行機に劣らず優秀だそうだ、といった話がまことしやかに語られる様子が写しとられている。日米戦が、現実味を帯びつつあったことをよく語っている場面である。

「ホノルル移民局」は、「三等渡布記」の続きで、検疫検査の後、下船し移民局の抑留所で過さざるを得なかった日々の出来事を書いていた。

三等船客は「米国領土、即ちハワイ、カリフオールニアへ移住した日本人と、その子弟の母国訪問の帰途が大部分」を占めていて、彼らは「ひたすら無事の上陸を念じ、アメリカ官憲の心証をよくしようがため、怯々として、長い航海中に人格を太平洋の海底深く投げ捨て、来たもの」のように見える。そして「猿紅色の顔したアメリカ人」の「屈辱に唯々諾々と甘んじ」「アメリカの独善国法に考察を廻す不逞の者」などいない。一時入国者である主人公の進登にしても「三等客であるからには三等的卑屈、屈辱に甘んじる美徳に醇化し、無事に上陸を願う心に変りはない」が、彼は上陸を許されず、移民局に送られる。

宮城は、抑留所の建物を、まさしく作家の目でもって、克明に描いていく。そして抑留された者たち——古参の「白地浴衣を着流した若者」「胴抜きのアンダーシャツにスポーツ猿股の若者」「中華民国人」「比島人」「痩せた老人」を含め新参者の進登たちとともに監視人や移民官、書記、通訳官などの動きも同様に細かく観察している。

宮城は、移民局の抑留所に閉じ込められた者たちの喜怒哀楽を描いていく中で「七重八重に堅めて東洋人を囚めるアメリカ移民局に、再び夜が来た」[26)]と進登の抑留がまだ続いていることを示し、作品を次のように閉じていた。

> 何時しか進登はアメリカの移民局を考へてみた。平素は温和な彼だが、むらむらとアメリカの独善政治、東洋人への人種的偏見に憤りを持ち出してゐた。
> ——移民局のないハワイ！ ダイヤモンドヘッドに砲台がなくなるハワイ！——。そして日本を想ひ、果てはまたハワイが蘭印や豪州と共に日本と同じ色に塗られた地図なども思ひ浮べるのであつた。

ハワイが、日本領になることを願う主人公の姿がここにも見られる。「三等渡布記」「ホノルル移民局」はともに、同じ事を「思ひ浮べる」主人公を描いて終わっている。

「アメリカの移民局」の三等船客に対する対応のひどさに発した憤りが、ハワイの占領を「思ひ浮べ」させるというのは突飛すぎるが、そのような飛躍を可能にする状況というのは確かにあった。それは、「蘭印や豪州」の占領に沸き立っていたというだけではない。渡布する日本人の多さと、ハワイに住む日系人たちの祖国日本への熱誠にひたすらなものがあったことによる。

連作作品最後の「ホノルル」は、進登が以前来た時に知り合った人たちが、移民局の抑留所から出てきた進登を迎えて、新聞社や領事館を案内したり歓迎会を開いたり、夜の街を探訪したりしたあと「寝静つて暗いカラハアヴエヌーを驀進してゐる」ところで終わるが、その終わりを「七人の日本人を乗せた車は、ギリシヤ神話のサンダルとなつ

て西の空を天翔り、彼等の魂を乗せて、愛する祖国日本へ突進してゐるのであつた」と閉じていた[27]。

　それは、ハワイで生活していても、その魂は日本人であることをことさらに強調しようとしたものであったといっていいだろう。「ホノルル」が、「三等渡布記」「ホノルル移民局」の後を受けて書かれた作品でありながら、進登を主人公にしてないことにもそれは現われている。

　作品の眼目は、進登が先にホノルルを訪ねた時「まだハイスクール在学中だった」上田が、日本映画「上海陸戦隊」を見たり、ラジオで「日本海々戦のあつた海軍記念日の日日比谷公会堂」で行われた講演の録音に耳を傾けたり、ラジオドラマ「海行かば」を聞いたり、「練習艦隊乗組みの従兄」を桟橋まで送っていったりするなかで、日米の比較をしながら、母国日本の「生死無我忠君殉国の精神」や「非常時国民の意気」や「日本の軍規の厳粛さ」に思い至るというもので、練習艦隊浅間、八雲をホノルルに迎えて沸き立つ日本人社会を背景にしていた。

　1935年（昭和10）6月15日付き『日布時事』は「帝国練習艦隊来る　海の宮様方三方の御機嫌いと麗はし　けふぞ迎ふる我等が海の勇士！　旭日旗を仰ぐ同胞の感激」の見出し[28]を掲げた特別号を出し、19日には「練習艦隊けさ抜錨　奉・歓迎の同胞一万　埠頭に描く感激の渦巻　畏し三宮殿下にはレイを懸けさせられホノルルに御名残りを惜ませ給ふ　万歳声裡に一路ヤルートへ」といった見出し[29]で15日から19日にかけて、あと1つの邦字新聞『布哇報知』とともに連日大々的に歓迎、送別の記事を出しその熱狂振りを伝えている。宮城は、その興奮を作品の背景にしていた。

　宮城は、ホノルルの日本人社会を熱狂させた練習艦隊来航を描く一方で、ホノルル中を震撼させた事件も取扱っていた。「アラモアナ事件」がそれである。

　1931年（昭和6）9月14日付き『布哇報知』が「非倫極道の不良団　白婦人を輪姦？　暴力沙汰で婦人を誘拐　アラモアナの藪中で　嫌疑者七名昨夜より厳重取調中」の見出しで報じた事件[30]を、その発端から犯人と思われるものたちの検挙、裁判の開始、公判での原告・被告両側証言、犯行現場検証、巡査証言、両方代言人による弁論を経て12月6日「ジューリーの意見不一致でミスツラル（未結審）になった」[31]こと、5人の被告は、ポンドを提供し自由になったが、原告は再審の準備に着手したこと、その後被告の1人の日系人が、水兵に拉致されリンチを受け気絶したが蘇生したこと、同じく被告の「ハワイ土人」1人が斬殺されたこと、犯行に及んだ中尉以下4人が拘留されたが1時間ほどで釈放されたといったことを新聞報道を参照しながら書いている。

　宮城は同事件を追っていく中で「主として白人は官憲とマッシー夫人の同情に傾き、有色人種は被告の無罪を信じた」と記し、事件をめぐって「白人」と「有色人種」が真っ二つに割れたとしている。

　宮城が「アラモアナ事件」を書いた意図は明確である。それは「実話」を締めくくるにあたって「アメリカの政治がアングロサクソン以外は人間でないと考える好見本であつた」と強調しているからである。

4. 故郷の懐かしさ——ハワイ紀行と随筆

　『ハワイ』に納められた「創作」及び「実話」は、アメリカ批判に主眼があったといっていい。それは「紀行」の中にも「アメリカ人は、最初のハワイ発見者はキヤプテンクックと云つてゐる。がこれは神を畏れぬ不遜の心の現れである。白人を誇り、有色人種と蔑げすみ、そして有色人種を獣類と同じく見下した傲れる心の現れである」[32)]といった箇所や「谷の景色に加ふるに川口の景色があり海浜もあり、市の眺めあり弦月湾の大展望がある。そして吾等の立つた背後の住宅の庭々の美しさもなか〳〵いゝ、しかし白人の特種部落で人種的の障壁を設けてあるといふのはやはり、アメリカ独善を感じさせた」[33)]といった箇所が見られないわけではないが、「紀行」は、必ずしもアメリカを批判するために書かれていたわけではない。

　「紀行」には日付がついている。「オアフ島紀行」が、七月三日から十八日、飛んで八月六日から九月七日までになっているのは、その間にハワイ島[34)]、マウイ島[35)]へ出かけていたことによる。「紀行」には、それぞれの島の素晴しさとともにそこに住む人々の人情の厚さを取り上げていた。

　宮城がハワイに引き付けられた由縁であるが、後1つ、そこには宮城を捕えて離さないのがあった。

　　夏になると、自分にはハワイや故郷の懐かしさが強く湧き出す。南の海、南の空の色が堪らなく偲ばれる。自分がハワイへ行つたのは、二度共初夏の日だつたが、横浜を出た船が、明日はホノルルに着くといふ日あたりからは、海の色を見て、はッと故郷へ来た感じに打たれた。
　　亜熱帯色の鮮かな群青に変つてゐるのである。変つてゐるのは海ばかりではない、空も深く透き徹つて鮮かである。
　　ホノルル郊外のワイキキビーチに坐つてゐると、涙が自然に湧き出た。

　「随筆」の部に収録された1編「夏日南を懐ふ」に見られるものである。そこにはまたコナの海について「銀白色の海は波がなく凝然と平かなので、成る程と思はれたが、沖縄の夏の夕暮れ時の凪ぎと全く同じ海だつた」と書いているように、ハワイは故郷沖縄を遥かに偲ばせるものがあった。

　宮城のアメリカへの違和も反感も、時代がしからしめたものであったが、それは、ハワイに寄せる思いが強かったからにほかならない。ハワイが「故郷へ来た感じ」を与えるものであったことによって、ハワイに寄せる思いはいよいよ強くなっていったのである。

おわりに

　宮城は「紀行」の中で「私の為めにホノルル同胞有志の一般歓迎会といふのを催して貰つた。それには、二つの大新聞の学術担当のMさんやFさんなども見え、ホノルルの潮音詩社同人の歌人や、文学愛好家も大勢見え、若い女の人なども四五人交り、先輩、同郷人、旧知、未知、随分賑かで、すつかり恐縮させられた」[36]といったことや、「夜になると、Mダクター夫妻は、私の歓迎の宴を開いて下さつた。新聞社やヒロ俳句会、銀雨社等の人々に私を紹介しようとの心遣ひに依つたもので、夫人は、朝の中からコックのXさんを始め家人を指揮され準備したらしいのである。夕方からは二階の床の間の大座敷でヒロの文学に縁故のある多くの知識人が集つた」[37]といったことを書いていた。

　宮城の2度目の渡布が、創作の素材を求めての旅であったことから、文学に関心のあるものたちとの交流が行われたのは自然だが、それ以上に、宮城が「新進作家」の1人として注目されるようになっていたことが、会を盛り上げる一助になったに違いない。

　ハワイの文学界は、新進作家の宮城を迎え、心からの応対をしたことがわかる。そして宮城は、そのことへの感謝を含めて、ハワイの文学状況を報告した「憶ひ出のハワイ歌壇」[38]、に続く「ハワイ短歌壇」[39]、「ハワイの日本文学」[40] 等の文章を発表していたが、『ハワイ』には、それらの文章を収録していない。

　戦勝に沸くなかで、ハワイの短歌会や俳句会に関する文章など見向きもされなかったであろうが、宮城の報告は、英語圏のなかでの日本語の表現活動を伝えるものとして価値があった。さらに付け加えておけば、沖縄系移民の表現活動に関心のあるものにとっても大切なものであった。比嘉静観、嘉数南星といった名前が見られるからである。

　しかし、宮城には、沖縄系移民たちが、ハワイでどのような表現活動をしていたかについて、特別関心があったように思われない。もし彼が、その点に関してもう少し眼が向いておれば、同じ作家として、ハワイで精力的に小説作品を発表していた外間勝美[41]について、何らかの形で触れたはずであるが、彼についての言及はない。それは『ハワイ』に収録した作品が、沖縄系移民を描こうとしたのではないことを端的に示すものでもあった[42]。

注

1) 「文学と私　連載14」(『新沖縄文学』第22、1972年6月1日)で、宮城は横浜を5月3日にたち、「十一日目」にホノルルについたと回想しているが、記憶違いかと思われる。宮城が、ホノルルについたのは、6月4日であることが、1927年6月4日付き『布哇報知』(「黒人野球団を乗せ　サイベリア丸入港　当地上陸客は二百二名である」乗船名簿)に見えているからである。

2) 「文学と私　連載14」『新沖縄文学』第22、1972年6月1日。

3) 1927年6月4日付き『布哇報知』は、「サイベリア丸　帰布者氏名　全部八十二名」の小見出しで「今朝入港のサイベリア丸の当地上り船客は一等七名、二等一名、三等七十四名、合計

八十二名にて県別氏名左の如し」として乗客名簿を出していて、「一等船客」の中に宮城久輝の名が見えている。船中で知り合った「山城ホテルの若旦那」とは、やはり一等船客の中に「山城松一」とある、その人であろう。ちなみに山城松一は「公人私人」の欄に「太平洋漁業会社の同氏単独にて同上帰布」とあるが「山城ホテル」の件は記されていない。

4) 注2と同。
5) 「文学と私　連載十八回」（『新沖縄文学』第26、1974年10月）に「足かけ十年間勤めたこの雑誌「改造」に一行でも自分の書いたものが採用される日があるだろうか、と、思い通して来た。折口信夫さんに、故郷の沖縄で、小説を書くために東京へ出て行きますといったが、余りに狭い門である作家の道をはっきり知った時、そう思った。しかしどうしてもやるのだという心はわたくしの体にしみ込んでいて、いわゆる夢寝の間も忘れてはいなかった」と書いていて、沖縄にいるときから、作家になることを夢見ていたことがわかるが、その思いを決定的なものにしたのがハワイであったといえよう。「琉球で知つた折口信夫」（『短歌研究』1935年1月1日）の中にも「ゆく／＼は作家として立つ積りだと答へた」といったのが見える。
6) 宮城は「一九二七年、三六年の再度のわたくしの渡布旅行が、偶然だが五月であった。三六年の時も、ホノルルの街は、九年前と変ってはいなかった」と「文学と私　連載15回――ハワイの思い出――」に書いているが、2度目の渡布は36年ではなく、35年である。
7) 注2と同。
8) 注5と同。
9) 『生活の誕生』（文生社　1946年10月25日）「あとがき」で宮城は「「生活の誕生」は師、里見弴の叱正数回の書き直しを経て1934年3月号『三田文学』に掲載された。それより少し前に、やはり里見弴の推薦で、東京日日新聞、大阪毎日新聞の夕刊に「故郷は地球」の題で、連載創作を発表したが、自分の処女作は、「生活の誕生」である」と書いている。
10) 注5と同。
11) 注5と同。
12) 宮城は「一九三五年の三月には東京日日（現在の毎日）と大阪毎日新聞の夕刊純文学作品の連載」（「文学と私　連載14回」）と書いているが、作品が連載されたのは1935年ではなく1934年である。
13) 岡本恵徳「脱出と回帰――沖縄の昭和初期文学の一側面」及び「沖縄の昭和期の文学の一側面――「生活の誕生」を中心に――」（『沖縄文学の情景　現代作家・作品を読む』2000年2月ニライ社）を参照。
14) 仲程昌徳「位牌と遺骨――二つの出郷作品をめぐって」（『日本東洋文化論集』第11号、2005年3月）。
15) 宮城は「週刊朝日」に発表したと回想しているが、『新青年』（1930年11月号、赤藤了勇氏のご教示による）の間違い。ハワイに取材した作品としても宮城の創作としても殆ど始めのころのものである。暴行を受けた白人女性が、犯行を黙認したにも関らず、あえて自首した現地人の行為を書いたもので、際物的で、習作の域を出るものではない。取上げるまでもないが、ハワイに取材した作品、とりわけ「アラモアナ事件」との繋がりなど、後の作品に見られる白人対ハワイ人の確執が描かれているという点で見落とせない作品だといえないわけではない。
16) 注5と同。
17) 注5と同。
18) 注2と同。
19) 注2と同。
20) 「生活困難なるが為に家庭の和楽も破れ行く子供達を連れて帰国す――父母に別れる子供の不幸さ」の見出しがある。
21) 「本婦人非常に多くなったぞ　亭主を嫌つて家出した女房住ふに家なく再び舞戻る昔の布哇であつたら独身者の横奪競争が始まるのだ　婦人の増加はすべて子供の増加なり」の見出しがある。

22）「姦夫姦婦処刑　沖縄県人の駆落騒ぎ」の見出しがある。
23）「ラナイ島」が「ニイハウ」へ、「新田」が「藤田」へといった地名、人名の変更、「注発音をハワイ地方に取る。例へば twenty third fivety seven をトワンテー、タード、ファイテー、セブンと云ふ、by and by をバンバイ、anather man をナダーマン、water をワダと云ふ如し、又、ワヒネ（妻）ヒラヒラ（恥じる）カウカウ（食事）などのカナカ語、併せてバケー（支那人）などの訛言などもそのまま使用する」といった注の削除、その他文章の増減など数多く見られる。
24）本稿では、『ハワイ』に収録された作品をテキストとして使用した。
25）『創作　ホノルル』（東京図書株式会社、1936年7月1日）所収「三等渡布記」では、ゴチック体の部分は伏字（「××××××××」）になっている。
26）「七重八重に堅めて東洋人を囚めるアメリカ移民局に、再び夜が来た」の箇所、そして以下引用した箇所等『ハワイ』に収録された際書き加えられたもので、初出の『三田文学』（1937年1月1日）には見られない。
27）本稿で引用した「三等渡布記」「ホノルル移民局」「ホノルル」の結末の文章は、『創作ホノルル』に収録されている作品には見られない。『ハワイ』に収録する際、書き加えられた箇所である。宮城のハワイ関連作品に関しては、真珠湾以前と以後という観点から、論じられる必要があるが、それは別稿にゆずりたい。
28）同日の『布哇報知』は「宮殿下御三方お乗組みの帝国練習艦隊来る　けさ八時四十五分「浅間」「八雲」の両艦堂々と第七号桟橋に入繋　海に陸に歓迎の大絵巻」の見出しになっている。
29）『布哇報知』は「万々歳轟く裡に練習艦隊けさ出港　皇国の将士に別れを　惜しむ同胞無慮一万　一路南洋統治領へ」の見出しになっている。
30）同日の『日布時事』は「痴漢横行時代　七人組不良の□め　白婦人凌辱さる　土曜日深夜アラモアナで　被害者は地位あり教養ある婦人　日曜夜にも一婦人襲はる」の見出しで報じている。
31）1931年12月7日付け『日布時事』は「アラモアナ強姦事件　九十四時間に亘り審議せるも陪審員の意見不一致　裁判は遂にミスツライアルに入る　昨夜十時五分ステッドマン判事はジュリーの解散を命じ原告側は再審の要求を発表す」の見出しで報じた。
32）「裏オアフの記」。
33）「ヒロ滞在記二」。
34）「ハワイ島紀行」7月10日〜24日。
35）「馬哇紀行」7月26日〜29日。
36）「ホノルル」。
37）「ヒロ行」。
38）『短歌研究』1935年7月1日。
39）『短歌研究』1936年1月1日。
40）『制作』1935年12月。
41）外間は、『実業之布哇』に1933年「さようなら」、34年「布哇狂想曲」、35年「春の序曲」「愛情に涙する者」、宮城が渡布した三六年には一月号から「移民地哀話」を連載中であった。ハワイの沖縄出身作家として数多くの作品を発表。外間加津美、絵島洋太郎のペンネームがある。
42）「ホノルル移民局」の中で、宮城は、主人公進登が「おやッ！」と思った出来事として「日本人側の隅のベッドから、異様なメロデーの俚謡が流れて来た。ベッドに横坐りで足を垂げてゐた進登は、おやッ！　と思ふとすぐに立ち上つてゐた。それは20年近く忘れてゐた一種独特のメロデーで、彼の故郷の民謡だつたからである。進登はその唄で故郷を共にする青年だと知ると、意外を感じながらそのベッドの前に行き、いきなり郡や村を尋ねた。すると安田兄弟もやつて来て、方言丸出しにベッドの青年に話しかけた。進登は安田達が兄弟であり、そして自分と同郷なのも初めて分り、これまた意外であつた。」といった箇所が見られるが、とりわけ「沖縄系移民」に関心があったというほどではない。

参考文献

岡本恵徳責任編集（1994）『ふるさと文学館　第54巻　沖縄』ぎょうせい、東京。
岡本恵徳（2000）『沖縄文学の情景　現代作家・作品をよむ』ニライ社、沖縄。
比嘉武信編著（1990）『新聞にみるハワイの沖縄人90年戦前編』若夏社、沖縄。
比嘉武信編著（1994）『新聞にみるハワイの沖縄人90年戦後編』文進印刷株式会社、沖縄。
神谷忠孝・木村一信編（2007）『〈外地〉日本語文学論』世界思想社、京都。
崎原貢（1980）『がじまるのつどい　沖縄系ハワイ移民達の話集』ハワイ報知社、ハワイ。
神村朝堅編（1951）『おきなわ　ハワイ特集』第3巻第10号、おきなわ社、東京。

"Unaiism" を拓く組踊『執心鐘入』の大団円
―― フェミニスト・エスノグラフィーの可能性 ――

勝方＝稲福　恵子*

"Unaiism" Manifested in the Denouement of *Syushin-Kaneiri*: Feminist Ethnography in Okinawa

KATSUKATA = INAFUKU Keiko

For the 25th anniversary of the Okinawan women's Unai-Festival, *Syushin-Kaneiri* (1719) was put on stage with a new dramatic interpretation. Since "Unai' means the Sister-Goddess, who protects her brothers in the Ryukyuan-Okinawan folk religion where women are regarded as living goddesses themselves, the "Unai" discourse has been used for the empowerment of women in their various activities.

The new interpretation of the denouement of this classic drama under female direction is that the metamorphosed woman-devil is given emphasis as a protagonist of the drama, and she leaves the stage not by expulsion but by her own independent will.

There are two grounds for this interpretation: one is the historical background of the drama (the religious reformation by the Regent Shou Jou-ken), which was caused by a feud between the side of Kikoe-Ohkimi and that of the King, and which is metaphorically expressed in the story of *Syushin-Kaneiri* where Wakamatsu is the embodiment of Confucianism and the Woman represents the native religion).

The other ground is the trinary system of the story—the Woman, Wakamatsu, and the Priest—which brings forth the tertiary to break through a dichotomy, and which presents "Unaiism" as a performative discourse on Okinawan women's activities.

はじめに

　もはやフェミニズム（feminism）は単数形ではなくなった。白人中産階級フェミニズムに代表されていた女性解放の運動が、1980年代も後半になると、黒人フェミニズムの台頭によって、相対化されたからである［勝方 2006: pp. 33-4］。つまり人種や民族、階級な

---

* 早稲田大学教授、琉球・沖縄研究所所長　Professor, Waseda University; Director, Ryukyu Okinawan Studies

どによって抑圧関係もさまざまに異なる女性の経験は、単一のイメージで括れるものではない、と言うわけで、フェミニズムは複数形（feminisms）が多用されるようになり、フェミニスト・エスノグラフィー［川橋・黒木2004: p. 39］が時代の趨勢となった。もちろん相対化によってもたらされた女性の多様性によって、女性運動が相対主義に陥ることがあってはならないし、エスニックな運動のゲットー化に組してもならない。もちろん、分派主義に拘泥するべきでもない。

しかし沖縄女性を論じるには、日本女性というカテゴリーでは一括りできない剰余が生じるので、どうしてもエスニシティの関数を起動させる必要がある。時代の趨勢となったフェミニスト・エスノグラフィーの水脈につながるためにも、ジェンダーとエスニシティの複眼的視点を持った女性運動には注目する必要がある。

とりわけ1985年のナイロビ女性会議以降、沖縄の先進的な女性運動の中で、伝統的な民俗信仰（うない信仰）がよみがえった例は看過できない。近代フェミニズムの観点からすると女性差別以外の何物でもない民俗宗教の根本疑念である「うない」を採用することに激しい反対意見があった中で、第一回の女性の祭典は、「うない」フェスティバルと命名された。ちなみに「うない」とは、姉妹を指す琉球語で、姉妹は兄弟の守護神であるとされる。

しかも、うないフェスティバルは2009年に25周年を迎え、プレうない「うないがひらく伝統の未来」と銘打って、国指定の重要無形文化財である組踊『執心鐘入』を、女性舞踊家・演出家の手で舞台に乗せるという画期的な所業を成し遂げたのである。

概して、民俗・芸能の世界では、男女が明確に区分されて、それぞれに固定的役割が付与されている。たとえば、村落共同体の根神（女性）と根人（男性）のように、あるいは綱引きにおける雄綱と雌綱のように、ジェンダーの二項対立は象徴的な域まで徹底している。しかも、女人禁制のような女性を排除した聖域空間が厳然と存在して、女性抑圧の温床のように考えられている。

しかし、沖縄では逆に、男子禁制の御嶽は存在しても、女人禁制は聞かない。世界史的に見ても、女性祭祀権が制度的に残っている珍しい地域とされる沖縄には、ジェンダーの区別が、女性排除や女性抑圧に直結するのではないような、めずらしい女性優位のシステムが機能しているとされる。そのシステムこそが「うない（信仰）」として呼び慣らされているものなのであろう。したがって「うない」の言説を纏うことは、女性抑圧のもう一つの極である近代合理主義に対する自己防衛のために、文化・伝統の本質に戦略的にこだわっていく、一種の民族運動であると考えることもできるだろう。

近代化による合理化・均質化の波をかぶると、「それはいやだ」とばかりに逆行現象が生じ、ことさら伝統的な民俗儀礼を纏って、対抗的客体化が起こることがある。西欧的近代化という啓蒙的な流れに掉さすしかないことを知りながら、それでもこの前近代的な民俗信仰を新しい文脈に置き換えて対抗的なアイデンティティを醸成し、当座のしのぎとする。たしかにこれは一種の物象化（objectification 客体化）を伴うものではあるが、「そのままでいいんだよ」とされる言説空間を構築することで、もう一つの自己認識・自

己肯定を許容することにもなる。

　「うない（姉妹）」という民俗信仰の概念を復活させた1985年以降の沖縄における女性運動、とりわけ「2009年うないフェスティバル」における組踊『執心鐘入』の新しい演出を考察することによって、「古琉球を取り戻すこと」と女性解放思想との親和性を考えたい。

1. うないフェスティバル（2009年）と佐藤太圭子演出の組踊『執心鐘入』

　1985年に第一回目が開催された「うないフェスティバル」は、2009年12月に25周年を迎えた。「うない」は、沖縄の民間信仰における「女神」のようなもので、霊力高い女性たちはそれぞれ兄弟の姉妹神（守護神）として位置づけられている。それは、沖縄女性の霊的優位性が顕著に現れている言葉であり、女性たちは、家においても、村落共同体においても、さらには門中行事においても、神女・神官として祭祀行事を執り行っている[1]。

　この「うない」という表現が、女性を鼓舞して主体性を取り戻させる言説として利用されたのは1985年。「国連婦人の10年」最終年で、第三回世界女性会議ナイロビ大会に参加した女性たちの帰国報告会「女から女たちへ」が開かれた年である。報告会を取材したラジオ沖縄の源啓美は、懸案だったラジオ沖縄開局25周年記念事業の一環として、女たちの祭典を提案した。第二波のフェミニズム運動が世界的に展開する契機となった「ナイロビの風」を受けて、「うないフェスティバル」は発案されたわけである。

　フェスティバルの名前をどうしようかと議論する段で、実行委員の一人だった源啓美は幼いころ祖母がよく口にしていた言葉を思い出した。幼い啓美をからかい半分にいたぶる兄たちを傍らで諌める時も、祖母は「あたら、うない！」と言っていた。「大切な守護神を粗末に扱って！」というような意味である。兄弟の守護女神としての姉妹の価値を、祖母は日常的に諭していたのである。その思い出がよみがえり、女たちの祭典に「うない」の名称を提案した。当初は、封建時代の遺物を感じさせるからと強く反発する参加者もいたが議論の末に決定した。古い言葉ではあるが、新しい意味を付与しようという意気込みで、女性史研究家の宮城晴美は、報告書「第1回うないフェスティバル'85」の冒頭の「うないフェスティバル実行委員会」宣言に、次のように記している。

　　　女たちが、胎動を始めました。「国連婦人の10年」最終年の今年、ウチナーでいま、女のパワーが爆発しようとしています。名づけてうないフェスティバル'85／古代「うない」は女きょうだいを意味し、家庭にあってうない神、共同体においては神女となって沖縄社会を司ってきたと言われます。いま、私達は「うない」の思いを受けつぎつつ、21世紀に向けて「うない」に新しい意味を見出そうとしています
　　　（略）

以来「うない」は、行為遂行的な言霊として、女性たちの主体化を支えてきたのである。沖縄の女性運動には、ナイロビで覚醒したフェミニズムの理論と、土着の「うない信仰」との絶妙な出会いが見られることが、大きな特徴と言えよう。

その具体例として、2009年開催の「うないフェスティバル」25周年を祝う舞台に、佐藤太圭子演出の組踊『執心鐘入』が選ばれたことを挙げたい。じつはこの作品には国指定の無形文化財として遵守されてきた伝統的演出があり、鬼女は座主の唱える真言（陀羅尼）の法力と熾烈な争いを展開しながらも、勧善懲悪の結末らしく奈落へ堕ちていく。ところが佐藤演出では、大団円が斬新に解釈しなおされ、組踊保存会とは別様の演出——鬼女は自らの意思で入端に向き直り静かに退場する——となる。しかも、比嘉いずみが「宿の女」を演じたほか、若松に皆川律子、座主に比嘉一惠をあてて全ての配役を女性舞踊家で演じたことも、御冠船踊の伝統に反するものだった。はからずも保存会とは異なる解釈に至ったことを、佐藤太圭子は、公演で配布された「演出ノート」に、次のように記している。

　　劇性を高めるために、座主と鬼女が丁々発止の争いを展開する場面も見受けますが、座主と小僧は、真言宗の宗旨に則り、手に印を結び悠揚迫らぬ態度で真言を唱えて鬼女に対峙すればいいと思われます。そうすることで真言のコトダマにより、次第に女の魔性は取り除かれ、本然の姿を取り戻して女の性に目覚めます。それが高位の僧格をもつ座主の姿と思います。［佐藤 2009: p.5］

これは、従来の勧善懲悪的な演出に対して、控えめではあるが、満を持しての言揚げであるように思われる。国の重要無形文化財に認定された組踊では、伝統芸能の仕組みに則って、女性が舞台で演じることは許されていない。いわんや「演出」においてをや、である。しかし敗戦後の荒廃した地において、琉球舞踊の伝統は男性芸能者から女性へと受け継がれてきたことで命脈を保ってきたという事実、つまり「戦前の男性舞踊家の芸を女の身体に写し取って」[2] 伝統を今に繋いできたという事実は否めない。しかし伝統芸能における女性排除のシステムは、この事実をすっかり覆い隠してしまうほどに徹底しているようだ。

佐藤太圭子は眞境名由康や島袋光裕から「組踊について厳しい薫陶を受け」[3] ており、他方、児玉清子は「（渡嘉敷）守良の手の継承」を託された唯一の直弟子である［波照間 2007: p.75］。しかし、自他ともに認める「継承者」であるにもかかわらず、組踊の保持者に認定されることはない。琉球舞踊においては、佐藤自身も国指定重要無形文化財保持者に総合認定され、伝統の型にこだわり続けているだけに、伝統からの逸脱と評されることへは葛藤も大きい。「国の『重要文化財』に認定された組踊りに演出が許されるのか？　しかも、女性のみの演じ手で。大きな自問です」［佐藤 2009: p.6］

しかし、島袋光裕を踏襲した「自問」を抱えながらのこの演出は、決して「逸脱」で片づけるべきではなく、むしろ玉城朝薫の時代状況を深く反映させたものであることを、

本論では歴史的に辿ってみたい。

2. 王府の宗教改革によって弱体化する女性祭祀組織

『執心鐘入』の大団円を解釈するには、作者・玉城朝薫が踊奉行に任ぜられた当時の時代状況を考慮することも必要であろう。折しも「聞得大君」の霊的権威を失墜させるような事件が次々と起こっていたからである。

佐喜真興英［佐喜真1969: p. 51］は、大正末に出版した著書『女人政治考』で、古代琉球における女君政治を進化論的に証明しようとした。たとえば「古琉球の女治」章では、「おもろさうし」に描かれた聞得大君に関する叙述を検討した上で、「女君は日の神の霊をもって古琉球を治めた」という仮説をたて、さらに、尚清王の冊封正使として1534年に来琉した陳侃の『使琉球録』を援用して「これらの材料でみると古琉球に女君が存在し、その霊力で島国を支配しておったことが分る」と確信し、「女君は第一次主権者で国王は第二次主権者」としての男女二重統治であったことを主張している。

佐喜真興英によるこの女性優位体制の主張は、進化論という普遍的なパラダイムから割り出したものであったが、比嘉政夫［比嘉1987: p. 162］は、後年『女人政治考・霊の島々—佐喜真興英全集』を組むにあたって、佐喜真の女君仮説は、伊波普猷の「をなり神」論考が出版される前に出された言葉足らずのものであるが、それでも「女性の呪術・宗教的力による優位と、それによる支配の形を前面に出し」たものと評価し、「沖縄の村落における根人と根神の関係…また、琉球王朝時代の国王と聞得大君の関係」に具体的に当てはめ、「根人や国王は、世俗的・政治的場のリーダーであるが、根神や聞得大君は、宗教・祭祀の場で、根人や国王より上位に立つからである」と解説している。

聞得大君を頂点として琉球処分期まで続いた神女組織は、大和にも類がなく、世界史的にも珍しい。伊波普猷をはじめ真境名安興や佐喜真興英など、沖縄女性論の古典をひも解くと、祭祀権をめぐる女性の地位は、按司・王国時代を通じて高かったことがわかる。これは、宮城栄昌の「沖縄の女性は、すべておなり神である」［宮城1967: p. 2］や「沖縄女性は生得的に二重三重の神であった」［宮城1979: p. 411］で、いっそう明らかにされる。在来宗教の神女／巫女として、祭祀権を掌中におさめていた沖縄女性は、祭政一致の政治体制のなかで強大な発言権を持っていたようである。

村落共同体に培われた根人・根神や尚真王の時代に頂点を極めた聞得大君体制は、このように琉球・沖縄社会における女性優位を説く根拠となっているが、高良倉吉［高良1980: p. 224］によると、公儀ノロへの「辞令書」が王府から発令されていることから、あくまで王府が主たる組織で、聞得大君体制はそれを裏から支える組織にすぎなかったということになる。たしかに聞得大君を頂点とする三十三君が尚真王の手によって制度的に整えられたからには、すでに聞得大君御殿は政治主導型の祭祀組織に堕していたことになる。それでも、うない神信仰に支えられた国王の守護神としての聞得大君の権力が、絶大なものであったことにかわりはない。

しかし、古琉球におけるこのような「祭政一致体制」がさらに崩壊して聞得大君の権威が失墜してしまった要因としては、佐喜真興英も、伊波普猷も、宮城栄昌も、高良倉吉も、おしなべて1609年の「薩摩の琉球侵攻」を挙げている。1611年（慶長16）9月19日に定められた「掟」十五条の中の一条に、「女房衆え知行被遣間敷之事」という経済封鎖を決められたことが最大の原因だった。「当時知行を受ける女房衆といえば、御内原に勤務する禁中女官や、王妃・王夫人・王女に仕えるもののほかは、聞得大君以下中央・地方の神女関係者であった。薩摩は彼女たちの経済的収入を絶つことによってその地位の低下をはかり、固有の宗教のもつ勢力を弱体化させようとしたのである。この経済的圧迫は奄美諸島の神女弾圧策にも執拗に続けられたものであった」［宮城 1979: pp. 147–8］。

　薩摩が琉球王府を傀儡するためには、伝統的な祭祀儀礼を盾にしてことごとく口を出してくる聞得大君御殿の勢力を断ち切る必要があったのであるが、その薩摩の狙いは、図らずも、王府自身の儒教的な教義のもとに因習的な祭祀儀礼を断ち切って自律をはかる合理化の動きと一致した。そもそも「神女組織」は、女の霊力を利用して王権の正統性を護り祭政一致体制を補強するために、尚真時代に確立されたもので、御嶽を護るノロ・ツカサばかりでなく在野のトキ・ユタなども重用され、土着の信仰に支えられたシステムだった。しかし薩摩侵攻いらいの琉球王府は、親島津の政権を擁立することで後ろ盾を得ることになり、もはや意のままにならない神女組織は不要ということで、為政者側の思惑は一致したわけである。女性が公的領域から排除されるシステムが作動しはじめたことになる。

　ことに1666年摂政となった向象賢（羽地朝秀）は、人心を一新し、財政の立て直しを図るために、いわゆる「黄金の箍」をはめる諸改革を実施した。とりわけ強化されたのが、政教分離策である。何よりも、聞得大君御殿の神女勢力の非合理的な浪費と要求を制御する必要を感じ、王妃の下位に聞得大君を置く。そうすることによって、聞得大君を頂点とする祭祀組織にピラミッド型に配置されている三十三君の女神官の勢力を殺ぐ政策がとられていたわけである。「『羽地仕置』政策で最高潮に達する17世紀の王府の宗教改革は、…大君の宗教的な役割を根本的に弱体化させることになる」［伊従 2005: p. 423］。さらに1673年、国王による久高島参詣も廃止された。「この御参詣を廃した時、政治家と宗教家との間に、即ち男子と女子との間に、大衝突が起こった」と伊波は言及している［伊波 1969: p. 196］

　向象賢が摂政を退いて後も、政教分離策は徹底的に継続され、王府と聞得大君御殿はことごとく対立することになる。たとえば、1713年、尚敬（第13代国王、在位：1713–1752年）の王位継承に基づき、1717年には聞得大君御殿から「御新下り」の要請があった。今こそ挙行しないと祟りがあるという主張に対して、三司官側は、二年後に控えた尚敬王冊封に莫大な費用を要するので、これまた御新下りに膨大な費用が嵩んでは財政上困難であることを理由に挙行を退けた。それに対し聞得大君側では、冊封の御願のためにも年内に挙行すべきであると主張した。互いに譲らず、結局は聞得大君御殿の再三の要請を三司官側がはねつけた形になった。これが、「御新下り」延期事件である[4]。

御新下りは、聞得大君の就任戴冠儀礼のことで、新国王に守護神として霊力を授け、王権の根拠を与えるために、聞得大君自身が王国最高聖地の斎場御嶽に赴いて霊力を高めるための儀礼を挙行する。王権授受の儀礼において何よりも先行して行われなければならない手続きである。「御新下り延期」事件は、儒教体制の確立と祭政一致システムの崩壊、そしてそれに伴う神女組織の失墜を象徴的に物語っていると考えることができる。

　しかも、政教分離策は、結局は薩摩の占領政策に棹さすことになり、皮肉なことに、芸能の源泉である民俗文化が枯渇しかねない事態を招いてしまった。というのも、無限抱擁の混沌にただよう女性原理よりも、意思や理性の力で屹立する男性原理を選ぶべき時代、言い換えれば、「色恋」よりも「忠義」を選ぶべき時代に移行することになったからである。恩納なべ（生没年不詳）が「姉べたやよかて　しのぐしち遊で　わすた世になれば　お止めされて」と、奔放なしのぐ遊びが禁止されたことへの恨みを詠い、また「恩納松下に　禁止の牌の立ちゅす　恋忍ぶまでの　禁止やないさめ」と、王府の締めつけによる失われゆくものへの惜別を詠んだのも、ちょうどこの時代である。

　じつは、1719年の冊封の祭典を任されたのが、踊り奉行に任命された玉城朝薫で、首里城内に広がった事件の波紋は、朝薫にも届いたと考えられる。宮仕えの朝薫は、向象賢から蔡温へと連なる政治改革に身を置き、政教分離の動きに連ならざるを得ない立場ながら、創作家としては、その改革を憂える気持ちに引き裂かれていただろう。朝薫は、目の前に繰り広げられている女性宗教家と男性政治家との確執を、すでに伝播していた「道成寺譚」を下敷きにして、独自の組踊に仕上げたと考えられる。

3. 『執心鐘入』における「若松 ⇔ 宿の女 ⇔ 座主」の三極構造

　日本各地の諸芸能に残る「道成寺譚」は、女人禁制の由来を説く物語ともいわれている。その背景には、女人の執心によって、煩悩を絶つはずの梵鐘の音色がピタリと止んでしまった説話［徳江 1982: pp.24］などがあり、女人の罪障の深さが恐れられて聖域から排除されていった歴史的プロセスがそこに見て取れるからである。また、宗教・政治の表舞台から女性の生命エネルギーが排除されることによって造形・形成される異端の鬼＝般若は、西洋中世の魔女像の形成とも重なるものがある。この点で、「道成寺」譚は、魔女物語と通底し、日本における女性排除の由来物語の一つとなっている。

　清姫の誘惑から逃れて道成寺の大鐘の中に身を隠す修行僧・安珍は、愛欲・怨恨・情念の蛇と化した清姫の吐く火炎によって焼き殺されるが、住職の唱える『法華経』の功徳によって、清姫と共に成仏する。この物語は沖縄にも、熊野修験僧らによって古くから伝播していたらしい。『執心鐘入』も、伊波普猷いらいの研究蓄積によって、大和芸能に伝承されている道成寺譚と出自を同じくするものと評価され、晴れて「道成寺もの」の一翼を担うようになった。したがって、その「道成寺」譚を下敷きにしたとされる『執心鐘入』もまた、女人禁制を説く物語にされている。

　従来の「執心鐘入」研究の目指すところは、琉球古典芸能の組踊も、歌舞伎や能のよ

うな大和芸能と肩を並べる作品だということを実証し確認することだった。いわば、大和芸能との同質論に立ち、大和の土俵にのせた上での比較検討だった。

したがって、「宿の女」が「中城若松」を焼き殺さずに「退場」した『執心鐘入』の結末が、「道成寺譚」の結末とはまったく異なっていることから展開する異質論、しかもその「異なり」が作品の価値であり独自性であるという異質論は、残念ながらまだ出てこなかった。

にもかかわらず、沖縄での文化講演に招かれた啓蒙思想家たちは、暁烏敏も茅原崋山も、人気のあるこの組踊を引き合いに出しては、「男を焼き殺さずに敗退した女の意気地なさ」として解釈してみせ、果ては「そういう弱い心では、目的を達することは出来ない」と聴衆に喝を入れる始末 [勝方 2006：p. 81]。これでは、啓蒙主義者の自文化中心主義である。「男を焼き殺すことが女の強さである」と短絡的なもの言いをする講演者の理屈に囲い込まれているかぎり、反論の糸口は見いだせない。

啓蒙思想家たちの素朴同質論には、重要な視点が欠落している。第一の欠落は、前節の「御新下り延期事件」で述べた歴史的視点。つまりこれは、当時あらわになってきた「王府と神女組織」との確執であり、さらには、王府を取り込んだ外来の儒教・仏教と土着の民族宗教との確執として敷衍することができる。

もう一つの欠落は、物語構造への視角である。「王府と神女組織」の確執を間近に見ていた躍奉行・玉城朝薫は、大和伝来の仏教を象徴する「座主」を軸に、一方の極には王府（向象賢・蔡温の日琉同祖論と儒教に基づく政治改革イデオロギー）を体現する「若松」と、他方の極には琉球固有の民族宗教を体現する「宿の女」を左右に拮抗させる三極構造の物語を展開したと考えられる。政治的に絶妙な均衡をとったのだ。

座主の役割は、矢野輝雄 [矢野 2001：p. 187] が戌の冠船の資料から読み取ったように、三極構造の一極を占めるものとしてもちろん重要である。「色恋」と「忠義」の葛藤を描き、女の情念を鬼の形に昇華させ、変身させ、仏教の法力で退場させる筋書きは、神女組織にくずぶる不満をねじ伏せようとする王府の意を汲んでいる。しかしそれでも「道成寺」譚の結末のように、《男が鬼女に焼き殺された後で、二者ともに法力で成仏する》ような、仏教の一方的な勝利に持っていくわけにはいかない。冊封饗応の御冠船踊りの場であるからこそ、結末は《若松は座主に助けられて王府へ向かう》ことにしなければならなかった。若松を焼き殺すわけにはいかなかったのである。

三極構造の二つ目の極である中城若松は、おもろ詩人・阿嘉武樽子が中城に遊んだ時に出会った孝行の誉れ高い若者で、『おもろさうし』に歌われ（「安谷屋の若松、あはれ若松、枝さらへ、浦おそふ若松」）、また章姓上間親方系譜には「始祖乃安谷屋之生名若松時人称安谷屋若松」と伝えられている人物である [当間 1969：p. 200]。つまり若松は仏僧ではなくて、首里へ出仕する元服前の14歳の美少年で、女の誘惑を振り切ってひたすら首里王府へ急ぐ儒教的イデオロギーの体現者として描かれている。

しかも、上位文化である中国からの冊封使を饗応する演目であるということも、筋書きに影響したはずである。冊封使たちには、漢訳された梗概が故事集として配布された

ようで、冊封副使の徐葆光（1671～1740）が『中山伝信録』に記録したところによると、初演時の梗概では、女は十六歳で妖麗な猟師の娘、年下の男は学問の師を求めて首里に上るとなっている。猟師の娘は、雪女伝説や山姥伝説にあるような里の若者を誘惑する山の精として、ことさら象徴化されているようだ。王府での立身を志向する男に立ちはだかる「誘惑する妖女」の構図は、男と女との二項対立を深めながらも、冊封使を意識すればするほど、やがては忠義を選ぶ若松の側に立った結末にならなければならない。

玉城朝薫が御冠船踊り（冊封使歓待の踊り）のためにつくった「組踊五番」（『執心鐘入』『二童敵討』『銘苅子』『女物狂』『孝行之巻』）は、おしなべて史実にもとづいたもので、忠義を重んじ、「たうたう躍て戻らうや」などと、「万事めでたし」の終わり方をする。『執心鐘入』も、忠義を重んじる者にとって「めでたし」の終わり方でなければならなかった。

さて、三極構造の三番目の極を支えるのは宿の女で、それに組するには、啓蒙思想家たちの素朴同質論に欠落している解釈を拓いてみる必要がある。

4. 女人禁制によって変貌した鬼女の主体性を読み込む—"unaiism"を拓く

能は「現在能」と「夢幻能」とに分けられ、夢幻能は「死者」が中心となった能とされる。しかし組踊は「現在能」に近い時間構造を持っており、直線的な時間にそって物語が展開する。幽玄を旨とする能の語りが、過ぎ去った出来事を回想することで「ここではないどこか」に収斂していくのに対し、『執心鐘入』では、「今ここ」に女人禁制の現場が舞台化されて、実況中継さながらに、政治社会の表舞台から排除される「魔女／鬼」が造形・形成される物語構造となっている。

夕闇の中にぽつねんと浮かぶ人里離れた民家に住まう女は、魑魅魍魎のけもの道を住処としている猟師の娘であり、もののけの気配を漂わせている。しかも、若松と知るなり情念を露わにする宿の女は、儒教的教えを逸脱し仏法とは相容れない女、として描かれる。さらに当時の宗教的対立の構図に当てはめれば、女は、渡来仏教や儒教になじまぬ琉球在来の民俗宗教の化身ということになる。宿の女と中城若松は、単に舞台上の登場人物であるばかりではない。二人はその身にあらんかぎりの象徴を引き受けて、二項対立として対峙する。

その対立をさらに際立たせるのが、二人の「つらね」の応酬：宿の女が「をとこ生まれても、恋しらぬものや、玉のさかづきの　底も見らぬ」と歌えば、即座に若松は「をんな生まれても、義理知らぬものや、これど世の中の　地獄だいもの」と返す。ここで、若松の恐れる「地獄」は、伊波普猷［伊波 1938: p.132］によると「地獄」＝「淫売婦」ということであるが、当間一郎［当間 1992: p.170］によると「地獄だいもの」は、「人間として理に反した、無軌道なことだ、まるで人道をふみはずした、理性を失ったおそろしいことだと、いうような意味」とされ、矢野輝雄［矢野 2001: p.185］も「悪の極み」の意味だとし、「祭温によると『女は地獄の使い』というのが中世の常識」であると解説してい

る。たしかに、琉球語にはなじみの薄い「地獄」という大和言葉を唐突に挿入することで、「悪の極み」というような強烈な意味合いを持たせていると考えられる。

　しかし加えて含意されていると思われるのは、「地獄」が女の変身する鬼の予兆でもあるということ。つまり、女人禁制の寺の中で女性性を否定された女が変身せざるを得ない「鬼」の前触れであるということ。「若松」が背を向ける「地獄」は、結果的には、女人禁制に阻まれて「女としてまるごと受容されない女」が否応なく変身させられる「鬼」を、逆に「若松」に呼び寄せる。排除したはずのものにつきまとわれる構図である。

　無限抱擁の地獄に引きずり込もうと迫る破滅的な誘惑者と、それに対して忠義心と克己心を持って懸命に自己を律しようとする理性とのせめぎ。その瀬戸際で吐く若松の台詞を砕いてみると、「忠義心と向上心をもって自己の悦楽・欲望を律することをせずに、無秩序な頽廃・堕落・停滞に身を任せるなんて、これではまるで俗にいう地獄の使い／鬼ではないか」ということになろうか。年上の女の一途な色恋に溺れまいとする若松少年の精一杯の儒教的・仏教的精神がここにある。

　さらにここには、女性原理と男性原理の奇妙なねじれが見えてくる。主人公若松は、世に聞こえた美少年。しかも元服前の慣わしで、目にもあでやかな紅型模様の振袖の衣装で登場する。そこには、たとえば元服前の王子が着用したと伝わる国宝「紅色地龍宝珠瑞雲文様紅型絹袷衣装」にも表現されているように、首里王府における儒教的な忠孝の世界と「清ら」の世界の併存がある。若松が象徴しているものの二重性――たとえば座主に助けを求める時の「すがり方」などに見られる女性性と、首里王府に奉公に上る男性性。だからこそ、幼さ・儚さ・美しさなどの女性原理がいかんなく発揮されたこの若松の「清ら」の世界は、女性性から排除されたはずの宿の女にとっても、守護する／されるべき世界となる。

　また宿の女にしても、欲望を直截に語り、誘惑する行為に及ぶなど、物語のプロットを主体的に創りあげる女として、女性原理を逸脱した側面が大きい。その逸脱が鬼への変身につながるわけだが、道成寺譚とは全く異なって、恋する若松を火炎で「焼き殺す」ことはしない。一気呵成に情念の焔となるのではなく、若松への思いを断ちがたく時にためらいを見せ、時に絶望と怒りを見せるところは、却って生身の人間らしい。固有名詞を与えられていない「宿の女」ではあるが、むしろ若松よりも主人公にふさわしい。そうなると、儒教の忠義も仏教の法力も作品の最終テーマではない、ということになる。

　座主が象徴するのは、仏教世界であり、仏法の力によって在来土着の宗教を駆逐する力である。首里への出仕ひとすじの若松が首里王府を象徴するとすれば、新たに現れた座主は、脆弱な首里王府の後見人として現れた薩摩権力かもしれず、それに対峙することになる鬼女は、法力によって退治されなければならない異教徒の悪や煩悩のすべてを背負わされることになる。それは同時に、薩摩によって弱体化させられる聞得大君御殿に他ならない。しかし、神女組織は現在までしぶとく残っている。三極構造が奇妙なバランスを保ちながらいずれも淘汰されずに残存している沖縄の現実社会を見わたすと、《鬼となった宿の女が、座主の唱える真言（陀羅尼）の法力に抵抗して激しい死闘を繰り

広げ、奈落へ堕ちて滅亡する》という勧善懲悪の演出では座りが悪い。

「若松⇔宿の女⇔座主」の三極構造は、儒教イデオロギー・首里王府⇔聞得大君御殿・琉球在来の民俗宗教⇔仏教・大和権力（薩摩）など、当時の政治的三極構造の寓話としても解釈できるし、現代社会を象徴する寓話としても読み込める。どこに力を入れるかという演出の在り方で、物語の奥行きはさま変わりする。玉城朝薫が提示したこの三極構造は、その構造を破綻させない限り、あらゆる演出に開かれていると考える。

うないフェスティバルで上演された佐藤太圭子の演出は、《大団円において自らの意思で入り端に向き直り、静かに退場する》という点で、三極構造が保たれている稀有な例である。「ダラニ（真言）の連唱で女の本性に目覚めた鬼女が無明の闇に灯りだした光に導かれ、自らの意思で修羅の場を退く静かな動きの中に、いまだ若松への執心を整除しきれていない砕動風の鬼を演出してみました」[佐藤2009: p.5][5]。この演出こそ、むしろ一層深く若松に思いを寄せる鬼女の心が読み取れて、作品が深くなる。

般若面は、女人禁制の場において、女性性を拒絶されることによって対抗的に造形されるものかもしれない。だからこそ般若面は、丸ごとの存在を拒否されたときに、素面に被膜のように物象化する愛の正身(むざね)のようなものだと言えよう。「うない」という言説もたしかに一種の物象化（objectification 客体化）を伴うものではあるが、守護神でありたいと願うまっすぐなこころは、むしろ近代化の邪気を払ってくれる。

古典芸能や民俗宗教を考えるに際しては、女性優位システムを遺していたとされる古琉球の歴史的現実に深く分け入れば分け入るほど、今を生きる私たちにとっても居心地のいい解釈を探り当てることになるのではないか。これを沖縄におけるフェミニズム・エスノグラフィーの作業仮説としたい。

注

1) 宮城栄昌は、「沖縄の女性は、すべてうない神である」（1967: p.2）と述べ、とくに「オナリ神」の節を設けて詳説している[宮城1967: p.48-54]。
2) 由井晶子（フェスティバル実行委員長）は、うないフェスティバル2009パンフレット『うないがひらく伝統の未来』に掲載した挨拶文「発展を担ってきた女性たち」に、そのように表現している。
3) 島袋光裕は、座主が鬼女と争う祈りの型は、歌舞伎の荒事風にではなく能風に（静かに）演ずるように指導した[矢野2001: pp.188-9]。
4) 伊波普猷や宮城栄昌によれば、この1717年の事件は「御新下り」の延期となっているが、実際には「御初地入り」延期事件であった、という貴重な指摘が、伊従勉[伊従2005: pp.411-425]によってなされている。たしかに1717に王府と聞得大君御殿との間にあった反目は、「御初地入り」に関することであったらしい。いずれにしても政教分離策による両者の反目が高まっていたことに変わりはない。
5) 佐藤太圭子は筆者のインタヴューでも「鬼女の心情をなぞるように流れる『伊野波節』によって女の魔性は取り除かれ、本然の姿を取り戻して女の性に目覚めることがわかります」と述べ、大団円の演出の根拠を示した（2009年12月28日 21:00）。

参考文献

伊波普猷（1969）「沖縄女性史」『沖縄女性物語』pp. 157–226、風土記社、沖縄。
伊波普猷（1992）『琉球戯曲辞典　復刻版』（1938 初版）榕樹書林、沖縄。
伊波普猷（1992）『校注　琉球戯曲集』（1929 初版、春陽堂、東京）。
伊從勉（2005）『琉球祭祀空間の研究：カミとヒトの環境学』中央公論美術出版、東京。
勝方 = 稲福 恵子（2006）『おきなわ女性学事始』新宿書房、東京。
川橋 範子・黒木雅子（2004）『混在するめぐみ』人文書院（叢書文化研究 4）、京都。
金城芳子（1985）『相思樹の花影——おきなわ女の群像』沖縄文化協会、東京。
佐喜真興英（1969）「女人政治考」『沖縄女性物語』pp. 49–108、風土記社、沖縄。
佐藤太圭子（2009）「組踊『執心鐘入』〜演出ノート〜」12 月 4 日公演配布資料。
高良倉吉（1989）『新版・琉球の時代——大いなる歴史像を求めて』筑摩書房、東京。
陳侃『琉球使録』、原田禹雄訳注（1995）『冊封琉球使録集成 1』榕樹書林、沖縄。
当間一郎他（1969）『劇聖・玉城朝薫——組踊上演 250 年記念誌』沖縄タイムス社、東京。
当間一郎（1992）『組踊研究』第一書房、東京。
徳江元正（1982）「『道成寺』譚成立考」『道成寺』小学館、東京。
波照間永子（2007）「舞踊家オーラル・ヒストリー——児玉清子の生涯」『琉球・沖縄研究』創刊号、pp. 61–88）、東京。
比嘉政夫（1987）『女性優位と男系原理——沖縄の民俗社会構造』凱風社、東京。
宮城栄昌（1967）『沖縄女性史』沖縄タイムス社、沖縄。
宮城栄昌（1979）『沖縄のノロの研究』吉川弘文館、東京。
矢野輝雄（2001）『沖縄舞踊の歴史』（1988 初版）築地書館、東京。
矢野輝雄（2001）『組踊への招待』琉球新報社、沖縄。
矢野輝雄（2005）「矢野輝雄芸能研究遺稿集」沖縄県立芸大附属研究所紀要『沖縄芸術の科学』第 17 号、沖縄。

北琉球方言における同化と異化

かりまた　しげひさ*

Dissimilation and Assimilation in Northern Ryukyuan Dialects

KARIMATA Shigehisa

This paper examines how "dissimilation" and "assimilation" have occured in phonological change in Northern Ryukyuan dialects. By dividing phonological changes in the Northern Ryukyus into "dissimilation" and "assimilation," I will examine how phonemic insert, loss, merger, and split occurred in the dissimilation and assimilation processes in the formation of compound/derived words and their grammatical structures, while pointing out that there are several types of these phonemic changes. Clarifying both the dissimilation and assimilation process, as well as analyzing how these processes interact with each other in phonemic changes, the present analysis will contribute to our better understanding of the past and present conditions of phonemic change in Northern Ryukyuan dialects.

1.　同化と異化

　北琉球方言には狭母音化や二重母音の融合などの母音変化がある。破裂音化・破擦音化・摩擦音化・鼻音化などの調音方法の変化、口蓋音化・唇音化などの調音位置の変化、喉頭音化などの声門の状態の変化などの子音変化がある。音韻変化の要因にもいろいろあるが、筋弾性的な条件がつよく関与した音韻変化があり、空気力学的な条件がつよく関与しておきる音韻変化がある[1]。特定のフォネームが隣接する他のフォネームの音韻的特徴（以下、韻質）や音環境に依存せず、すべてのアロフォンが音韻変化するばあいもあるし、音環境や結合するフォネームの韻質に依存した特定のアロフォンにおきる音韻変化もあるし、特定の単語にだけみられる音韻変化もある。さまざまにみられる琉球方言の音韻変化は、おおきく同化と異化の二つにわけることができる[2]。
　同化とは、前後するふたつのフォネームの一方から他方への、あるいは相互の影響のもとに、一方のフォネームの韻質の一部あるいは全部がもう一方に付与されて韻質に変

---

* 琉球大学教授 Professor, University of the Ryukyus

化をもたらしたり、あるいは二つのフォネームが相互に韻質を交換して変化したりする音韻変化である。同化は、前後に配置されたフォネームの韻質におおきく依存した相互作用によって生ずるさまざまな音韻変化を総称したものである。

　琉球方言の同化には隣接同化と遠隔同化がある。隣接同化と遠隔同化は、付与される韻質の方向によって進行同化、逆行同化、相互同化にわかれている。それぞれの同化には影響をあたえる韻質の程度によって完全同化と部分同化とがある。

　いっぽう、ある特定のフォネームが前後に配置された別のフォネームから相対的に独立して変化し、異なる韻質をもつようになる音韻変化を「異化」とよぶ。「異化」のこのような使用は、「同一ないし類似した音が音連鎖のなかで隣接ないし近接した場合に、一方が他方とは異なった音に変わる現象で、同化に対立する[3]」という一般的な使用とは少し異なり、さししめす現象の範囲はひろい。しかし、「同化に対立する」という異化の説明を拡大して使用するものである。同化によらないさまざまな音韻変化を異化と総称することにする。

　異化が前後のフォネームから相対的に独立した音韻変化であるとはいっても、単語を構成する音節構造のなかで個々のフォネームが孤立して存在しているわけではなく、前後に配置されたフォネームは、相互に密接にむすびつき、当該のフォネームが音韻変化するための音環境を提供していて、間接的に影響をあたえている[4]。

　異化と同化は、性格のことなる音韻変化であるが、特定の音環境をもった単語のなかで同化と異化が連続しておこり、一方がもう一方をひきおこすための条件や前提をつくりだしているばあいもある。異化と同化の結果、単語の音節構造のなかでのフォネームのふるまい方、あるいはフォネーム同士の関係のし方に変化が生じるが、それを音挿入[5]、音消失[6]、音分割[7]、音融合[8]のタイプにわけることができる。

2. 母音の異化

　琉球方言には多様な異化がみられるが、狭母音化は、琉球方言の代表的な異化であり、おおくの子音変化にも影響をあたえていて、琉球方言を本土諸方言から区分する音韻論的な特徴をうみだした。琉球方言において異化をひきおこした要因もさまざまあるが、呼気流の増減という空気力学的な条件の関与した異化がおおい。

　北琉球方言の狭母音化 *o＞u、*e＞ï＞i も呼気流のつよまりという空気力学的な条件が優勢にはたらいたもので、先行、後続の子音の如何をとわず独立しておきている[9]。

2-1　奥舌半狭母音 *o の奥舌狭母音化

　奥舌半狭母音 *o の奥舌狭母音 u への変化は、声道をながれるつよい呼気によって舌の盛り上がりによる声道のせばめの位置が軟口蓋後部から軟口蓋中央部へとおしやられ、口のひらきもせまくなったものである。*o の円唇性もひきつがれている。その結果、もとから存在した u と統合している。沖縄島中南部諸方言、沖永良部与論沖縄島北部諸方

言では *o は u に変化しているが、奄美徳之島諸方言では u に変化せず o のままあらわれる語がみられる。

ʔuja（親）、mutʃi（餅）、t'uri（鳥）、k'udzu（去年）、nudu（喉）、duru（泥）、k'imo（肝）、mado（間）、k'oro（心）、moho（婿）、momo（腿）　　奄美大島龍郷町瀬留

ʔutu（音）、ʔuja（親）、ɸudu（去年）、ɸuri（これ）、kumu（雲）、kimu（肝）、pu:（帆）、puʃi（星）、pitʃu（人）、tui（鳥）、tudʒi（妻）、'utu（夫）、'uba（叔母）、miʃu（味噌）、duru（泥）、mumu（腿）、juru（夜）　　与論町城

ʔuja（親）、ʔut'u（音）、k'uk'uru（心）、mu:k'u（婿）、suk'u（底）、suwa:（側）、t'ui（鳥）、mat'u（的）、duru:（泥）、madu:（間）、nuk'ugiri:（鋸）、mumu:（腿）、mutʃi:（餅）、k'imu:（肝）、junawi（夜なべ）、juk'u（横）　　沖縄島名護市幸喜

2-2　前舌半狭母音 *e の前舌狭母音化

前舌半狭母音 *e の中舌狭母音 ï への変化、および、前舌狭母音 i への変化は、つよい呼気流によって舌全体とそのもりあがりの最高点が前寄りに移動し、口のひらきも狭くなったものである。中舌狭母音 ï は、奄美徳之島諸方言であらわれ、沖永良部与論沖縄島北部諸方言、沖縄島中南部諸方言では舌面が前寄りに移動し口の開きのせばまった前舌狭母音 i があらわれている。奄美徳之島諸方言では *e のおおくは ï にとどまっている。また、竜郷町瀬留方言には warabë（童）、ʃiragë（白髪）、ʔjemë（夢）などのように半狭の中舌母音であらわれる単語もある。奄美徳之島諸方言の狭母音化は完了していないのである。

ʔamï（雨）、k'ï（毛）、k'ït'a〜k'ët'a（桁）、t'ï（手）、t'ïŋ（天）、ʔudï（腕）、nï（根）、ɸïra（箆）、ʔasï（汗）、k'adzï（風）、nabï（鍋）　　龍郷町瀬留

ʔibi（エビ）、ʔami（雨）、na:bi（鍋）、ki:（毛）、saki（酒）、ka:gi（陰）、ti:（手）、ʔudi（腕）、ɲi:（根）、ʔaʃi（汗）、kadʒi（風）　　沖縄島西原町小那覇

前舌歯茎を調音点にもつ子音 t、d、n と結合する ï は、前寄りのアロフォンであらわれ、i に統合しつつある。奥舌軟口蓋や両唇を調音点にする子音 k、g、p、b、m、ɸ と結合する ï は、やや奥よりのくらい音色をもったアロフォンであらわれる。唇音 m、ɸ と結合した mï、ɸï は 70〜60 代以降の世代では ʔamu（雨）、mamu（豆）、ɸura（箆）、nabu（鍋）のように、u に統合しつつある。前者の tï＞ti、dï＞di、nï＞ni は、沖永良部与論沖縄島北部諸方言、沖縄島中南部諸方言とおなじく狭母音化が進行しているともみることができるが、後者は、狭母音化とはことなる、聴覚的な印象の近似に起因する異化だと

かんがえる。

　沖縄南部阿嘉島方言、慶留間島方言では短母音 e は狭母音化して i であらわれるが、長母音は、狭母音化しない e: があらわれる[10]。ほとんどの下位方言で e ＞ i の狭母音化が完了している沖縄諸島方言にあって阿嘉島方言と慶留間島方言で狭母音化しない e: がみられる詳細な理由はわかっていない。

　　ke:（毛、木）、me:（目）、ka:me:（亀）、he:（屁）、te:（手）　　座間味村阿嘉

3.　子音の異化

　北琉球方言の子音の異化には、無声破裂音の喉頭音化、破裂音の摩擦音化（*p＞ɸ＞h、*k＞h、*t＞s、*t＞λ[11]）、破擦音の摩擦音化（*ts＞s）、接近音のゆるやかな声だてへの変化（*w＞'）がある。

3-1　破裂音の喉頭音化と非喉頭音化

　奄美徳之島諸方言、沖縄島北部諸方言で無声の喉頭音化した破裂音は、狭母音化をひきおこした呼気流によってひきおこされたものである。狭母音 *u、*i と結合した無声破裂音 *k は、せまい声道をながれる相対的につよい呼気流によって声帯筋が緊張し、喉頭音化したアロフォン k' としてあらわれる。いっぽう、広母音 *a、半狭母音 *o、*e とむすびついた *k は、ひろめの声道をながれる相対的によわい呼気流に照応して声帯筋が弛緩した喉頭音化しないアロフォン k' としてあらわれる。

　狭母音化が進行して k'o が k'u に変化すると、喉頭音化した k' と喉頭音化しない k' は、フォネームとしての対立に移行し、無声破裂音に喉頭/非喉頭のあらたな音韻的な対立が生じることとなる。同様に *ki＞k'i と *ke＞k'ï＞k'i、*pu＞p'u と *po＞p'o＞p'u、*pi＞p'i と *pe＞p'ï＞p'i のあいだでも喉頭/非喉頭の対立が生じたとかんがえる。無声破裂音に喉頭/非喉頭の対立が確立されると、k'a、p'a のように *a と結合する喉頭音化しないアロフォンの k'、p'、同じく t'a、t'u、t'ï（沖縄島北部諸方言では t'i）のように *a、*o、*e と結合する喉頭音化しないアロフォン t' をフォネームとして編成する。なお、奄美大島諸方言のばあい、語中の破裂音でも喉頭/非喉頭の対立がみられる。

　　k'umï（米）、k'uï（声）、ʔik'i（池）、k'ï（毛）、k'asa（笠）、k'amï（亀）、k'o（皮）、k'umi（組）、k'ubi（首）、k'ura（倉）、k'iŋ（衣）、ʔik'i（息）　　龍郷町瀬留

　今帰仁村方言のばあい、*po も *pu も p'u に統合され、そこでは喉頭/非喉頭の対立は失われているが、*pe 由来の p'i と *pi 由来の p'i は喉頭/非喉頭の対立を維持している。今帰仁村方言の p' は、破裂がやわらかく、服部四郎（1951）が「琉球語今帰仁村与那嶺方言の [p'ana:]〈花〉〈鼻〉の [p] は息の閉鎖音であるが、呼気が弱く、気圧がよわく、し

たがって出わたりの破裂も弱い」と記している。かたい響きの印象をうける喉頭音化した破裂音と破裂のよわい喉頭音化しない破裂音とのちがいははっきりしている。

 p'ana:（花、鼻）、p'ak'a:（墓）、p'aɸu:（箱）、p'ama（浜）、p'o:tʃi（箒）、p'o:tʃa:（包丁）、p'e:（灰）、p'e:（蠅）、p'e:（南）、p'u:（帆、穂）、p'uɲi（骨）、p'ira（箆）、p'iri:（縁）、p'udi:（筆）、p'uju:（冬）、p'uɲi（船）、p'idʒi:（髭）、p'idʒi:（肘）、p'iru:（昼）、p'ima:（暇）、p'iru:（蒜）、p'idʒai（左）　　沖縄島今帰仁村謝名

3-2　両唇破裂音の摩擦音化

　笠利町佐仁方言、与論島方言、今帰仁村方言、名護市方言、恩納村恩納方言は、pを保存しているが、おおくの北琉球方言ではpの摩擦音化が進行している。

　沖縄島北部大宜味村大宜味方言では *a、*o、*e と結合した *p は、注意ぶかく観察していないと上下の唇がふれていることをみのがしてしまうほど唇の閉鎖がとてもやわらかく、ᵖɸと表記するような破裂音で、ᵖɸ～ɸでゆれている。今帰仁村方言や与論方言のpよりもさらにやわらかい。両唇摩擦音ɸに変化しきってしまう直前の状態なのであろう。摩擦音化していないpは、喉頭音化したp'であらわれることもあるし、喉頭音化しないp'であらわれることもあって、対立する一方の音声（p'）が摩擦音化することによって、もう一方の音声（p'）は、喉頭音化が必ずしも義務的ではなくなっていくのであろう。喉頭/非喉頭の対立から破裂音/摩擦音の対立へと移行していっているようである。

　ᵖɸana（鼻）、ᵖɸana（花）、ᵖɸai（針）、ᵖɸabu（ハブ）、ᵖɸagama（羽釜）、ᵖɸa:（歯）、ɸuni（骨）、ɸu:（穂）、ɸu:（帆）、ɸuʃi（星）、ᵖɸira（箆）、puʃi（節）、piru:（昼）、pigi（髭）、pi:（火）、pidzai（左）、pi:（屁）　　大宜味村大宜味

　沖縄島北部の国頭村宇嘉方言、辺野喜方言では擬声擬態語以外の名詞、動詞の語頭のpは、結合する母音の如何をとわず摩擦音化してɸであらわれる[12]。

　ɸa:（葉）、ɸama（浜）、ɸana（鼻）、ɸigi（髭）、ɸigai（左）、ɸira（箆）、ɸuʃi（節）、ɸu:（穂）、ɸuni（骨）、ɸo:ta（包丁）、ɸe:（灰）、ɸe:（蠅）　　国頭村宇嘉

　奄美大島諸方言、徳之島諸方言、沖縄島中南部諸方言では、p＞ɸ＞hの変化が進行し、完了している。ただし、u、ï、ëと結合するばあいは両唇摩擦音ɸのアロフォンがあらわれ、iと結合するばあいは歯茎摩擦音çのアロフォンがあらわれる。

　ha:（歯）、hatʃi（蜂）、hat'ë（畑）、ɸunï（舟）、ɸunï（骨）、çigi（髭）、çikjusï（挽臼）、çu:ri（日和）、ɸï（屁）、ɸë（蠅）、ɸë（灰）　　龍郷町瀬留

ha:(歯)、hatʃi(蜂)、hataki(畑)、ɸuɲi(舟)、ɸuda(札)、ɸuɲi(骨)、çidʒi(髭)、çitʃiʔu:ʃi(挽臼)、çi(屁)、çi:ra(箆)、he:(蝿)、he:(灰)　西原町小那覇

3-3 奥舌軟口蓋破裂音の摩擦音化

　喜界島方言、沖永良部島方言、与論島方言、沖縄島北部諸方言で *a、*o、*e と結合した語頭の軟口蓋破裂音 k の声門摩擦音 h への異化がみられる。

　hadi(風)、hanï(金)、hanï(銭)、hama(鎌)、ho:bï(頭)、hat'ana(包丁・刀)、haŋami(鏡)、hi:(毛)、hi:(木)、hibuʃi(煙)、humï(米)、huʃi(腰)、k'imu(肝)、k'iɲu:(昨日)、k'ubi(首)、k'umu(雲)　喜界町佐手久

　hata(肩)、hagi(影)、hama(鎌)、hari(舵)、hagami(鏡)、hi:(毛)、hibuʃi(煙)、hu:(粉)、humi(米)、hui(声)　国頭村宇嘉

　語頭での *k ＞ h のみられない奄美大島南部諸方言でも広母音 *a、半狭母音 *e、*o にはさまれた語中の軟口蓋破裂音 k の声門摩擦音 h への異化がみられる。

　naha:(中)、mahar(椀)、sëhë:(酒)、dëhë:(竹)、hat'ë:hë(畑)、t'oho:(蛸)、k'oho:ro(心)、k'oho:not(九つ)、wehë:(桶)　奄美瀬戸内町芝

　奄美大島北部諸方言、徳之島諸方言でも語頭ではkの摩擦音化はみられないが、語中ではkがhに変化し、さらに、母音間で有声音化して消失している。

　na(中)、ma:ri(椀)、së(酒)、dë:(竹)、t'ë:(丈)、hat'ë:(畑)、wëŋ(分ける)、t'o:(蛸)、k'oro(心)、k'onotʃi(九つ)、wë:(桶)　龍郷町瀬留

3-4 歯茎破裂音の摩擦音化

　国頭村宇嘉方言、辺野喜方言で *a、*e、*o と結合した語頭の歯茎の無声破裂音 *t の無声摩擦音 s への異化がみられる。

　sa:(田)、saɸu(蛸)、sabaku(煙草)、satami(畳)、sui(鳥)、suha(十日)、suʃi(年)、ʃi:(手)、ʃi:(樋)、ʃira(太陽)、so:ɸu(豆腐)、ʃe:ɸu(台風)　国頭村宇嘉

　沖縄久高島方言で *a、*e、*o と結合した無声の歯茎の破裂音 *t の無声歯茎側面摩擦音 ƛ への摩擦音化がみられる[13]。宇嘉方言、辺野喜方言の *t ＞ s とはことなり、久高島方言の *t ＞ ƛ は、語頭だけでなく語中でもおきている。ただし語中での摩擦音化のみられる語例はすくなく、破裂音 t であらわれるものがおおい。

ɬa:（田）、ɬa:bi（足袋）、ɬaɬa:（砂糖）、ɬaɬaŋ（畳）、ɬi:（手）、ɬindʒo:（天井）、ɬippu:（鉄砲）、ɬui（鳥）、ɬira（太陽）、ɬu:（十）、ɬo:pu（豆腐）

　久高島方言では *a、*e、*o、*u と結合した無声歯茎摩擦音 *s の無声側面摩擦音 ɬ への異化がみられる。この異化は、歯茎音から側面音への調音点の変更である。この変化も語頭、語中でみられる。

ɬaɬa:（砂糖）、haɬa:（傘）、ɬa:ju:（白湯）、kuɬa（草）、ɬi:（巣）、ɬiɬi（煤）、ɬina（砂）、kuɬui（薬）、ɬiŋ（千）、aɬi（汗）、ɬuba（側）、kuɬu（糞）、ɬo:（竿）

3-5　歯茎破擦音の摩擦音化
　沖縄島名護市幸喜方言で無声破擦音 ts、tʃ が摩擦音化して ʃ、s であらわれる例がみられる。tsu ＞ ʃi、tʃu ＞ su のように母音が u のばあいに限定され、しかも後続の子音が無声子音に限定される。

ʃik'iʔusu:（搗き臼）、ʃik'idʒik'i（月々）、ʃik'imunu（漬物）、ʃik'ahaŋ（近い）、ʃik'aiŋ（使う）、suk'iri（一切れ）、suk'abu（一株）、suk'utʃi（一口）、suk'oibana:（造花）、sut'awai（一束）、sut'uk'uru（一所）、sup'a:ku（一箱）、sup'i:ru（一尋）

3-6　歯茎破擦音の破裂音化
　国頭村宇嘉方言、辺野喜方言では歯茎破擦音 ts、dz の歯茎破裂音 t、d への変化がみられる。

ti:（血）、kuti（口）、ɸati（蜂）、timi（爪）、tira（顔）、tika（柄）、tiŋ（角）、mati（松）、sutiti（蘇鉄）、ta:（茶）、tagwaŋ（茶碗）、ho:ta（包丁）、tu:（人）、ti:ti（一つ）、ta:ti（二つ）、ititi（五つ）　　国頭村宇嘉

　国頭村宇嘉方言、辺野喜方言では語頭、語中での d と r の区別がなく、ru:（胴）、surana（戸棚）、ruru（泥）などのように、すべて r であらわれる。したがって、有声破擦音 dz から破裂音化した d も r であらわれる。

ra:（座）、ara（痣）、ri:（地、陸）、ɸiri（肘）、hari（舵）、suri（妻）、miri（水）、kiri（傷）、ho:ri（麹）、amaraki（酢・＜甘酒に対応）、hari（風）、ɾo:（門）、aʃira（足駄）、huru（去年）　　国頭村宇嘉

3-7　接近音のゆるやかな声だてへの異化
　両唇の丸めと奥舌面の軟口蓋へのもちあがりとを特徴とする唇軟口蓋接近音 w は、円

唇奥舌狭母音 u の特徴と近似する。*wo ＞ wu の狭母音化が進行すると、w は u に吸収されるが、w から o への持続部にみられたわたり的な特徴は、母音 u の入りわたりのゆるやかな声だてへと移行する。母音の入りわたりのゆるやかな声だてを「'」と表記する。*woba ＞ wu̜ba ＞ 'uba（叔母）。

いっぽう、語頭の母音単独音節 o、u に自然に挿入されるかるい？は、*w の音消失によって発生した母音の入りわたりのゆるやかな声だての /'/ と音韻論的に対立するフォネーム /ʔ/ として確立された。/ʔ/ は、/'/ との音韻論的対立のなかで語頭の母音のまえに音挿入されたのである。

'u（緒）、'uba（叔母）、'udʒi（叔父）、'unagu（女）、'unari（姉妹・をなり）、'ugi（甘蔗・「荻」に対応）、'uduri（踊り）、'u:duri（雄鶏）　竜郷町瀬留

*wi（*we から変化した wi を含む）が唇音退化して /'i/ になり、/ʔi/ との音韻的対立も発生している。*jui（結・相互扶助）＞ 'i: などのように、j のばあいにもやわらかな声だて /'/ への異化が進行したとかんがえる。

'i（亥）、'irjuŋ（坐る）、'idzï（絵図）、'içiri（兄弟・ゑけり）、'i:（柄）、'i:（良い）、'iri（襟）、'irjuŋ（貰う、「得る」に対応）、

3-8　両唇音の歯茎音化

沖縄伊江島方言で *i と結合した両唇破裂音 *p、*b、両唇鼻音 *m の歯茎破裂音 t、d、歯茎鼻音 n への調音点の変更という異化がみられる。この異化は、t'ja:hu（百）、t'ja:i（旱魃）、asidjuŋ（遊ぶ）、juɲuŋ（読む）などの語例にみるように、口蓋音化した両唇音 pj、bj、mj も口蓋音化した tj、dj、ɲ に変化している。この異化は、*i と結合した *p、*b、*m を含む口蓋音化した両唇音の口蓋音化した歯茎音への調音点の変更であり、声道の形が似ていることによる聴覚的な特徴の近似に由来する変化であるとかんがえる[14]。pj ＞ tj、bj ＞ dj の異化は伊江島方言以外にはほとんどみられないが、mj ＞ ɲ、mi ＞ ɲi は個別的、散在的だがあちこちの方言にみられる。

t'i:（火）、t'iru:（昼）、t'idʒai（左）、t'idʒi（髭）、t'ja:hu（百）、t'ja:i（旱魃）、k'udi（首）、t'adi（旅）、ʔidi（エビ）、hadi（紙）、ʔasidjuN（遊ぶ）、naradjuŋ（並ぶ）、ɲiɲi:（耳）、ɲitʃi（道）、ɲidʒi:（右）、naɲi:（波）、ʔuɲi（海）、juɲuŋ（読む）

3-9　両唇音の軟口蓋音化

沖縄伊江島方言で *u と結合した両唇破裂音 *p の軟口蓋破裂音 k への異化がみられる。この異化は調音点の変更であるが、奥舌円唇狭母音 u と結合した両唇破裂音 p と k とは、その声道の形がよく似ており、したがって聞こえの相対的な近似に由来する変化ではな

かったかとかんがえる。上述の *pi ＞ ti、*bi ＞ di、*mi ＞ ni の異化と類似の変化である。

　k'uni（舟）、k'uda（札）、k'ubui（陰嚢）、k'uk'uɲuŋ（含む）、

　国頭村宇嘉方言、辺野喜方言では唇軟口蓋接近音 w の唇軟口蓋破裂音 gw への異化がみられる。宇嘉方言、辺野喜方言の g および gw の破裂はやわらかく、有声軟口蓋摩擦音 ɣ で発音されることもあった。
　a:（泡）、a:（粟）、ha:（皮）、na:（縄）など語中の *wa、*ha ＞ wa では w が音消失しているにもかかわらず、語中に wa を有した借用語「茶碗」では tagwaŋ（茶碗）のように wa の gwa への変化がみられる。また他の方言にみられる喉頭音化した唇軟口蓋接近音 ʔw も喉頭音化しない w とおなじく gwa に変化している。ʔw は、「ʔi、ʔu の音消失」の項で述べるように *uhabe ＞ ʔuwabe ＞ ʔwa:bi の過程を経て生成されたフォネームだが、宇嘉方言では ʔw と w の対立がうしなわれたのちに w ＞ gw の変化がおきたものとかんがえられる。

　gwata（腹）、gwata（綿）、gwaki（脇）、gwara（藁）、tagwaŋ（茶碗）、gwahasa:ŋ（若い）、gwassa:ŋ（悪い）、gwarabi（童・子供）、gwa:bi（上・上辺に対応）、gwa:tiki（天気）、gwa:（豚）、gwaŋ（私）、gwe:ku（櫂）、gwe:kintsu（金持ち）、gwe:ha（親戚）、gwe:ntu（鼠）、gwahanati（若夏）、

4. 同化

　母音と母音のあいだでおきる北琉球方言の同化には隣接同化と遠隔同化がみられる。遠隔同化とはいっても子音の持続部ですでに結合する母音の口がまえがとられていて、先行音節の母音と後続音節の母音は、相互に影響をあたえあう条件があり、隔たっているようにみえてもじっさいには隣接同化に同じだといってよいだろう。
　これまで調査した範囲で子音と母音の隣接同化はあるが、遠隔同化による子音変化はみられなかった。開音節の CV 構造を基本とする北琉球方言にあって、子音と子音のあいだには母音がはさまるので、母音を介して子音同士が子音としての調音上の特徴を付与することはない。

4-1　母音の同化

　北琉球方言の母音の隣接同化には相互同化がみられ、遠隔同化には相互同化、逆行同化、進行同化がみられる。隣接同化には部分同化の例がみられ、遠隔同化には完全同化と部分同化がみられる。
　北琉球方言では二重母音の隣接相互同化とそれにともなう音融合がおきている。*ao ＞ o:、*ae ＞ e:、*ai ＞ e:、*eu ＞ u: などの同化は、祖形を日本祖語の *awo、*awe、*awi、

*api、*ape、*epu とみると、*awi、*awe、*awo では語中接近音 w の唇音退化による音消失が先行し、*api、*ape、*epu では語中両唇破裂音 p の摩擦音化、有声音化 w、唇音退化による音消失が先行していたとみられる。

4-1-1　母音の隣接同化
*au、*ao の隣接相互同化
　*au ＞ o: は、a の広母音性と u の奥舌円唇性・狭母音性が影響をあたえあった相互部分同化で、円唇の奥舌半狭母音の o: に音融合（au ＞ o:）している。*au ＞ o: とおなじように、*ao ＞ o: の相互部分同化がみられる。

　k'o:dʒi（麹）、bo:（棒）、gumbo:（牛蒡）、p'o:tʃi（箒）、ʔutʒato:（茶湯）、so:（竿）、ʔo:ʔiru（青色）、t'o:suŋ（倒す）、no:suŋ（治す）　　今帰仁村謝名

*ai、*ae の隣接相互同化
　北琉球方言で *ai ＞ ë: ＞ e: の相互部分同化がみられる。a の広母音性と i の前舌性・狭母音性が影響をあたえあった相互部分同化で、奄美徳之島諸方言では半狭の中舌母音 ë:（あるいは ə）に音融合している。沖永良部与論沖縄島北部諸方言では前舌半狭母音 e: に音融合している。*ai ＞ ë: ＞ e: とおなじように、*ae ＞ ë: ＞ e: の相互部分同化がみられる。奄美徳之島諸方言の ë: は、歯茎音 t、d、n、r、s、ts、dz と結合するとき前舌寄りに発音されて e であらわれ、両唇音と結合するとき奥舌寄りに発音されて œ であらわれることがある。

　në:（地震）、ɸë:（灰）、t'arë（盥）、më:（米）、mimë:（見舞い）、ɸë:（蠅）、ɸë:（南）、më:（前）、në:（苗）、瀬戸内町諸鈍

*iwa、*ewa の隣接相互同化
　沖縄島中南部方言では語末に *e、*i を有する名詞にとりたて助辞 *wa が後接するとき、相互同化による音融合 *-iwa ＞ -ia ＞ -e:、*-ewa ＞ -iwa ＞ -ia ＞ -e: がおきている。

　mame:（豆は）、sake:（酒は）、hane:（羽は）、ʔaʃe:（汗は）、ʔare:（あれは）、mime:（耳は）、muʃe:（虫は）、kutʃe:（口は）、tudʒe:（妻は）、kudʒe:（釘は）、midʒe:（水は）、ʃi:ʃe:（煤は）、rikutʃe:（理屈は）　　西原町小那覇

*uwa の隣接相互同化[15]
　沖縄島中南部諸方言で語末に *u、*o を有する名詞にとりたて助辞 *wa が後接するとき相互同化による音融合 *-uwa ＞ -ua ＞ -o:、*-owa ＞ -uwa ＞ -ua ＞ -o: がおきている。

muːko: (婿は)、duro: (泥は)、'uto: (夫は)、kado: (角は)、nuno: (布は)、majo: (眉は)、kudʒo: (去年は)、habo: (ハブは)　　西原町小那覇

4-1-2　母音の遠隔同化
遠隔相互同化

　奄美大島南部瀬戸内町の加計呂麻島の芝方言の sëhëː (酒)、hatʼëːhë (畑)、dëhëː (竹)、wëhëː (桶)、tʼohoː (蛸) などは、h の両側の a と e、o と e、a と o が遠隔相互同化をおこして、ë、o に変化したものである。*sake (酒) ＞ sahe ＞ sëhëː、*woke (桶) ＞ wohe ＞ wëhëː、*tako (蛸) ＞ taho ＞ tʼohoː は、摩擦音化によって k から変化した語中の h の両側が広母音 a、半広母音 e、o という、音環境に依存した遠隔相互同化である。この遠隔相互同化は、加計呂麻島をふくむ奄美大島南部諸方言にみられる。

　加計呂麻島の諸鈍方言のばあいも同様の遠隔相互同化がみられるが、諸鈍方言は、高低アクセントと強弱アクセントを並存させる方言であり、弱強型のリズム＝アクセント構造をもつ単語の第1音節めの弱音節の母音は、ë が ï になり、o が u になってあらわれる傾向がある。この狭母音化は、単語のリズム＝アクセント構造に依存した異化である。

　　dïhëː (竹)、juːjihëː (夕焼)、wïhëː (桶)、tʼuhoː　　瀬戸内町諸鈍

　奄美大島北部諸方言では、遠隔相互同化ののちに、語中の h が音消失して母音の融合した sëː (酒)、hatʼë (畑)、dë (竹)、wë (桶)、tʼo (蛸) などの例がみられる。

　名護市幸喜方言では paru (畑) ＞ pʼoroː、ʔupuhaŋ ＞ upʼohoŋ (多い) の遠隔相互同化の語例がみられる。後述するように名護市幸喜方言は、遠隔進行同化、遠隔逆行同化もみられる方言である。

遠隔進行同化

　瀬戸内町諸鈍方言では *e に対応して ï が規則的にあらわれるが、çigi (髭)、ʔikʼi (池)、ʔiɲi (稲)、kʼiʃir (煙管) の語の第2音節めの母音は i があらわれている。先行第1音節めの母音 i の前舌狭母音性が遠隔進行同化によって第2音節めの母音に付与されて中舌狭母音 ï が前舌狭母音 i に変化した結果である。おなじ現象が他の奄美大島の諸方言でもみられる。

　名護市幸喜方言では pʼagohoŋ (汚い)、magehaŋ (大きい)、sakohaŋ (脆い) のような遠隔進行同化もみられる。pagohaŋ ＞ pʼagohoŋ (汚い) は第2音節めの母音 o の影響による第3音節めの母音の完全同化の例だが、magihaŋ ＞ magehaŋ (大きい)、sakuhaŋ ＞ sakohaŋ (脆い) では第1音節めの広母音 a の影響によって第2音節めの母音の前舌性はそのままに口のひらきの広狭の変化 i ＞ e、u ＞ o がみられる。juːsuwai (寝小便・夜しばり) も第1音節めの母音 u の影響によって第2音節めの母音 i が u に変化した完全同化の例である。juːʃibai ＞ juːsuwai。

遠隔逆行同化

　名護市幸喜方言にはつぎの遠隔逆行同化の語例もみられる。puta（蓋）＞p'at'a、sikoiŋ＞sok'oiŋ（作る）、ja:so:dʒimuja:＞ja:so:dʒimaja:（ヤモリ・清水守）。

　名護市幸喜方言には遠隔相互同化、遠隔進行同化、遠隔逆行同化がみられる。しかし、奄美大島南部諸方言の遠隔相互同化が特定の条件のもとで規則的におきるのに対して、幸喜方言のばあい規則的に遠隔同化がおきているわけではないようである。現段階で確認できた語例がすくないので、調査をすすめて、どのような条件のもとで同化がおこなわれるのか検討したい。

4-2　口蓋音化

　南琉球方言のばあい、母音の音消失によって発生した成節的な子音 m、n、f、v、s、ts、dz が後続の子音を変化させるさまざまな子音の同化がみられるし、いちじるしい狭母音化による母音の摩擦音化によって生成された音節主音的な子音 s、z も隣接の子音を同化させる。それに対して、北琉球方言のばあい、子音同士の同化の例をみつけられていない。

　瀬戸内町諸鈍方言では、ika（烏賊）＞ʔik'ja、mino（蓑）＞miɲo などのように、i に後続するあらゆる子音が口蓋音化する。また、ito（糸）＞ʔitʃu では口蓋音化にともなって、破擦音化もみられる。前舌狭母音 i の特徴が後続の子音に付与される進行部分同化である。おなじ変化が他の奄美大島南部諸方言でおきている。

　　ʃirjam（虱）、ʔuʃrjo（後ろ）、çidʒar（左）、mik'jadïk'i（三日月）、çigjaʃ（東）、ɲigjaʔuri（苦瓜）、ʔiʃgjak（石垣）、k'iɲu（昨日）、dʒirju（地炉）　　瀬戸内町諸鈍

　çigi（髭）、ʔik'i（池）、ʔiɲi（稲）、k'iʃir（煙管）の単語の第2音節めの子音も先行音節の母音 i の影響で口蓋音化している。同時に母音も ï から i に狭母音化している。

　西原町小那覇方言では、先行音節 i の影響で口蓋音化した子音のうち、kj、gj、k、g が破擦音化している語例がみられる。おおくの沖縄島中南部諸方言でもおなじ破擦音化がみられる。

　　ʔitʃa（烏賊）、'ndʒana（苦菜）、ʔitʃi（池）、çidʒi（髭）　　西原町小那覇

　西原町小那覇方言の ʃiraŋ（虱）、dʒi:ru（地炉）tʃinu:（昨日）、'nnu（蓑）、ʔiʃigatʃi（石垣）などのように非口蓋音化（直音化）している語例も少なくない。

5.　音消失

　単語を構成する複数個のフォネームのうち、単語内の特定の位置のフォネームが脱落

する現象を音消失 lost of phoneme という。脱落するフォネームの位置によって語頭音消失 aphaeresis、語中音消失 syncope、語末音消失 apocope がある。北琉球方言には語頭音消失、語中音消失、語末音消失がみられる。

1個のフォネームが音消失することによってさまざまな音韻現象がおきている。子音の音消失によって新たな二重母音が発生したり、母音連続が音融合したり、母音の音消失によって新たなフォネームがうまれたり、成節的な子音がうまれたり、閉音節構造の単語がうまれたり、音韻体系に大きな変化をもたらすこともある。

5-1　語頭音消失

北琉球方言の語頭音消失の代表的な例は、語頭の無声子音 *pi、*pu の消失であろう。また、喉頭破裂音をふくんだ語頭音節 ʔu、ʔi が脱落し、それにともなって喉頭音化した鼻音 ʔm、ʔn、接近音 ʔw、ʔj、流音 ʔr があらたなフォネームとして生成されることも北琉球方言にみられる音消失の代表的な例であろう。

5-1-1　*pi、*pu の音消失

竜郷町瀬留方言の t'a:tzï（二つ）、今帰仁村謝名方言の t'a:tʒi（二つ）は、語頭音節 *pu の音消失によってできたものである。

無声子音と狭母音の結合した語頭音節に無声子音が後続するとき、語頭音節の狭母音は無声音化する。そのとき、語頭の無声子音と無声化母音の持続部でおおくの呼気がながれてしまうが、後続の破裂音の調音に際して声門をせばめたり、閉鎖したりして呼気の浪費をふせいだ結果、第2音節めの破裂音が喉頭音化したアロフォンとしてあらわれる。この現象は、ひろくみられる。

第2音節めの喉頭音化した子音は、はじめは語頭音節の無声音化にともなう音環境に依存してあらわれるアロフォン *pu̥t'atsï であったが、語頭音節の狭母音が弱化・消失して、重子音 *tt'atʃi が発生し、そののちに消失し延長代償として第2音節めの母音がながくなって t'a:tʃi の語形があらわれる。音環境に依存しないフォネーム /t'/ があらたに生成される。

竜郷町瀬留方言の tʒui（一人）、tʒu（人）、今帰仁村謝名方言の tʒui（一人）、tʒu:（人）では語頭の *pi が音消失した語形であり、t'a:tzï（二つ）のばあいとおなじ変化を経たものである。語頭 *pi は、第2音節の子音を口蓋音化させたのちに音消失している。

竜郷町瀬留方言の t'ï:tzï（一つ）、今帰仁村謝名方言の t'i:tʒi（一つ）も同様の変化を経ているが、第2音節めの子音が口蓋音化（破擦音化）していないことから、語頭音節は *pu であったと推定される[16]。

喉頭音化した t'、tʒ がフォネームとして確立されると、喉頭音化しない t、tʃ とのあいだに音韻的な対立が生じ、無声破裂音に喉頭/非喉頭音の対立が発生して音韻体系の改変が行われる。

5-1-2 ʔi、ʔu の音消失

　今帰仁村謝名方言の ʔwa:ʃiba（上唇）、ʔwa:bi（上・上辺）、ʔwa:nai（嫉妬）などの語形にみられる ʔw は、語頭の音節の ʔu の母音が弱化によって音消失するさい、語頭音節の喉頭の緊張が後続の接近音 w に付与され、音融合によって生成されたフォネームである。他の沖縄島北部諸方言、西原町小那覇方言などの沖縄島中南部諸方言でも ʔu の音消失によって生成された ʔwa:bi（上・上辺）などの単語がみられる。

　沖縄島中南部諸方言では末尾に母音 u を有する名詞にとりたて助辞 *wa が後接するとき、隣接相互同化をおこして -uwa > -o: が発生しているが、おなじ音連続 -uwa をふくむ ʔuwabe > ʔwa:bi は、母音の隣接相互同化ではなく、音消失と音融合がおきている。ʔuwa > ʔwa: の音消失が北琉球方言全体にみられるのに対して、uwa > o: の隣接相互同化が沖縄島中南部諸方言にしかみられないことから、名詞末尾母音 u ととりたて助辞 wa の相互同化のおきた時期がおそいこと、異なる変化過程をへたであろうことが予想される。

　龍郷町瀬留方言の ʔju:（魚）、ʔjaŋ（言わない）も喉頭音化した歯茎接近音 ʔj も語頭の母音 ʔi の弱化よって音消失するさい、語頭音節の喉頭の緊張が後続の接近音 j に付与されて音融合し、あらたに生成されたものである。語頭音節の母音が i であったために、後続の子音が口蓋音化して歯茎接近音 ʔj であらわれている。

*iwo > ʔiju > ʔju:（魚）、*iwanu > ʔijanu > ʔjaŋ（言わない）

　龍郷町瀬留方言の ʔɲi:（稲）、ʔɲa:dama（稲霊）、ʔɲu:tʃi（命）などの単語にみられる喉頭音化した歯茎鼻音 ʔɲ は、語頭の母音 ʔi が弱化によって音消失するさい、語頭音節の喉頭破裂音の喉頭の緊張が後続の鼻音 ɲ に付与されて音融合し、あらたに生成されたものである。語頭音節の母音が i であったために、後続の子音が口蓋音化した ɲ であらわれている。ʔma:（馬）、ʔma:ga（孫）、ʔma:re（生まれ・素性）などの単語にみられる喉頭音化した両唇鼻音 ʔm も、語頭の ʔu の母音の弱化によって音消失するさい、語頭音節の喉頭破裂音の喉頭の緊張が後続の鼻音 m に付与されて音融合し、あらたに生成されたものである。

　今帰仁村与那嶺方言にも、喉頭音化した歯茎鼻音 ʔn を有する ʔna:gara（稲株）、喉頭音化した両唇鼻音 ʔm を有する ʔma:（馬）、ʔma:ri（生まれ・素性）、ʔme:ʃi（箸）、ʔmenʃeŋ（いらっしゃる）、ʔmo:ruŋ（いらっしゃる）などの単語がみられる。

　伊江島西江上方言の ʔra:（おまえ）は、与論島城方言の ura、伊平屋村我喜屋方言の ʔura の語頭音節の ʔu の母音の弱化によって音消失するさい、語頭音節の喉頭の緊張が後続の r に付与され、音融合によって生じた語形である。ʔr は、伊江島方言だけにみられるフォネームである。

5-2 語中音消失

語中の音消失には北琉球方言全体にみられる、*sawo（竿）＞ sao ＞ soː、*nawi（地震）＞ nai ＞ neː などの語中 *w の消失、*napa（縄）＞ naɸa ＞ nawa ＞ naː、*mape（前）＞ *maɸe ＞ mawe ＞ mae ＞ meː（以上、西原町小那覇方言）などの語中 *p の消失がある。また、奄美大島北部諸方言の *naka（中）＞ naha ＞ na、*tako（蛸）＞ taho ＞ tʻoː、take（丈）＞ tahe ＞ tʻëː（以上、龍郷町瀬留方言）などの語中 k の音消失などがある。本稿では語中破裂音 b の音消失、語中鼻音 m の音消失、語中流音 r の音消失についてのべる。

5-2-1 語中 b 音の消失

沖縄島名護市幸喜方言で語中の両唇破裂音 b の接近音化とそれにつづく音消失がみられる。幸喜方言では *soba（側）＞ suba ＞ suwa、*dabi（煙草）＞ dawi、sawani（サバニ）、のように b の接近音 w への異化がみられるが、さらに、*pabu ＞ pau、*nabe（鍋）＞ nabi ＞ nawi ＞ nai のような脱唇音化の進行した音消失がおきている単語もみられる。接近音化するまえに bu ＞ βu、bi ＞ βi、ba ＞ βa のような摩擦音化を経たであろうとかんがえる。語中 b の接近音化と唇音退化による音消失は、先行、後続の母音の韻質をとわない音韻変化である。ただし、語中の b がすべて消失するわけではなく、b のままあらわれる語例もおおいし、接近音 w であらわれる語例もある。どのような条件で b の接近音化と音消失がおきるのかについては不明である。

 sawa（鮫）、sawani（サバニ）、tʻawakʻu（タバコ）、tʻuwasuŋ（飛ばす）、hawahaŋ（香ばしい）、tʻawi（旅）、kʻui（首）

5-2-2 語中 m 音の消失

奄美大島北部笠利町佐仁方言では語中の両唇鼻音 m の音消失した結果、鼻母音ができている。語中で m の両唇の閉鎖が開放されて鼻音化した唇軟口蓋接近音 w̃ が生成される。その後、両唇での丸めがとれて唇音退化して鼻母音 ã、õ、ĩ がうまれる。

 pʻaã（浜）、jaã（山）、haã（鎌）、taãgo（卵）、ʔaãkʻa（甘い）、kʻjoõ（肝）、kʻoõ（雲）、moõ（腿）、ʔoõgë（おもがい）、ʃoõ（鳥）、haw̃ĩ～haĩ（亀）、ʔaw̃ĩ～ʔaĩ（雨）、maw̃ĩ～maĩ（豆）、huw̃ï～huĩ（米）、tziw̃ï～tziĩ（爪）

5-2-3 語中 r 音の消失

伊江島西江上方言では語中の流音 *r が弱化した音消失がみられる。tsaː（面）、kʻuː（黒）、ʃaːni（虱）、ʃuː（白）、ʔaitʃuN（歩く）、unai（をなり）、wikʻiː（ゑけり）、tʻui（鳥）、nai（実）、tʻidʒai（左）、pʻujuN（降る）。おおくの語例は、i に先行する r、あるいは口蓋音化した rj の音脱落である。a、o、u、e と結合する r の音消失は、先行母音が i のときに限定されておきる。

sui（鳥）、kusui（薬）、hannai（雷）、ɸugui（陰嚢・ふぐり）、nuɸugi（のこぎり）、sa:mi（虱）、mussu（筵）、sa:gi（白髪）、su:mi（脂肉・白身）、ɸe:（坂・ひら）、be:（葱・＜bira）伊江村西江上

他の沖縄中南部諸方言でも語中のrが母音iと結合するときにかぎってrの音消失がみられる。ただし、nukudʒiri（鋸）のように、語中riの先行音節の母音がiのとき、rの音消失はおきていない。

tui（鳥）、kusui（薬）、ha:i（針）、ma:i（毯）、tai（二人）　　西原町小那覇

5-3　語末音消失

奄美大島南部諸方言では2音節名詞、3音節名詞の語末の狭母音 *i、*u の弱化による音消失がみられる。加計呂麻島の諸鈍方言のばあい、「国語アクセント類別対応表」の2音節名詞1類、2類の語末に狭母音 *i、*u を有する単語にほぼ限定され、3類、4類、5類の名詞の語末の *i、*u は消失していない。諸鈍方言の1、2類名詞は下降調の acute accent で、第一音節目は高く強く、第2音節目は低く弱く発音され、筋肉の弛緩とともにピッチが下降する[17]。狭い声道での共鳴を特徴とする i、u は、音響管としての効率の悪さから、相対的におおきい呼気流によって声帯を振動させるにもかかわらず聞こえはちいさく、つよさもつよくない母音であるが、下降調の acute accent のばあい、その傾向は顕著になり、*i、*u が弱化して消失したとかんがえる[18]。

諸鈍方言をはじめとする奄美大島南部諸方言の語末音消失は、母音 i、u の調音上の特徴と空気力学的な特徴の相互作用、語末にあらわれるフォネーム構造、下降調の acute accent という条件がそろっておきている。*i、*u と結合する子音が破裂音、破擦音、摩擦音、鼻音、流音でも音消失がみられる。諸鈍方言の破裂音、破擦音にみられる有声・無声の対立も喉頭・非喉頭の対立も閉音節をつくる子音では中和している。

juk（雪）、mik（右）、k'up（首）、k'utʃ（口）、mït（水）、t'utʃ（妻）、ʔin（犬）、mim（耳）、t'ur（鳥）、çir（昼）、sakra（桜）、apra（油）

6.　音分割と音挿入

1個のフォネームが前後に連続する2個のことなるフォネームに syntagmatic に分割される音韻変化を音分割という。北琉球方言にはいくつかの音分割の例がみられる。音分割の結果、語頭、語中、語末にあらたなフォネームが挿入される。

北琉球方言には、単語の語頭に別のフォネームが挿入される語頭音挿入 prothesis、単語内の連続する2個のフォネームの中間に別のフォネームが発生して挿入される語中音挿入 epenthesis、語末に別のフォネームが挿入される語末音挿入 epithesis がみられる。

6-1 語頭音挿入

今帰仁村西部地区方言では haʤike:（扱い[19]）、çik'usa:（戦）、ɸuʃi:（牛）のように語頭の母音音節が ha、çi、ɸu であらわれ、語頭に h、ç、ɸ が挿入されたようにみえる。語頭の母音音節に無声摩擦音が音挿入されるには、語頭音節の無声音化があったであろうとかんがえる。

この語頭の音挿入は、第2音節めが無声子音ではじまる音節であるばあいにかぎられている。語頭の母音音節に無声子音がつづき、呼気流がよわまると、後続の無声子音の影響とあいまって語頭の母音音節が無声母音化して u̥ になったのではないかと考える。無声音化した母音は、その後、u̥ の無声性が子音 h になって u と分割し、語頭に h が挿入されたみることができる。

haʃi:（汗）、hat'a:（肩）、hak'a:（赤）、çiʤa:（烏賊）、çiʧi:（いつ）、çit'u:ma（暇）、ɸuk'i（桶）、ɸut'a:（歌）、ɸuʤi:（内）、ɸup'uʔami（大雨）　今帰仁村与那嶺

6-2 語中音挿入

大宜味村大宜味方言などにみられる /'iNsu/（味噌）を那覇市泉崎方言などの /'Nsu/ くらべると、語頭に i が挿入されているようにみえる。語頭の i はどのように挿入されたのか。

沖縄島北部諸方言の *miso の語頭音節の母音 i が弱化して消失すると、鼻音だけになるが、m は後続する s のために、s とおなじ口がまえで発する鼻音化した歯茎接近音 ɹ̃ になる。mi から変化した N/'N:su/ も 'ɹ̃:su とかんがえるが、語頭の持続部の立ち上がりで鼻音性がなくなって 'ɹ̃su となり、さらに 'ĩsu/'iNsu/ になったとかんがえる。語頭 'n: の持続部の立ち上がりで鼻音化した舌先母音 ɹ̃ の鼻音性が前後で分割されて、iñsu になったものである。分割された結果、語頭に 'i が挿入されたとみれば、後述する語頭音挿入である。

*miso ＞ 'ɹ̃su ＞ 'ɹ̃:su ＞ 'ɹ̃su ＞ 'iñsu

沖縄島北部の北山原方言にみられる *hune（船）＞ çiɲi/hini/ では、*hu ＞ hi という琉球語において例外的な音韻変化がおきているようにみえる。しかし、沖縄島西方の粟国島方言や渡名喜島方言にみられる ŋ̊ni（船）を介すると、*hune（船）＞ hiɲi の変化過程がよく理解できる。語頭の無声摩擦音 h の影響で母音が無声音化 hu̥ し、さらに後続の鼻音 n の逆行同化によって無声音化したまま鼻母音化 ũ̥ する一方で、さらに同化が進行して舌先での閉鎖がおきると、渡名喜島方言の ŋ̊ni とおなじ形に変化する。後続の母音が i なので口蓋音化した鼻音 ŋ̊ɲi である。無声音化した鼻音は呼気を浪費する不安定な発音であり、呼気の流出を制御するため、あるいは、呼気流のよわまりによって鼻腔へ呼気がながれなくなって、語末の母音 i の影響で i が語中に挿入（çɲi ＞ çiɲi）されて çiɲi の語形

になったとかんがえる。çɲi の ç の無声音性と口蓋性が分離したとみれば音分割であろう。

*pune（船）＞ɸuɲi＞ɸu̥ɲi＞ɸɲ̥ɲi＞ɲ̥ɲi＞çiɲi＞çiɲi

6-3　語末音挿入

語末音挿入には、名護市幸喜方言の *tʃawan（茶碗）＞tʃawanuː、sun（損）＞sunuː にみられる語末の u の挿入、今帰仁村謝名方言に dʒiniː（銭）などの i の挿入などがある。

*tʃawan（茶碗）＞tʃawanuː、　　*son（損）＞sun＞sunuː

7.　音融合と音分割と音挿入

沖永良部島の和泊町国頭方言の ɸjuː（今日）、国頭以外の沖永良部島の集落の方言の çuː（今日）は、相互同化による音融合とその後の音分割によって生成された語形である[20]。国頭方言 ɸjuː の ɸj は両唇の摩擦音 ɸ が口蓋音化したもの、あるいは歯茎摩擦音 ç が唇音化したもので、唇音化と口蓋音化を同時に実現した摩擦音である。第二次基本母音 y の半母音化（接近音化）した ɥ が無声音化して摩擦音になったものであるが、これをあらわす音声記号がないので、仮に ɸj と表記する。

祖形を *kepu とみると、語中 p の摩擦音化 p＞ɸ、有声音化と唇音退化 ɸ＞w＝u、狭母音化 e＞i を経て発生した二重母音 iu の i の前舌狭母音性と u の奥舌円唇狭母音性が隣接相互部分同化によって融合して第二次基本母音の円唇前舌狭母音 y が生成されて *ɸyː ができたとかんがえる。その後、国頭方言では母音 yː の前舌狭母音の特徴がきえて奥舌円唇母音 u となり、口蓋音性は ɸj として子音にのこって分割された語形である。沖永良部島の他の集落の方言では ɸj の唇音退化した ç に変化している。

　　*kepu＞keɸu＞keu　　　異化・語中 p の摩擦音化、有声音化、w 音消失
　　*keu＞heu＞hiu　　　　語頭 k の摩擦音化、e の狭母音化
　　*hiu＞*ɸyː　　　　　　隣接相互部分同化による音融合
　　*ɸyː＞ɸjuː＞çuː　　　口蓋音性と円唇奥舌母音の音分割、脱唇音化

8.　課題

北琉球方言の異化と同化の代表的な例を概観し、音挿入、音消失、音融合、音分割に異化と同化がかかわっていることをのべた。個々のフォネームが他のフォネームとの相互作用のなかで自らの韻質をどのように変化させたか、音節構造のなかで他のフォネームに対するふるまいをどう変えたかをみた。しかし、本稿の記述は、個別的、羅列的で

ある。個々の方言内での他の音韻変化との関連性や音韻体系のなかでの位置づけをおこなっていない。個々の音韻変化が北琉球方言の他の下位方言のそれとどう関連するか記述できていない。

　国頭村宇嘉方言の破裂音 p、k、t は摩擦音 ɸ、h、s に変化しているが、それぞれの摩擦音化には共通点とちがいがある。それぞれの摩擦音化を比較しながらその要因を検討するとともに、宇嘉方言におきた破擦音 ts、dz の破裂音 t、d (r) への異化、唇軟口蓋接近音 w の唇軟口蓋破裂音 gw への異化との関連性の有無を検討する必要があるが、本稿ではそれを果たせていない。琉球方言におきた e＞i、o＞u、i＞ɿ などの狭母音化をひきこし、変化に方向性をあたえた発生拘束として呼気流のつよまりを想定できるのだが、宇嘉方言の摩擦音化や破裂音化にも発生拘束が存在するのか検討できていない[21]。宇嘉方言を周辺方言と比較検討し、沖縄島北部諸方言内での位置づけも、とおくはなれた久高島方言で類似の異化がおきる理由の検討も[22]、北琉球方言内での宇嘉方言の位置づけなどもおこなっていない。

　本稿は、北琉球方言でおきた音韻変化の体系を記述し、音韻変化の詳細を明らかにするための準備的なものである。かりまた (2010) で南琉球方言についても記述したが、琉球方言全体の体系的な記述が必要であろう。

注

1) 琉球方言でおきた音韻変化の要因については、上村幸雄 (1989)、かりまた (2009)、かりまた (2006) を参照。
2) 南琉球方言の同化と異化については、かりまた (2010) を参照。
3) 亀井孝・河野六郎・千野栄一編著 (1996)。
4) 同化を「条件変化 conditioned change」とよび、異化を「自生的変化 spontaneous change」あるいは「無条件変化 unconditioned change」とよぶこともできそうであるが、「異化」のなかには、語頭や語中にかぎっておこるものがあって、単語内での位置を音韻変化の条件とみることもできる。現段階では保留しておく。
5) addition of phonemes。添加ともいう。
6) lost of phonemes。音脱落、無音化、黙音化ともいう。
7) cleaving。本稿でいう音分割を日本語音聲學会編 (1976) で「分裂 cleaving」とよんで解説している。亀井孝・河野六郎。千野栄一編著 (1996) の「分裂 split」は、1個の一部のアロフォンが音韻変化して、2個のフォネームに paradigmatic に分裂することをあらわす。
8) contraction。縮約、凝縮、収約ともいう。
9) 狭母音化の要因について詳しくは上村幸雄 (1989)、かりまた (2009)、かりまた (2006) を参照。
10) 詳しくは、名嘉順一・かりまたしげひさ (1989)、琉球方言研究クラブ (1990)、高橋ユキ (2008) を参照。
11) かりまた (2000) を参照。
12) 辺野喜方言については琉球方言研究クラブ (1991) を参照。
13) 久高島方言については、かりまた (1993)、琉球方言研究クラブ (1980) を参照。
14) 名護市史編さん委員会編 (2006) pp. 318–319、358–359、生塩睦子 (1999) を参照。
15) 語中の唇軟口蓋接近音 w は、唇音退化によって消失していた可能性がある。uwa の同化のばあい、w と先行の u は韻質が近似するので同化の結果をおおきくかえないとかんがえる。なお、

aと結合するばあいもふくめて語中のwは、消失しているが、先行母音がuのばあいはおそくまでのこっていた可能性もある。

16) 屋比久浩・かりまた（2006）は、沖縄島北部諸方言の「一つ」「二つ」のさまざまな語形やその変化過程について記述している。
17) acute accent については上村幸雄（1992）を参照。
18) くわしくは、かりまた（1995）、かりまた（1996）を参照。
19) 喉頭音化した無声の破擦音を tz、tʒ のように表記する。
20) 同じ相互同化が大神島方言、宮古島方言でもおきている。大神島方言の ky: も宮古島平良下里方言の kju:（今日）も *keu > ky: > kju: のように隣接相互同化による音融合とその後の音分割によって生成された語形である。
21) 琉球方言における発生拘束については、かりまた（2009）でのべているが、さらに詳細な検討が必要だろう。
22) かりまた（2007）では、はなれた地点の類似する音韻変化を比較するとき、由来する形式と変化後の形式の韻質、変化の要因と過程、変化を条件づける音環境、音韻体系内での位置、他の音韻変化との整合性などを総合的に検討する必要があることについてのべた。

参考文献

上村幸雄（1992）「acute accent と grave accent」『琉球列島における音声の収集と研究』、沖縄言語研究センター、pp. 44–48、沖縄。

上村幸雄（1990）『日本語の母音、子音、音節　調音運動の実験音声学的研究』国立国語研究所報告100、東京。

上村幸雄（1989）「音韻変化はどのようにしてひきおこされるか（2）——琉球列島諸方言のばあい——」『沖縄言語研究センター資料 No.79』、沖縄言語研究センター、pp. 1–16、沖縄。

上村幸雄（1978）『X線映画資料による母音の発音の研究、フォネーム研究序説』国立国語研究所報告60、東京。

生塩睦子（1999）『沖縄伊江島方言辞典』伊江村教育委員会、沖縄。

亀井孝・河野六郎・千野栄一編著（1996）『言語学大辞典（術語編）』三省堂、東京。

かりまたしげひさ（2010）「南琉球方言の同化と異化」『日本東洋文化論集』第16号、琉球大学法文学部紀要、pp. 159–196、沖縄。

かりまたしげひさ（2009）「琉球語音韻変化の研究」『ことばの科学12』、むぎ書房、pp. 276–354、東京。

かりまたしげひさ（2007）「琉球方言音韻研究の現況——音韻変化の体系の研究をめざして」『国文学解釈と鑑賞』第72巻7号、pp. 28–38、東京。

かりまたしげひさ（2006）「琉球語のせま母音化の要因をかんがえる——空気力学的な条件と筋弾性的な条件——」『沖縄文化』第40巻2号100号、pp. 234–253、沖縄。

かりまたしげひさ（2000）「北琉球方言における破裂音の摩擦音化」『音声研究』第4巻第1号、pp. 19–27、東京。

かりまたしげひさ（1999）「音声の面からみた琉球諸方言」『ことばの科学9』、むぎ書房、pp. 14–85、東京。

かりまたしげひさ（1996）「鹿児島県大島郡瀬戸内町諸鈍方言のフォネーム（下）」『日本東洋文化論集』第2号、琉球大学法文学部紀要、pp. 1–57、沖縄。

かりまたしげひさ（1995）「鹿児島県大島郡瀬戸内町諸鈍方言のフォネーム（上）」『日本東洋文化論集』創刊号、琉球大学法文学部紀要、pp. 1–23、沖縄。

かりまたしげひさ（1993）「久高島方言——その音声的な特徴からみた位置づけ——」『沖縄・久高島のイザイホー』、砂子屋書房、pp. 112–131、東京。

名嘉順一・かりまたしげひさ（1989）「第5章言語伝承第1節　言語」『座間味村史』、沖縄。

仲宗根政善（1983）『沖縄今帰仁方言辞典』角川書店、東京。
名護市史編さん委員会編（2006）『名護市史本編10言語——やんばるの方言』、沖縄。
高橋ユキ（2008）「阿嘉島方言の音韻」『琉球アジア社会文化研究』第11号、pp. 1–22、沖縄。
日本音聲學編（1976）『音聲學大辞典』三修社、東京。
服部四郎（1951）『音声学』岩波書店、東京。
屋比久浩・かりまたしげひさ（2006）「第10節数詞」『名護市史本編10言語——やんばるの方言』、pp. 524–543、沖縄。
琉球方言研究クラブ（1991）『琉大方言第6号——辺野喜方言の音韻体系』、沖縄。
琉球方言研究クラブ（1990）『琉大方言第5号——阿嘉方言の音韻体系』、沖縄。
琉球方言研究クラブ（1980）『琉球方言第15号——久高方言の音韻と語彙』、沖縄。

[Book Review]

Stewart, F., & Yamazato K. (Eds.). (2009).
Voices from Okinawa: Featuring three plays by Jon Shirota.
Honolulu: U of Hawai'i P. (213 pages)

KINA Ikue（喜 納 育 江）

The shifting critical paradigm from modernism to postmodernism and postcolonialism redefines the meaning of Okinawa in a global context. Once called the "Keystone of the Pacific," Okinawa served a function of postwar strategic importance for the U.S. military. Today, however, the "keystone" has an alternative implication in terms of Okinawa's new role as an intellectual center responding to the research interests of the postcolonial scholars inside and outside Okinawa.

It should be noted, however, that flourishing "Okinawan Studies" constantly face the danger of orientalism, by which Okinawa and Okinawans are viewed and treated as an exotic and yet intriguing Other. In orientalist gaze and interpretation, Okinawa and Okinawan culture are subject to romanticization, which may eventually lead to either negative or positive stereotypes. Whereas we, Okinawan scholars, have been resisting the negative stereotypes of the Okinawan people and culture, we tend to remain less critical about the positive stereotypes. Nevertheless, this is a process of self-orientalization or self-colonization in which Okinawans remain unaware that we are appreciated, preferred, and accepted only because of our uncritical compliance to colonizers' institutions rather than claiming our agency. One of the problematic assumptions consciously or unconsciously held by Okinawan Studies scholars is that the Other, Okinawa, is eventually part of them, the Self, and is supposed to *belong to* the Self, playing the role of the object of their studies in their attempt to *discover* the Other within themselves.

At this moment, one question arises in terms of my own situation as a scholar who lives and feels responsible for the future of Okinawa: whose studies are Okinawan Studies? In other words, how do we speak of what it means to be Okinawan today when globalization allows more and more people—indigenous and non-indigenous, part- or full-Okinawan, those located inside or outside the Ryukyu Islands—to participate in this interpretative process of an emerging academic practice? What kind of "license" is required in order to speak of one's concern and interest in Okinawa, and how can we get it, or is such "license" necessary at all? This kind of dilemma occurs in any situation where indigenous people and cultures are exposed to contact with those outside of indigenous communities. How do we develop our approaches to studying Okinawa while assisting Okinawa to become a decolonizing subject rather than to remain an object of a colonizing orientalist gaze?

It seems to me *Voices from Okinawa* offers its readers a potential answer to those questions. Published as a biannual series of the volumes of the acclaimed journal from the University of Hawai'i, *Mānoa: A Pacific Journal of International Writing*, *Voices from Okinawa* is doubtless a groundbreaking publication. It is the first literary anthology of Okinawan American literature, attesting to the fact that Okinawan voices have always existed in the U.S. but have only been unheard. While Japanese American writers were recognized as a part of Asian American literature and gained their position in the field of American literature as early as the 1970s, Okinawan American writers and their literary heritage have remained underrepresented or worse yet, invisible, in the shadow of the American literary mainstream. Katsunori Yamazato, one of the editors of *Voices from Okinawa* and a critic who has recognized the significance of Jon Shirota for more than three decades, points out in his preface to this volume that "Okinawan writers have been seen as a small group within the larger category of Japanese American literature" (viii). Yamazato further states that being thus marginalized even within the category of Japanese American literature, "these [Okinawan American] writers have generally been overlooked by scholars and editors" (viii).

Featuring three works and one essay by Jon Shirota, one of the most outstanding but underrated voices in American literature, *Voices from Okinawa* finally enables Okinawan American writers to make an initial step toward becoming an agent in articulating their voices to the English-speaking audience. Besides Shirota's featured three plays—*Lucky Come Hawaii*, *Leilani's Hibiscus*, and *Voices from Okinawa*—the volume also includes other Okinawan voices that are following Shirota's creative works. The second half of the volume contains the autobiographical and non-fictional narrative voices of five prominent "Uchinanchu (Okinawans)": Mitsugu Sakihara, Seiyei Wakugawa, June Hiroko Arakawa, Jon Shirota, and Philip K. Ige. One of the editorial efforts of *Voices from Okinawa* is found in this multivocality, embracing diverse voices while being aware of the differences among those voices. In his Afterword, Frank Stewart, another editor of the volume, refers to the "heterophonic" and "polyphonic" nature of Okinawan folk music and concludes: "In Okinawan American literature such as Jon Shirota's, folk music and dance are integral to the polyphonic spirit," that is, "a lively 'mixing' both literally and metaphorically, of many voices" (207).

The sense of heterophony and polyphony that is central to Shirota's theatrical stages is shared by other voices in *Voices from Okinawa*. Though the autobiographical stories in the second half of the volume may seem to play the role of providing background information for understanding Shirota's plays, they should not be regarded merely in that context. Those non-fictional discourses are texts as well, as they are narratives that tell us the diverse life experiences of Okinawans as vigorously as Shirota's plays do. Every author in this book tells what it means to be Okinawan American through their own story or their ancestors' stories, e.g., the stories of coming to the U.S. from Okinawa to become farm workers or students, of being in the U.S. as a prisoner of war from the Battle of Okinawa, and of being born in the U.S. as children of Okinawan immigrants and moved between two nations as *kibei*. The polyphonic voices of five Okinawans tell us that Okinawan identity is not monolithic but diverse and multifaceted even though they are all based in Hawaii.

Having immigrated all over the world, Okinawans have a long history of diaspora. Some Okinawans came home, others found their new homes to be rooted, and there are those still migrating. No matter where they move, however, there is a shared sense of heritage and communal consciousness that can connect the diverse and polyphonic voices of Okinawans. A new Okinawan story is told in each new location, and the collection of those stories forms an Okinawan tradition in a new place. The "Tinsagu nu hana," an emblematic Okinawan folk song about the profoundness of parents' love and wisdom, for example, is as poignant to diasporic Okinawans as to Okinawans at home. In other words, "Tinsagu nu hana" connects Okinawans all over the world emotionally. Wesley Ueunten's translation of this song on the opening page of *Voices from Okinawa*, therefore, is thematically critical for this book, and the meaning of its lyrics becomes even more compelling as readers go on reading and realize the message that this book is trying to transmit: a bond exists between different generations and among Okinawan communities. This emotional understanding is thus distilled into the words in the song: "Dye the teaching of your parents / Onto your heart" (Ueunten).

Shirota's plays, too, express the playwright's appreciation for Okinawans who came before him. It is this sense of desire to make ancestral voices heard that provides the foundation of Shirota's narrative. Kama Gusuda, an iconic Okinawan character both in *Lucky Come Hawaii* and *Leilani's Hibiscus*, for instance, represents Shirota's appreciation of the ancestral voices in Okinawan traditions. Kama's life stories as the "number one pig farmer in all Maui" (2) and an immigrant father become quintessential to Shirota's imagination as an Okinawa American storyteller. Shirota is primarily an empathetic listener who creates voices based on his sympathetic understanding of the voices of his parents' generation. His imagination essentially comes from his respect for the voices of the generations of Okinawan immigrants, including Shirota's parents, whose "teaching" he had "dyed onto his heart." Locating his own voice and sense of who he is in connection with Okinawan traditions is significant for Shirota in coming up with an Okinawan American tradition, a tradition to which he belongs.

The non-fictional autobiographical accounts of other writers in this book can also be read as their acts of creating an Okinawan American tradition. They attempt to pass on their "teaching" to later generations, in their cases, by speaking in their own words. Their essays convey a similar sense of urgency to Shirota's that the understanding of younger generations will be crucial for the continuation of an Okinawan American heritage. Wakukawa's life story, told in form of a letter to his son, and other autobiographical writings by Sakihara, Ige, and Shirota as well come from their hope to pass on the stories of their life experiences to future generations of Okinawan American communities. As precisely put in the title of Arakawa's life story, as told to Kinuko Yamazato, a young Okinawan scholar, just before Arakawa passed away, these writings are indeed "gifts" to be passed on for the survival of the cultural and spiritual traditions of Okinawan American people and communities.

However, throughout the volume of *Voices from Okinawa*, it is suggested that there is also a challenge in handing down the spirit of "Tinsagu nu Hana." The geographical distance between Okinawa and the Okinawan American communities, the different social environments, and the language barrier make it difficult for Okinawan Americans to be connected with their ancestral homeland. Okinawan American people and communities face adversity in fully appreciating their ancestral heritage. Shirota's plays manifest this challenge through his presentation of conflicting values between Okinawan Issei and Nisei generations, e.g., Kimiko's ambivalence about her ethnic identity in *Lucky Come Hawaii* and Yasuichi's romantic involvement with Leilani, an indigenous Hawaiian woman, in *Leilani's Hibiscus*. The uncompromising values among Okinawan Americans complicate the process of cultural communication between different generations.

Nevertheless, this is a moment of heterophony among the voices of the Okianwan American people. Shirota's other challenge as an Okinawan American writer is in his exploration of further polyphony by expressing a new Okinawan voice that even he may not have heard in his life. In his essay also published in this volume, "The Dawning of an Okinawan," Shirota addresses to his father how contemporary Okinawa has changed from what it used to be. His most recent play, *Voices from Okinawa*, exemplifies Shirota's challenge of expressing the new awareness that mediates voices that he listened to during his stay in Okinawa in 2005. According to LiAnn Ishizuka's article, "Guests in Okinawa," Shirota was "inspired to write a play about the relationship between Okinawans and the American GIs that are stationed there [in Okinawa]." Presenting Kama Hutchins, a great-grandson of Kama Gusuda, Shirota in this play attempts to go beyond the traditional image of Okinawa held by Hawaiian or Okinawan communities in the U.S. In so doing, he creates Kama Hutchins as an Okinawan American learner of the contemporary culture and society of Okinawa.

Creating characters that resist common stereotypes is another strategy of Shirota's expressing new Okinawan voices. Kama's Caucasian-Okinawan mixed heritage, for instance, works successfully in representing a new type of Okinawan American character in which racial implications make audiences' perceptions of Okinawan identity more complex. Another character in the play, Keiko Oshiro, an educated young Okinawan woman principal of the "Naha English School" where Hatchins teaches, also projects Shirota's resistance against long held negative stereotypes of Okinawan women as the exotic objects of American GIs' sexual interest. Along with Namiye Matsuda, another Okinawan woman who is found to be a rape victim toward the end of the play, Shirota compassionately listened to voices he had never heard before and expressed his new understanding of Okinawa through the creation of new types of characters.

While I understand that these Okinawan characters came out of the playwright's good intentions to "speak for" Okinawans in Okinawa and to bring the American audience a cross-cultural perspective on what it is like to live in Okinawa, I do, however, have to raise a question in terms of whether or not Shirota's description of Okinawan women was perfectly appropriate. I would argue that creating a dramatic moment by implying a romance for Keiko, a professional woman, whose attitude could be perceived as "bossy" by Kama (106), is not necessary, since it casts a reflection on Keiko's presumed non-stereotypical representation as an Okinawan woman by confining it within the traditional gender role in the matrimonial institution governed by heterosexism and patriarchy. Likewise, Namiye's revealing of her past experience—being raped by an American GI—in a speech to an English classroom seems awkward and unlikely in reality because rape victims are usually known to refuse to describe or even remember the horrifying moment of the sexual assault. The rape case is not merely a politically but also emotionally sensitive issue for Okinawan women, and it thus requires a careful dramatic process that can justify Namiye's determination to make a confession about the most traumatic experience in her life *in class*.

The play *Voices from Okinawa* is nonetheless an ambitious work that informs American audiences of the base-related issues in contemporary Okinawa and makes them, as Americans, aware of their responsibility for the involvement of the U.S. in what is going on around the world. As this new work demonstrates, Shirota's imagination and creativity continue to explore further heterophony in Okinawan voices. Meanwhile, his classic 1965 novel *Lucky Come Hawaii* was also reprinted by University of Hawai'i Press in 2009 as another volume from the *Mānoa* series, and this signals that Shirota's literature is now going through a new phase of evaluation, especially in a new critical paradigm that the editors of this volume propose: Okinawan American literature. *Voices from Okinawa*, the first anthology of Okinawan American literature, is a model outcome of Okinawan Studies. It presents "teaching" in which Okinawans and Okinawan Americans are required to speak out as agents as well as listen earnestly to the voices of Okinawans all over the world.

References

Stewart, F., & Yamazato K. (Eds.). (2009). *Voices from Okinawa: Featuring three plays by Jon Shirota*. Honolulu: U of Hawai'i P.

Ishizuka, L. (2008, February 8). Guests in Okinawa. [Review of the book *Voices from Okinawa: Featuring three plays by Jon Sihrota*]. *Asia Pacific Arts*. Retrieved January 15, 2010, from the USLA Asia Institute Website http://www.asiaarts.ucla.edu/080208/article.asp?parentID=86959

(University of the Ryukyus)

[書 評]

北村　毅（KITAMURA, T.）著
『死者たちの戦後誌──沖縄戦跡をめぐる人びとの記憶』
お茶の水書房　2009年　428ページ

山　城　新（YAMASHIRO Shin）

　最近の沖縄関連研究において、歴史的主体を批判しつつ、新たな主体性を再考するための研究書が出版されるようになってきた。本書も沖縄の戦後についてこれまでの研究とは違った視角から第二次世界大戦後の沖縄と日本を提示しようと企図する意欲的な研究書である。具体的には、「遺骨収集、記念碑の建立、慰霊祭、戦死者供養、戦跡巡礼（巡拝）、戦跡観光など、1940年代後半から2000年代までに沖縄の戦跡で行われてきた諸実践」が分析の対象となり、その析出のために、これまでの戦後研究ではあまり扱われることのなかった様々な私的・公的記録を駆使している。そうして、死者と生者を含む「戦死後」の人々の営みを「関係史」としてとらえ直すことが、本書の主題となっている。

　生存者たちの証言を基に沖縄戦直後の廃墟と荒野の中に散乱していた死体や遺骨の風景描写から始まる第1章「さまよえる遺骨──戦死者が『復帰』する場所」では、沖縄で亡くなった戦死者の遺骨の扱われ方の経緯が詳説されている。戦後復興とともに遺骨はやがて人々の生活空間から物理的に切り離され、日本国家の一元的管理下におかれることになるが、しかし同時に政治的な遺骨処理問題として社会の中にたち現れる。本章ではその一連の問題の発生経緯と構造を多様な史料を基に分析していく。例えば、1952年以降、日本政府はサンフランシスコ講和条約発効後の戦後処理の問題として国民の要請に応える必要があったし、戦後の救護法の適用を受け経済上の恩恵を受けるために、当時の琉球政府はいわゆる「祖国復帰」の契機として戦死者の慰霊と追悼を政治的に利用したいという思惑も絡んでいたと指摘する。その政治的文脈の中で、日本の大手新聞紙上で多数の日本兵の遺骨が沖縄の地で「野ざらし」になっているという報道に端を発し、繰り広げられる遺骨処理問題について、戦後沖縄思想史で展開された日本同祖論に似た構図の中で論じつつ、当時のぎくしゃくした日本と沖縄の関係史を「戦死後」から読み直している。

　第2章「『復帰』へといたる『病』──ひめゆりの塔と『沖縄病患者』」では、1960年代以降沖縄文化が本土資本に消費される過程で蔓延する「沖縄病」について、「ひめゆり学徒隊」の心象イメージがどのように造られ流布したかを解説する。ひめゆりの塔をめぐって展開する小説、映画、観光業などがいかに「哀悼共同体」を形成し、「復帰運動においてひめゆりの自己犠牲のイメージのうえにみずからの自画像を重ね合わせたか」と論じる。更に、沖縄病の罹患プロセスにおけるバスガイドの「語り」の機能分析を行い、戦後日本で母性の果たした役割と同様に「無垢」なひめゆり学徒の戦死者が戦後日本社会に「犠牲者」として召還されることによって、戦死者全員の無垢性に置き換えられ」、また「戦後日本社会はひめゆりのイメージを流用＝領有することによって、戦死者一般の戦争責任をも冤罪していた」と考察する。

　第3章「『父』を亡くした後──遺児たちの戦跡巡礼と慰霊行進」では、ヒット曲「さとうきび畑」の歌の分析からはじまり、さとうきび畑の中を「父親たちの死の痕跡にみちた場所」として訪れる遺児たちの慰霊の日をめぐる巡礼のなかに「自分たちの来歴」と「父の痕跡」の両方の探

求があったとし、日本遺族会の沖縄戦跡をめぐる実践の歴史的経緯と遺児の自己探求プロセスを重ね合わせる。その過程において「『血』のイデオロギー」が戦死者と遺族の間の身体的経験を同一化するものとして稼動し、同時に「『平和』のイデオロギー」と連動していくことによって遺族共同体の形成に大きく作用し、沖縄戦の戦跡は、それらの諸力学が効果的に働く場所として、あるいは、遺族の求める父親の呼びかける声を提供する場所として機能していたと分析する。

第4章「戦死者の魂(マブイ)が語り出すとき――戦後沖縄の心象風景」では、組織体制の変遷史あるいは思想史的な分析とは対照的に、沖縄戦の二四万余の戦死者と残された遺族の関係性はどのように構築されていったのかという個人レベルの戦死後に焦点が当てられる。「生き残った者が、死者の存在をどのように観念していたのか」という問いを立て、戦死者の供養や祭祀においてユタが生活空間と精神世界をどのように繋いでいたのかということを、一人のユタのライフヒストリーを中心に展開し、民俗的慣行「ヌジファ」の実践について解説している。しかしながら、論は単なる実践報告にとどまらず、靖国神社をはじめとする「国家的慰霊システムから取りこぼされた戦死者を救い上げ、さらには、そこに囲い込まれた(すなわち靖国神社に『合祀』された)戦死者一人一人を家族のもとに取り環していく過程であった」とし、そのほかにもユタの口寄せを介さず、各々で戦跡や戦没地を巡礼しながら悲しみを癒す人々の私的な戦死者供養のあり方の重要性についても指摘することによって、本論を沖縄民俗風習の固有性や特異性にのみ回収する危険性を注意深く回避している。

第5章「風景の遺影――摩文仁の丘の戦後」では、摩文仁の丘の物理的風景が荒野からさとうきび畑そして平和祈念公園へと変化する過程を示しながら、そこにどのような政治的取捨選択がなされてきたかを「風景の遺影」をめぐる問いとして展開している。第1章でも言及されている1960年代の霊域整備事業によって開発が進められる過程の中に、慰霊塔・碑の維持管理をめぐって台頭してきた「奉賛会」が霊域管理事業を取り仕切る過程で摩文仁の指定霊域が「靖国神社の支部、地方出張所として、『護国の神』を祀る場所」になったと論じる。更に多くの記念碑や公園で「平和」の名を冠する全国的な当時の傾向について述べながら、記念碑が「復興」や「繁栄」など言葉と並びつつ高度成長期の日本を形象化し、同時に敗戦の記憶と「日本人」を言祝ぐ傾向があったとし、摩文仁の丘にも「沖縄を国民国家の外延として再定義しようとする欲望」が発動していたと指摘する。そのようなナショナリズムの危険性への警戒心を持って「平和の礎」の建設は始められるが、一九九九年の稲嶺恵一県政下の新資料館の展示改ざん問題に見られるように、「ポジティブな沖縄」を演出するような政治的介入があったり、2000年に来沖したクリントン元大統領の演説の中で沖縄問題を隠蔽するような文脈に置かれたり、絶えず忘却と隠蔽の政治的力学に利用されてきたとする。しかしながら、一方で、平和の礎の特徴として「あくまでもローカルに(家族単位で)戦死者を想起しようとする点に特色があるのではないか」とし、礎に刻まれた「名は、戦死者の固有性を保たせつつ、生者の前に確固たる存在証明を証しているのである」と本章を結び、グローバル時代に果たしうる礎の役割も確認する。

以上、本書の議論の要点と流れを確認した上で、更に筆者のアプローチについてまとめてみたい。何よりも、本書の価値はそこでの議論や解説される史実にのみあるのではなく、論じ方にも示唆的なものがあると思われるからである。まず、著者がその名を著書の中でもしばしば用いているように、ミシェル・フーコーの規律=訓練や監視といったテクノロジーの分析の実践例として本書をみることができる。つまり、身体がどのように権力によって規律化され、用立てられ、再編されるような従順さをつくりだすように働きかけられているかについての分析である。本書では、具体的に骨や血という身体部分あるいは遺品に身体が分割され、全体的な管理と効率化に役

立てられていたということを明らかにしている。遺骨や死者という生者の社会の匿名性の中に作用した権力とその組織化が沖縄の戦後には主に「復帰運動」や国家的ナショナリズムと折衝しながら稼働していたかを批判的に論じる。しかしながら、一方で、筆者はそのようないわゆる近代的個人と権力システムの二極で沖縄の戦後を単純化することには警戒感を持っている。例えば戦跡巡礼において、ユタという間主観的存在によって果たされた慰霊の役割について指摘している一方で、先述したように逆にユタの口寄せを介することなく個別に執り行われた個人的な慰霊儀式の存在に言及しているし、その他にも様々な個人的な悼みの在り方を取り上げているからである。また、遺骨や戦死者、旧植民地出身者の遺骨処理問題や「無名戦没者」の存在を指摘することによって、従来の戦後沖縄研究であまり言及されることのなかった沖縄戦の更なる暗部に光を当て、今後の沖縄研究の可能性も示唆しているといえる。

　本書で展開される沖縄戦を対象として戦死者の死後をめぐるさまざまな問いは、しかしながら、大きな悲しみの上に成り立っている。それは、24万人余の多数の戦死者を出した沖縄戦を語る上で不可避の感情であり、その数を上回る遺族の悲しみと共鳴しており、更に、今の時代の危機感に支えられているのだろう。「戦争の痕跡の一切合切が消失していこうとする現在において、せめて失われた戦争の痕跡のささやかな目録をつくろうとする試みともなろう。」序章で語られる「戦争の痕跡のささやかな目録」として献上される本書は、死者へ寄り添う視点がある一方で、その悲しみを、今とこれからを生きる者たちへと伝えていこうとする試みである。序章の第2節は「本書の議論をより理解するために」では、沖縄戦と本書を理解する上での基本的な問題構造と歴史背景を概説すると同時に、「慰霊の日」や「終戦の日」の違いや、「沖縄」と「日本」のそれぞれの戦後処理の違いと問題点などを丁寧に説明しているのは、そのような筆者の態度の表れとも読める。これからの世代にとって「戦後」という時代理解が今後ますます学問的課題になることを考慮に入れると、このような沖縄研究における基本的背景としての知識や情報の扱い方は、一つの参考例としても考えられるだろう。

　したがって、本書で照射されるのは直接的には戦死者をめぐる戦後史であるが、本質的には「死」という私的で個別に絶対的な出来事が過去と未来の共同体を巻き込み、存続させていくという側面である。死は一人では完結させることはできず、また、死に限っては、社会の成員の誰も欠落させることもできない。しばしば言われるように、私たちは、自分の死を経験することはできない。できるのは他人の死のみであり、そこに他者性を認識し、顧みて自己の来たる「死」に擬似的に直面し、結果的に他者と自己との離れがたき関係性を理解するのである。本書はそのような意味において、究極的には「わたしたち」についての本である。もちろん「わたしたち」は誰を指すのかについては、読者に委ねられているのだが。

　読後にふと『ニューヨークタイムズ紙』に掲載された "Okinawa: The Bloodiest Battle of All"（1987年）という短いエッセイを思い出した。シュガーローフの激戦を経験した米国従軍者の視点から、美化された戦争体験や戦死について批判的に書いている作品であるが、たとえば、この作品に間接的に言及されているような米軍人たちの戦死後はどのように考えられるべきだろうか。本書で血のイデオロギーは主要概念であるが、マンチェスターのエッセイに奇しくも "bloodiest" な戦闘として再び現れる「血」と「沖縄」の並列は、単に戦争という名詞に付随する形容詞としての統語的な関係によるものだろうか。戦後処理の諸問題において、敵としての米軍人の死は、あるいは、米国側の政治的、文化的価値観はいかなる影響を与えただろうか。本書の議論では1955年に米国民政府が遺骨処理をめぐる過程において示した政治的懸念に言及しており、その情報のみに依拠するならば、米国民政府をはじめとするアメリカの存在は、沖縄の戦死後にそれほど影響を

与えなかったように読むこともできる。

　沖縄戦の、そして沖縄の戦後の特徴の重要な部分に米軍の存在がある以上、「アメリカ」は今後の戦死後の議論の課題として避けられないであろう。何よりも戦死後や遺骨や血といった本書の主要概念が魅力的なのは、それらが匿名性を帯びているが故に、私たちの価値観がそこに映し出されるということ、そして本書の議論が示しているとおり、それらは私たちに亡霊のごとく憑依し、陵駕してしまうということである。もちろん断っておくが、本書の主題は日本と沖縄の関係を戦死後の人々の営みを「生者」と「死者」の「関係史」として捉えなおすことであるので、「アメリカ」という存在を戦死後の思考に持ち込むことは、本書の意図するものではないだろう。むしろ、本書によって明らかにされた沖縄研究の新たな可能性であり、戦後を考え創っていく者たちに突きつけられた今後の課題として捉えるべきである。ちなみに本書は2009年度タイムス出版文化賞（正賞）を受賞している。

（琉球大学）

Submission Guidelines

IJOS: International Journal of Okinawan Studies

IJOS: International Journal of Okinawan Studies, a peer reviewed journal published by IIOS (International Institute for Okinawan Studies) at the University of the Ryukyus, seeks papers 20 to 30 pages in length on issues, areas, and topics related to Okinawa. Please contact *IJOS* editors IIOS@w3.u-ryukyu.ac.jp for submission details and manuscript style in English.

Manuscript Submission
1. The title of the paper, author's or authors' name(s), affiliation(s), and full postal and e-mail addresses should be submitted on a separate sheet.
2. Contributors should submit one copy of their manuscript to the editor-in-chief of *IJOS* (the name and address are given on the inside front cover). They should also submit a copy of the manuscript either on a floppy disk, CD-ROM, or other form of digital storage. Submission by e-mail attachment will be accepted.
3. Copyrights of accepted manuscripts belong to IIOS (International Institute for Okinawan Studies).
4. English manuscripts for *IJOS* generally follow the APA (American Psychological Association) Style. Only cited works may be included in the reference list. When using APA format, the author's last name and the year of publication for the source should appear in the text, e.g., (Karimata, 1998), and a complete reference should appear in the reference list at the end of the paper. Do not use footnotes.
5. Manuscripts should be printed on A4 paper or on letter-size paper with the following format: (a) a margin of 2.5 cm (1 inch) should be set for every edge; (b) Text should be double-spaced.
6. Manuscripts should be no longer than 30 pages. Manuscripts should have an abstract (limited to 200 words in English and 300 characters in Japanese), a body, endnotes, and references. If contributors cannot prepare an abstract in Japanese, ask the editors for assistance.
7. The title of the paper should be in 14-point type and centered. A subtitle, if any, should be in 12-point type and centered.
8. The abstract, body, endnotes, and references should be in 10-point type. However, independent quotations should be in 9-point type.
9. The terms "Abstract," "Endnotes," and "References," as well as section headings, should be in boldface; subsection headings should be in boldface and italics.

IJOS: International Journal of Okinawan Studies 投稿規定

1. 琉球大学国際沖縄研究所は *IJOS: International Journal of Okinawan Studie* を年 2 回発行する。
2. 投稿論文等は研究論文及び書評論文とする。
3. 論文等の内容は、沖縄および沖縄に関連する地域の人文科学、社会科学、自然科学等の分野のものとする。
4. 論文等の投稿者は、論文等のタイトル、氏名、連絡先住所、及び電子メールアドレス等を記した文書を添付することとする。
5. 投稿は随時受け付ける。投稿論文の採否は査読者による評価を参考にし、*IJOS* 編集委員会が決定する。
6. 投稿者は論文等のハードコピー 1 部と電子メールの添付書類として提出するものとする。原稿は Microsoft Word の形式あるいは PDF 形式で保存すること。
7. 論文の著作権は国際沖縄研究所に属する。
8. 執筆言語は日本語あるいは英語とし、使用ソフトは原則として MSWord とする。
9. 用紙は A4 またはレターサイズを使用し、ページ設定等は次のとおりとする。上下左右に 3.0 cm の余白をとる。1 ページあたりの行数は 35 行とし、1 行あたりの文字数は 39 字とする。
10. 原稿は横書きとし、論文名（日本語および英語で論文名を付すこと）、要旨、本文、注記、参考文献（本文及び注で引用された文献等のみ）から構成される。なお、論文名、氏名、所属、要旨、および本文の間はそれぞれ 1 行空ける。
11. 日本語の論文には英語の要旨（200 語以内）を、英語の論文には日本語の要旨（300 字以内）をつけること。書評論文には要旨は付けない。
12. 章節番号については、章は算用数字 1 から、節は 1–1 という順に記載する。「はじめに」、「おわりに」および「まとめ」などは番号を付さない。
13. 研究論文のページ数は上記 8)、9)、10) の設定で、要旨、注記、参考文献、表、図、をふくめて 12 ページ以内とする。
14. 書評論文のページ数は上記 8)、9)、10) の設定で、注記、参考文献、表、図、をふくめて 6000 字程度とする。
15. 注記は脚注とはせず、本文中に通し番号を付し、本文の末尾にまとめて示す。
16. 図、表は、本文とは別の用紙に作成する。図は原則としてそのまま印刷するので、レーザープリンタ等を利用して鮮明に印刷すること。また、本文中に図表の挿入位置を指示すること。
17. 参考文献は注記の後に記載し、形式（書籍、ジャーナル論文）に係わりなく 50 音順に列挙する。文献は、著者名（発行年）「論文名」『書名』巻、号、ページ、出版社名、出版地をこの順に示す。外国語の文献に関しては以上の日本語文献の記載の仕方に準ずる。英語の文献はアルファベット順に列挙する。

    （例）

    参考文献

    狩俣繁久（2000）「北琉球方言における破裂音の摩擦音化」『音声研究』第 4 巻、第 1 号、pp. 19–27、東京。

    島袋幸子・狩俣繁久（2009）「沖縄今帰仁村謝名方言のアスペクト・テンス・ムード」『日

本東洋文化論集』第 15 号、pp. 1–29、沖縄。

　　仲宗根政善（1983）『沖縄今帰仁方言辞典』角川書店、東京。

18. 本文中、および注記中に参考文献を示すときは、［著者名字　発行年：pp. x–x］、のようにすること。

　　（例）

　　中本正智［中本 1976: p. 100］は、琉球語全体におこった音韻変化とその変化過程について論じるなかで、せま母音化の要因を機能論的な観点から述べた。

19. 論文投稿に関する質問などは、下記の窓口へ問い合わせ下さい。

　　〒903–0213　沖縄県中頭郡西原町字千原 1
　　　　　　　琉球大学国際沖縄研究所
　　　　　　　IJOS 編集委員会
　　　　　　　Email: IIOS@w3.u-ryukyu.ac.jp
　　　　　　　Tel/Fax: 098–895–8475
　　　　　　　URL: http://www.iios.u-ryukyu.ac.jp

IJOS: International Journal of Okinawan Studies　Premier Issue

2010 年 3 月 19 日発行

編集　琉球大学国際沖縄研究所
〒903-0213　沖縄県中頭郡西原町字千原 1
TEL・FAX: 098-895-8475／E-mail: IIOS@w3.u-ryukyu.ac.jp
Website: http://www.IIOS.u-ryukyu.ac.jp/

所長　山　里　勝　己

出版　株式会社 研究社
〒102-8152　東京都千代田区富士見 2-11-3
TEL: 03-3288-7777／FAX: 03-3288-7799

印刷所　研究社印刷株式会社
〒352-0011　埼玉県新座市野火止 7-14-8
TEL: 048-481-5901／FAX: 048-481-5947

IJOS: International Journal of Okinawan Studies
Edited by the International Institute for Okinawan Studies, University of the Ryukyus
Published and distributed by Kenkyusha Co., Ltd.
March 2010